## Prentice Hall LITERATURE

PENGUIN  EDITION

# Unit Six
# Resources

*Grade Seven*

**PEARSON**

Upper Saddle River, New Jersey
Boston, Massachusetts
Chandler, Arizona
Glenview, Illinois

**BQ Tunes Credits**
Keith London, Defined Mind, Inc., Executive Producer
Mike Pandolfo, Wonderful, Producer
All songs mixed and mastered by Mike Pandolfo, Wonderful
Vlad Gutkovich, Wonderful, Assistant Engineer
Recorded November 2007 – February 2008 in SoHo, New York City, at
Wonderful, 594 Broadway

**PEARSON**

ISBN–13: 978-0-13-366441-6
ISBN–10:    0-13-366441-4

3 4 5 6 7 8 9 10    12 11 10 09

# CONTENTS

For information about the Unit Resources, assessing fluency, and teaching with BQ Tunes, see the opening pages of you Unit One Resources.

## BQ Tunes

### **Solidarity,** performed by the Fake Gimms

We have a **common** goal to achieve
Yea, what we want is the same.
We share a place, our home, our **community**.
We have a stake in the game.

It's bigger than you.
It's bigger than me, too.

Just a single **individual** trying to succeed.
It's not so easy by yourself,
You've got to work as a **team**.

It's bigger than you.
It's bigger than me, too.

Part of the **culture** stems from **tradition**.
The ways that we're defined.
These are the things that bring us together,
The things that **unify**.

It's bigger than you.
It's bigger than me, too.

Our **duty** and obligation,
Stand as one, a **group** of many in solidarity.
A **family** with a **unique** plan.
More effective than a single man.
To make a change when it matters.
Now.

Now.

I am a product of my surroundings,
Of my **environment**.
I have a **custom** and it defines how I live.

It's bigger than you.

It's bigger than me, too.

**Ethnicity** and identity might show them where we're from,

But **diversity** and difference will serve to make us strong.

It's bigger than you.

It's bigger than me, too.

---

Song Title: **Solidarity**

Artist / Performed by the Fake Gimms

Vocals & Guitar: Joe Pfeiffer

Guitar: Greg Kuter

Bass Guitar: Jared Duncan

Drums: Tom Morra

Lyrics by the Fake Gimms

Produced by the Fake Gimms

Studio Production: Mike Pandolfo, Wonderful

Executive Producer: Keith London, Defined Mind

Name _____ Date _____

# Unit 6: Themes in the Oral Tradition
## Big Question Vocabulary—1

**The Big Question: Community or individual: Which is more important?**

**common:** *adj.* shared with others, such as mutual ideas or interests

**community:** *n.* a town or neighborhood in which a group of people live; other forms: *communal, communities*

**culture:** *n.* the ideas, beliefs, and customs that are shared by people in a society; other forms: *cultural, cultured*

**individual:** *n.* a person; other form: *individually*

**unique:** *adj.* single, one of a kind

**A. DIRECTIONS:** *Follow each direction.*

1. Explain the difference between something that is **common** and something that is **unique.** Provide an example of each. _____

   _____

2. Explain the relationship between an **individual** and his or her **community.** _____

   _____

3. Provide three examples of **culture**—ideas, beliefs, or customs shared by people living in your community or in the United States at large.

   _____

   _____

   _____

**B. DIRECTIONS:** *Provide an example of each of the following.*

1. a common interest shared by you and a friend: _____

   _____

2. a community in which you would like to live someday: _____

   _____

3. a foreign culture of your family, neighbors, or friends: _____

   _____

4. an individual whom you admire: _____

   _____

5. a characteristic or feature that makes you unique: _____

   _____

Unit 6 Resources: Themes in the Oral Tradition

# Unit 6: Themes in the Oral Tradition
## Big Question Vocabulary—2

### The Big Question: Community or individual: Which is more important?

**custom:** *n.* a tradition shared by people from the same culture; other form: *customary.*

**diversity:** *n.* a variety of different ideas, cultures, or objects; other form: *diverse*

**environment:** *n.* the setting in which an individual lives; other form: *environmental*

**group:** *n.* several people or things that are together; other forms: *grouping, grouped*

**duty:** *n.* conduct due to parents and superiors; tasks, conduct, service, or functions that arise from one's position; other from: *dutiful*

**DIRECTIONS:** *Answer each question.*

1. Many snakes and colorful birds reside in a rain forest. Which vocabulary word **best** describes where they live? Explain your answer. _____
   _____

2. Sally takes care of her sisters every day when she comes home from school. Which vocabulary word **best** describes this situation? Explain your answer. _____
   _____

3. Every May 1, my sister and I make May baskets. Then we deliver them to our neighbors. Which vocabulary word **best** describes this annual event? Explain your answer.
   _____

4. Everyone interested in running the marathon got together to share their ideas about training. Which vocabulary word **best** describes these individuals? Explain your answer.
   _____

5. The restaurant serves Italian, Spanish, English, African, and German foods. Which vocabulary word **best** describes the menu? Explain your answer. _____
   _____

Name _____ Date _____

# Unit 6: Themes in the Oral Tradition
# Big Question Vocabulary—3

**The Big Question: Community or individual: Which is more important?**

**ethnicity:** *n.* the race or national group to which an individual belongs; other form: *ethnic*

**family:** *n.* a group of people who are related to each other; other forms: *families, familiar*

**team:** *n.* a group of people who work together to achieve a common goal

**tradition:** *n.* a belief or custom that has existed for a long time; other form: *traditional*

**unify:** *v.* to combine two or more things to form a single unit; other form: *unified*

**DIRECTIONS:** *Answer each question.*

1. Which vocabulary word is an **antonym** for the word *separate* ? Explain their opposite meanings.

   _____

2. Chico and Manny's family came to this country from Spain. Which vocabulary word **best** describes their family's roots? Explain your answer. _____

3. The students in my class broke into small groups to create radio plays. Which vocabulary word **best** describes each group? Explain your answer. _____

   _____

4. On Valentine's Day each year, my mother and her friend Mrs. Ortiz make delicious heart-shaped cookies. Which vocabulary word **best** describes this annual event? Explain your answer. _____

   _____

5. I have four brothers and fifteen cousins. Which vocabulary word **best** describes this group? Explain your answer. _____

   _____

Name _____ Date _____

# Unit 6: Themes in the Oral Tradition
# Applying the Big Question

## Community or individual—which is more important?

**DIRECTIONS:** *Complete the chart below to apply what you have learned about the importance of the community and the individual. One row has been completed for you.*

| Example | What does the individual want? | What does the community want? | Who won or lost | What I learned |
|---|---|---|---|---|
| **From Literature** | Ixtla wants to marry Popo | Ixtla to rule the kingdom | Nobody, because Ixtla dies of a broken heart | Sometimes individuals cannot be forced to do what others wish of them |
| **From Literature** | | | | |
| **From Science** | | | | |
| **From Social Studies** | | | | |
| **From Real Life** | | | | |

Name _____

# Unit 6: Themes in Oral Tradition  Skills Concept Map—1
## Community or individual: Which is more important?

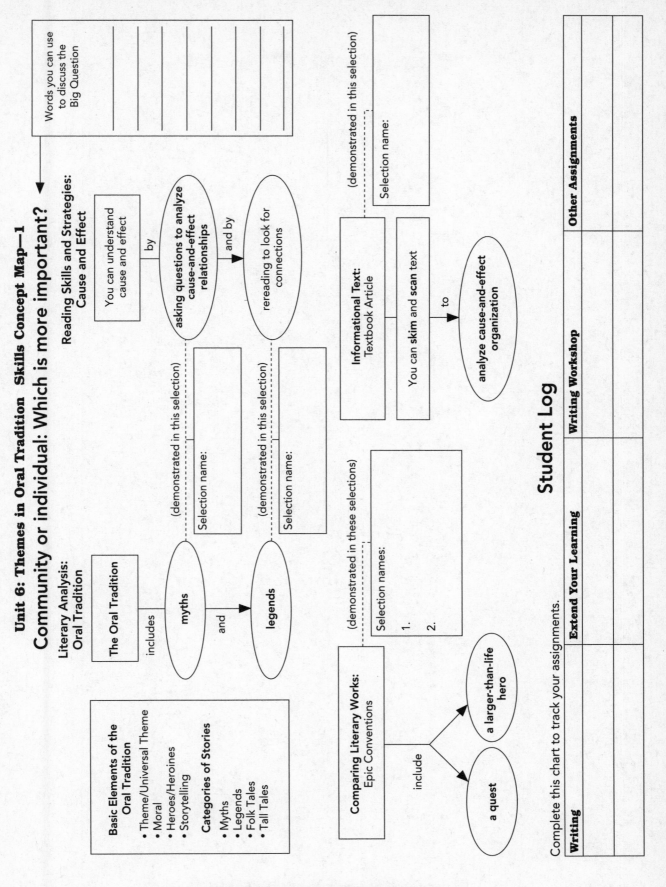

**Literary Analysis:**
Oral Tradition

The Oral Tradition → includes → myths → and → legends

(demonstrated in this selection)
Selection name: _____

(demonstrated in this selection)
Selection name: _____

**Basic Elements of the Oral Tradition**
• Theme/Universal Theme
• Moral
• Heroes/Heroines
• Storytelling

**Categories of Stories**
• Myths
• Legends
• Folk Tales
• Tall Tales

**Reading Skills and Strategies:**
Cause and Effect

You can understand cause and effect → by → asking questions to analyze cause-and-effect relationships → and by → rereading to look for connections

Words you can use to discuss the Big Question
_____
_____
_____
_____

**Informational Text:**
Textbook Article

You can skim and scan text → to → analyze cause-and-effect organization

(demonstrated in this selection)
Selection name: _____

**Comparing Literary Works:**
Epic Conventions → include → a larger-than-life hero / a quest

(demonstrated in these selections)
Selection names:
1.
2.

## Student Log

Complete this chart to track your assignments.

| Writing | Extend Your Learning | Writing Workshop | Other Assignments |
|---|---|---|---|
|  |  |  |  |

**5**

## "Grasshopper Logic," "The Other Frog Prince," and "duckbilled platypus vs. beefsnakstik®" by Jon Scieszka and Lane Smith
# Vocabulary Warm-up Word Lists

*Study these words from the selections. Then, complete the activities that follow.*

# Word List A

**bragged** [BRAGD] *v.* boasted
   The proud grandmother <u>bragged</u> about her talented grandchildren.

**fur** [FUR] *n.* the soft, thick hair covering many mammals
   The rabbit's <u>fur</u> was white with black spots.

**hopped** [HAHPT] *v.* jumped in a short, springing motion
   At the zoo, the kangaroo <u>hopped</u> over to its shelter.

**moral** [MAWR uhl] *n.* a lesson that is taught by a story, situation, or fable
   The <u>moral</u> of the story is to always tell the truth.

**pathetic** [puh THET ik] *adj.* causing feelings of pity
   The weak, hungry kittens were a <u>pathetic</u> sight.

**plenty** [PLEN tee] *n.* a lot of something
   We have <u>plenty</u> of milk and cheese in the refrigerator.

**promptly** [PRAHMPT lee] *adv.* quickly or without delay
   Billy <u>promptly</u> reported to work at seven in the morning.

**wiped** [WYPD] *v.* rubbed with something in order to clean something else
   We <u>wiped</u> the grime off the windshield wipers of the car.

# Word List B

**history** [HIS tuh ree] *n.* a class on recorded past events
   In <u>history</u>, we are learning about the Revolutionary War.

**logic** [LAHJ ik] *n.* a way of reasoning
   Mary used faulty <u>logic</u> to figure out how to read the map.

**mammals** [MAM uhlz] *n.* warm-blooded animals that have hair and nurse their young
   Camels are <u>mammals</u> that live in the desert.

**princess** [PRIN ses] *n.* the daughter of a king or queen
   The <u>princess</u> wore a beautiful gown to the ball.

**production** [pruh DUK shuhn] *n.* a work produced on the stage
   The Broadway <u>production</u> of the musical *Oklahoma* was a big success.

**rewrite** [ree RYT] *v.* to write again, often in a new form or using new words
   For English class, we must choose a story and <u>rewrite</u> the ending.

**spell** [SPEL] *n.* a charm or words that have magical power
   The good queen arrived and broke the magic <u>spell</u>.

**wicked** [WIK id] *adj.* evil, morally bad or wrong
   In the fairy tale, a <u>wicked</u> king ruled the land.

Name _____ Date _____

### "Grasshopper Logic," "The Other Frog Prince," and "duckbilled platypus vs. beefsnakstik®" by Jon Scieszka and Lane Smith
## Vocabulary Warm-up Exercises

**Exercise A** *Fill in each blank in the paragraph below with an appropriate word from Word List A. Use each word only once.*

Mark proudly [1] _____ to Al that he could beat him in a long bicycle race. Mark knew his fancy bike with [2] _____ of gears and a soft seat covered with [3] _____ could go fast. Mark thought that Al's bike was a [4] _____ piece of junk compared with his own bicycle. Al realized his bike was a simple one, but he was used to riding long distances on it. He agreed to race and both boys [5] _____ on their bicycles. Mark [6] _____ took the lead, but then mud splashed up and clogged his gears. He [7] _____ them off the best he could, but Al passed him and won the race. The [8] _____ of the story is that sometimes simple is best!

**Exercise B** *Revise each sentence so that the underlined vocabulary word is used in a way that makes sense. Be sure to keep the vocabulary word in your revision.*

**Example:** In <u>history</u>, we are learning many interesting facts about math equations.
*In <u>history</u>, we are learning many interesting facts about past events.*

1. When the <u>princess</u> arrived, the photographers didn't want to take her picture.
   _____

2. <u>Mammals</u>, such as horses and dogs, are cold-blooded animals.
   _____

3. The <u>wicked</u> boss always treated his employees fairly.
   _____

4. The <u>logic</u> of the witches' <u>spell</u> was easy to comprehend.
   _____

5. If you <u>rewrite</u> your assignment, it is a first draft of your work.
   _____

6. The <u>production</u> of the play is meant to be seen on film.
   _____

**8**

### "Grasshopper Logic," "The Other Frog Prince," and "duckbilled platypus vs. beefsnakstik®" by Jon Scieszka and Lane Smith
## Reading Warm-up A

*Read the following passage. Pay special attention to the underlined words. Then, read it again, and complete the activities. Use a separate sheet of paper for your written answers.*

Here is a very old fable from a storyteller named Aesop. It is the tale of "The Ant and the Grasshopper."

One hot day, a merry grasshopper sat in the shade sipping a cool drink and singing happily. He loved his idle life. Sometimes, as he sang a song, he also <u>hopped</u> about, doing a dance to celebrate the easy life of summer.

As the grasshopper played, a small ant crawled by. The ant was sweating and working very hard. The tiny insect was busily dragging an entire ear of corn down the road. "Stop a moment and rest," said the grasshopper to the ant. "It is a hot day. Why are you toiling away?" The ant <u>wiped</u> the sweat from his brow. He said, "A cold winter is coming. You had better get busy storing up some food for the days ahead." The grasshopper laughed and said, "Look around you. There is <u>plenty</u> to eat." The ant shook his head and continued on his way.

The grasshopper awoke from a pleasant nap only to find the ant dragging a huge chunk of rabbit <u>fur</u> down the road. "What have you there?" asked the grasshopper. "I found this fur in an old rabbit's nest," said the ant. "It will help me keep warm during the cold days of winter. You should go get some, too." The grasshopper said he saw no need for that. "My comfortable hammock and shady home are just perfect," he <u>bragged</u>. The ant shook his head and <u>promptly</u> continued on his way.

The warm days of summer gave way to fall. The cool fall days turned to cold, winter ones. The <u>pathetic</u> grasshopper shivered in the cold. He could find no food anywhere. The ant, however, was cozy, warm, and well fed in his house beneath the frozen ground.

<u>Moral</u>: Plan ahead for the days of necessity.

1. Circle the words that tell what the grasshopper did as he <u>hopped</u> about. Define *hopped*.

2. Circle the words that tell what the ant <u>wiped</u>. Use *wiped* in a sentence.

3. Underline the words that tell of what the grasshopper said there was <u>plenty</u>. What things do you think there are *plenty* of?

4. Circle the words that tell why the ant wanted the rabbit <u>fur</u>. What is *fur*?

5. Underline the words that tell what the grasshopper <u>bragged</u> about. Use *bragged* in a sentence.

6. Circle the words that tell what the ant <u>promptly</u> did. What have you ever done *promptly*?

7. Underline the words that describe more about why the grasshopper was <u>pathetic</u>. Use *pathetic* in a sentence.

8. Underline the words that tell the <u>moral</u> of the story. What is a *moral*?

Name _____   Date _____

# Reading Warm-up B

*Read the following passage. Pay special attention to the underlined words. Then, read it again, and complete the activities. Use a separate sheet of paper for your written answers.*

Are you familiar with fairy tales and legends? As little children, we often hear and read make-believe stories that have been handed down through time. These fantastic stories may have human characters in them. There may be a princess and a wicked witch; there may be a wizard who can cast a magic spell. Yet other fairy tales and folktales have animal characters. These animals talk and have other human traits. The Br'er Rabbit stories of African-Americans are an example of these. The main characters are mammals, such as a rabbit and a fox. In these tales, the two always try to outsmart each other.

Many people have studied fairy tales and legends from around the world. In presenting this topic's history, these scholars have found that many similar stories come from different parts of the world. People have tried to figure out how this occurred. Some believed that the tales spread from various parts of the world as explorers and conquerors moved from place to place. Perhaps their travels brought and mixed the tales of various cultures. The logic of this theory, however, has never been proved.

Other scholars believe that people throughout the world, despite having different cultures, religions, and histories, are alike. They all have the same basic need to express themselves through storytelling. These scholars believe the stories that grow out of this need show how much all people have in common.

Even today, many old stories that are based on legends and folktales are retold. Authors rewrite them and present them as novels and movies. The next time you see a production of a play that is based on a fairy tale or legend, enjoy it—and marvel at the idea that a story from long ago is still a part of today's culture.

1. Underline the words that tell where a character such as a princess may be found. What is a *princess*?

2. Circle the word that wicked modifies. Use *wicked* in a sentence.

3. Circle the words in the story that tell who might cast a magic spell. Who else might cast a *spell*?

4. Underline the words that give two examples of mammals that are main characters. Name a few other kinds of *mammals*.

5. Underline what scholars who have presented this topic's history have found. Define *history*.

6. Circle the words that tell whether the logic of the theory has or has not been proved. Use *logic* in a sentence.

7. Circle the words that tell what authors sometimes rewrite. Tell about something you have had to *rewrite* for a class project, or just for fun.

8. Underline the words that tell more about what a production is. Name a stage *production* that you have seen or would like to see.

**10**

**Jon Scieszka**
# Listening and Viewing

## Segment 1: Meet Jon Scieszka
- How did Jon Scieszka choose his audience? Scieszka reads all different types of literature.
- How do you think this helps him come up with writing ideas?

_____

_____

_____

_____

## Segment 2: Themes in the Oral Tradition
- Why is Jon Scieszka "amazed" by fairy tales, myths, and legends?
- Why do you think that the retelling of these stories over time is important?

_____

_____

_____

_____

## Segment 3: The Writing Process
- Who is Lane Smith, and how is he involved in Jon Scieszka's writing process?
- Why are illustrations important in fairy tales, myths, and fables like the stories that Jon Scieszka writes?

_____

_____

_____

_____

## Segment 4: The Rewards of Writing
- Why is being a writer rewarding to Jon Scieszka?
- Why do you think that reading is a valuable activity for young people in today's age of technology?

_____

_____

_____

_____

# Learning About the Oral Tradition

The sharing of stories, cultures, and ideas by word of mouth is called the **oral tradition.** Here are common elements of the oral tradition.

- The **theme** is a central idea, message, or insight that a story reveals.
- A **moral** is a lesson about life that is taught by a story.
- **Heroes** and **heroines** are larger-than-life figures whose virtues and deeds are often celebrated in stories from the oral tradition.
- **Storytelling** calls on the talents and personality of the teller to bring the narrative to life. Storytelling techniques include **hyperbole,** or the use of exaggeration or overstatement, and **personification,** the giving of human characteristics to a non-human subject.

Many stories have been written down for readers. Categories of stories in the oral tradition that have been committed to paper include the following.

- **Myths** are ancient tales that describe the actions of gods, goddesses, and the heroes who interact with them.
- **Legends** are traditional stories about the past. They are based on real-life events or people, but they are more fiction than fact.
- **Folk tales** tell about ordinary people. These stories reveal the traditions and values of a culture and teach a lesson about life.
- **Tall tales** are folk tales that contain hyperbole.
- **Fables** are brief animal stories that contain personification. Fables often end with a moral or lesson.
- **Epics** are long narrative poems about a hero who engages in a dangerous journey.

**A. DIRECTIONS:** *The following items are elements of stories in the oral tradition. Decide which of the two terms matches the preceding description. Underline your choice.*

1. A woman spins cloth out of gold.                    hyperbole   personification
2. The god Apollo drives his chariot across the sky.                    myth   legend
3. Baseball great Babe Ruth hits the ball into another state.                    fable   legend
4. The sun refuses to shine on an evil character's birthday.     personification   theme
5. It is best to be prepared.                    moral   hero

**B. DIRECTIONS:** *On the lines below, write a plot summary for an original fable. Include one or more animal characters, and include an example of personification. End your fable with a moral. Use a separate sheet of paper if more space is needed.*

_____

_____

_____

## "Grasshopper Logic," "The Other Frog Prince," and "duckbilled platypus vs. beefsnakstik®" by Jon Scieszka and Lane Smith
# Model Selection: The Oral Tradition

Jon Scieszka entertains readers with his comical versions of traditional **fairy tales** and **fables. Fables** are brief animal stories that contain personification. Fables often end with a moral or lesson. These three short selections are humorous examples of stories in the **oral tradition**—the sharing of stories, cultures, and ideas by word of mouth. Elements of the oral tradition include the following.

- The **theme** is a central idea, message, or insight that a story reveals.
- A **moral** is a lesson about life that is taught by a story. An example of a moral is "Hard work leads to success."
- **Hyperbole** is a deliberate exaggeration or overstatement. It is often used to create humor. For example, a man might be as strong as an ox.
- **Personification** is the granting of human characteristics to a nonhuman subject. This would include a talking fox or an angry tree.

**A. DIRECTIONS:** *Answer the following questions.*

1. Give an example of hyperbole from "Grasshopper Logic." Tell why it is a hyperbole.

_____

_____

2. How does the ending of "The Other Frog Prince" differ from the ending of the traditional "Frog Prince" fairy tale?

_____

_____

3. What types of characters are in "duckbilled platypus vs. beefsnakstik®," and in what specific ways are they examples of personification?

_____

_____

**B. DIRECTIONS:** *On the lines below, describe the specific ways in which the grasshopper and his mother talk and act like humans.*

_____

_____

_____

_____

_____

**"Grasshopper Logic," "The Other Frog Prince,"** and
**"Duckbilled Platypus vs. BeefSnakStik®"** by Jon Scieszka and Lane Smith

# Open-Book Test

**Short Answer** *Write your responses to the questions in this section on the lines provided.*

1. You are listening to a story that describes a difficult journey across the country taken by a family. What might be the theme of this story? Explain your answer, using your understanding of the concept of *theme.*

   _____

   _____

   _____

2. You are telling a tall tale in which the main character "eats 20 pancakes as a snack before sitting down to breakfast." What technique is being used in the tall tale to describe the character's behavior? Define the technique in your answer.

   _____

   _____

3. In a famous fable, one animal has prepared for winter by storing away food, but the other animal is completely unprepared. What device will probably be used to end this fable? Include in your answer an explanation of the device's purpose.

   _____

   _____

4. Imagine hearing a tale called "The Talking Stones of Ancient Rome." What techniques of the oral tradition would you expect to hear in the tale? Give and define two techniques.

   _____

   _____

   _____

5. In "Grasshopper Logic," Grasshopper's mother "freaked out." Is her reaction reasonable? Explain your answer, using details from the fable.

   _____

   _____

   _____

6. What about "Grasshopper Logic" makes it a good story to tell orally? Use examples from the fable to explain your response.

   _____

   _____

   _____

Name _____  Date _____

7. Why does the princess respond positively to the frog in "The Other Frog Prince"? Support your response with a detail from the fable.

_____

_____

_____

8. Early in "The Other Frog Prince," the writer gives a clue that shows the frog may be up to some trickery. Find the phrase that tells you that the frog is working hard to gain the princess's sympathy.

_____

_____

_____

9. Use details from the story to compare the duckbilled platypus and BeefSnakStik. List qualities that are alike and different. Then, explain why you find one character more admirable than the other.

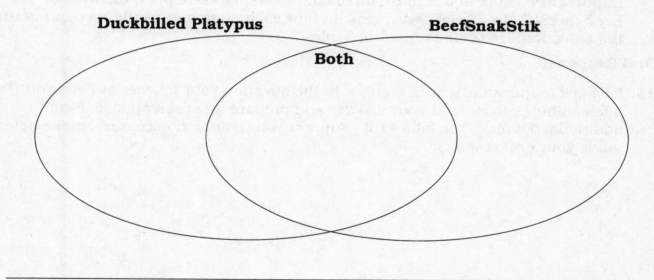

**Duckbilled Platypus**          **Both**          **BeefSnakStik**

_____

_____

10. Reread the moral of "Duckbilled Platypus vs. BeefSnakStik®." What other moral could be applied to the tale? Consider what kind of "stuff" each character has.

_____

_____

_____

## Essay

*Write an extended response to the question of your choice or to the question or questions your teacher assigns you.*

11. Personification is giving human characteristics to nonhuman subjects. In a brief essay, discuss John Scieszka's use of personification in "Grasshopper Logic" and "Duckbilled Platypus. . . ." Explain how personification in the stories adds to the humor. Use details from both tales.

12. Imagine "The Other Frog Prince" told from the princess's point of view. In a brief essay, tell how the fairy tale would be different. Include details about what the princess would be thinking and feeling. Then, write a moral for the tale.

13. John Scieszka says he uses humor in his work to keep listeners connected to the story. In a brief essay, explore the use of humor in "Grasshopper Logic," "The Other Frog Prince," and "Duckbilled Platypus. . . ." Explain which story you found most humorous, and why. Use details from the stories to support your ideas.

14. **Thinking About the Big Question: Community or Individual: Which is more important?** Think about these three characters: Grasshopper, the frog, or BeefSnakStik. In a brief essay, explain how each character would respond to the Big Question. Use details from the fables.

## Oral Response

15. Go back to question 1, 5, 9, or 10 or to the question your teacher assigns you. Take a few minutes to expand your answer and prepare an oral response. Find additional details in the fables that support your points. If necessary, make notes to guide your oral response.

Name _____ Date _____

"Grasshopper Logic," "The Other Frog Prince,"
and "duckbilled platypus vs. beefsnakstik®" by Jon Scieszka and Lane Smith
## Selection Test A

**Learning About the Oral Tradition** *Identify the letter of the choice that best answers the question.*

_____ 1. Which term names the central idea or message that a story reveals?
   A. theme
   B. legend
   C. personification
   D. myth

_____ 2. Which term names a lesson about life that is taught by a story?
   A. myth
   B. legend
   C. moral
   D. conflict

_____ 3. Which storytelling technique allows an animal to talk and act like a human?
   A. personification
   B. metaphor
   C. hyperbole
   D. onomatopoeia

_____ 4. Which of the following is an example of hyperbole?
   A. a story about ancient gods
   B. a bird that builds a cozy nest
   C. a man who solves a big problem
   D. a man who is as tall as a tree

_____ 5. Which statement about stories that are part of the oral tradition is true?
   A. All of these stories appear in books.
   B. Each one features a talking animal that learns an important lesson about life.
   C. Each one has been passed down by word of mouth.
   D. Each one features a magical or evil character, such as a wicked witch.

## Critical Reading

____ 6. In "Grasshopper Logic," what did Grasshopper want to do right after school?
   A. go out with his friends
   B. finish his homework
   C. rewrite some myths
   D. spend time with his mother

____ 7. What hyperbole, or exaggeration, occurs in "Grasshopper Logic"?
   A. Grasshopper's height
   B. Grasshopper's homework assignment
   C. Mom Grasshopper's angry words
   D. Grasshopper's friends

____ 8. In "The Other Frog Prince," why does the frog speak to the princess?
   A. He wants to become a prince.
   B. He thinks she is very beautiful.
   C. He is lost and needs directions.
   D. He is really a wicked witch in disguise.

____ 9. Why does the princess help the frog?
   A. He promises her money.
   B. She wants to trick him.
   C. She feels sorry for him.
   D. He is covered with slime.

____ 10. What happens after the princess kisses the frog in "The Other Frog Prince"?
   A. They live happily ever after.
   B. He turns into a wicked witch.
   C. He turns into a handsome prince and rewards her with a necklace.
   D. He says that he was only kidding and jumps back into the pond.

____ 11. Which statement about "duckbilled platypus vs. beefsnakstik®" is true?
   A. It is a fable.
   B. It is a myth.
   C. It is a folk tale.
   D. It is a legend.

____ 12. What are Platypus and BeefSnakStik® doing during this story?
  A. competing in a race
  B. bragging about their features
  C. listening to a story
  D. trying to improve themselves

____ 13. According to this story, what is true about BeefSnakStik®?
  A. He has webbed feet.
  B. He is a hyperbole.
  C. He is under the spell of a witch.
  D. He contains many food additives.

____ 14. The platypus brags and the frog plays a trick on the princess. What type of storytelling technique do these characters exemplify?
  A. hyperbole
  B. metaphor
  C. moral
  D. personification

____ 15. Which statement is true about "Grasshopper Logic," "The Other Frog Prince," and "duckbilled platypus vs. beefsnakstik®"?
  A. Two are fables, and one is a folk tale.
  B. Two are legends, and one is a fable.
  C. All three are myths.
  D. All three are folk tales.

**Essay**

16. In a brief essay, describe how you think the princess feels at the end of "The Other Frog Prince." What did the princess expect would happen? Did the ending differ from her expectations?

17. What characteristics of the oral tradition can be found in "Grasshopper Logic"? In a brief essay, describe these characteristics and techniques using examples from the story. Think about what category the story falls under. Does the story teach a lesson or moral? If so, what is it?

18. **Thinking About the Big Question: Community or individual: Which is more important?** Think about these three characters from this section: Grasshopper, the frog, or BeefSnakStik. In a brief essay, explain how each character would respond to the Big Question. Use details from the fables to support your answer.

**"Grasshopper Logic," "The Other Frog Prince," and "duckbilled platypus vs. beefsnakstik®"** by Jon Scieszka and Lane Smith

## Selection Test B

**Learning About the Oral Tradition** *Identify the letter of the choice that best completes the statement or answers the question.*

____ 1. An ancient tale about Ares, the god of war, is an example of a
   A. fable.
   B. folk tale.
   C. legend.
   D. myth.

____ 2. Which statement is true about every story's <u>theme</u>?
   A. It is a creative explanation, such as "why leopards have spots."
   B. It teaches a lesson, such as "Always tell the truth."
   C. It is a central idea, message, or insight about life.
   D. It is an exaggeration, often used to add humor to the story.

____ 3. A dog who wears a suit and works in an office is an example of
   A. personification.
   B. moral.
   C. hyperbole.
   D. theme.

____ 4. This type of literature is called the <u>oral</u> <u>tradition</u> because it includes stories that
   A. are about animals.
   B. teach lessons about traditional values.
   C. have been passed down through word of mouth.
   D. often include magical or evil characters.

____ 5. The lesson about life that is taught by a story is called the
   A. hyperbole.
   B. moral.
   C. legend.
   D. instruction.

____ 6. Which is the BEST definition of a <u>tall</u> <u>tale</u>?
   A. a myth that contains personification
   B. a legend that features an evil character
   C. a folk tale that has animal characters
   D. a folk tale that contains hyperbole

**Critical Reading**

____ 7. In "Grasshopper Logic," Grasshopper tells his mother that he has
   A. a large assignment due tomorrow.
   B. a small assignment due tomorrow.
   C. no school tomorrow.
   D. no homework due tomorrow.

____ 8. Grasshopper's mother got upset because
    A. Grasshopper was late for dinner.
    B. Grasshopper lost his backpack.
    C. Grasshopper did a sloppy and incomplete job on his homework.
    D. Grasshopper's homework assignment was very large.

____ 9. When Grasshopper's mom asks him how long he has known about the assignment, he says,
    A. "I don't know."
    B. "Since last week."
    C. "Since this morning."
    D. "I can't remember."

____ 10. "The Other Frog Prince" is an example of a
    A. legend.
    B. epic.
    C. myth.
    D. fable.

____ 11. When the frog speaks to the princess in "The Other Frog Prince," she starts to jump up and run because
    A. he is ugly and covered with warts.
    B. she is frightened by the witch.
    C. she is very surprised that a frog can speak.
    D. she has a feeling that he will try to trick her.

____ 12. In "The Other Frog Prince," the princess feels sorry for the frog because
    A. she knows how wicked the evil witch is.
    B. he speaks in such a sad and pathetic voice.
    C. he is covered with frog slime.
    D. most frogs have very lonely lives.

____ 13. The humor at the end of "The Other Frog Prince" is caused by
    A. the unexpected ending, in which the frog says that he was only kidding.
    B. the unexpected ending, in which the frog turns into an ugly prince.
    C. the joke that the princess plays on the frog.
    D. the funny joke that the princess tells.

____ 14. The story "duckbilled platypus vs. beefsnakstik®" is an example of a
    A. legend.
    B. fable.
    C. myth.
    D. hyperbole.

____ 15. The realistic elements in "duckbilled platypus vs. beefsnakstik®" involve
    A. the facts and details about what each character has or can do.
    B. the voices of the characters.
    C. the way in which the characters argue and reason with each other.
    D. the proud attitude of the platypus.

_____ 16. Which statement *best* sums up the lesson of "duckbilled platypus vs. beefsnakstik®"?
  A. The platypus is a very strange animal.
  B. BeefSnakStik® is a wholesome and delicious snack food.
  C. Animals must be careful regarding what they eat.
  D. Do not be too proud about how "special" you are.

_____ 17. Which statement *best* describes BeefSnakStik®'s attitude toward the platypus?
  A. He is not impressed with what the platypus says about himself.
  B. He thinks that the platypus is really weird.
  C. He thinks that the platypus is under the spell of a witch.
  D. He knows that the platypus has more important features than he has himself.

_____ 18. Which is the *best* example of personification from Scieszka's tales?
  A. a sympathetic princess who is easily fooled
  B. a platypus who brags
  C. a frog who jumps out of the water
  D. a beefsnakstik® that contains soy protein concentrate

_____ 19. Which character from Scieszka's tales has the *best* reason to feel surprised and tricked at the end of the story?
  A. the platypus
  B. the grasshopper
  C. the princess
  D. the beefsnakstik®

**Essay**

20. Write a summary of "The Other Frog Prince" from the princess's point of view. Make sure that you show her thoughts and feelings about the frog and what takes place in the story.

21. If "Grasshopper Logic" were to continue, what do you think would happen next? How will Mom Grasshopper react? Will Grasshopper learn his lesson? Describe your prediction in a brief essay and support it with details from the story.

22. In a brief essay, describe the moral of "The Other Frog Prince." Use details from the story to support your response.

23. **Thinking About the Big Question: Community or individual: Which is more important?** Think about these three characters: Grasshopper, the frog, and BeefSnakStik. In a brief essay, explain how each character would respond to the Big Question. Use details from the fables.

# Vocabulary Warm-up Word Lists

*Study these words from "Icarus and Daedalus." Then, complete the activities that follow.*

## Word List A

**attempt** [uh TEMPT] *n.* an effort; a try
Jan was finally successful in her <u>attempt</u> to score a goal.

**captive** [KAP tiv] *adj.* held prisoner
The <u>captive</u> soldier was held in a prison camp until after the war.

**delay** [di LAY] *n.* a length of waiting time
The sick woman needed to see a doctor without <u>delay</u>.

**fashioned** [FASH uhnd] *v.* made or created
The potter <u>fashioned</u> a beautiful vase out of clay.

**favor** [FAY ver] *n.* an approving or supportive attitude
Everyone hoped to win the king's <u>favor</u>.

**glimpse** [GLIMPS] *n.* a brief, quick view
We caught a <u>glimpse</u> of the president through the window of the train.

**liberty** [LIB er tee] *n.* freedom
Americans have the <u>liberty</u> to move around the country.

**thirst** [thurst] *n.* a longing or strong desire for something
People who have a <u>thirst</u> for fame are often overachievers.

## Word List B

**aloft** [uh LAWFT] *adj.* up in the air
The hot air balloon was <u>aloft</u> high above the trees.

**architect** [AHR ki tekt] *n.* someone who designs buildings
The <u>architect</u> examined the plans for the new building.

**cautions** [KAW shuhnz] *n.* words of warning
Will listened to his mother's <u>cautions</u> about driving too fast.

**imprisoned** [im PRIZ uhnd] *v.* put in prison; locked up
The criminal was <u>imprisoned</u> for 20 years to pay for her crime.

**overtook** [oh ver TOOK] *v.* caught up to; came upon suddenly
The cowboy <u>overtook</u> the runaway bull and roped it.

**quench** [KWENCH] *v.* to satisfy
Drinking a glass of cold lemonade is a great way to <u>quench</u> your thirst.

**sustained** [suh STAYND] *v.* carried the weight of; supported
The freight elevator <u>sustained</u> a maximum load of 1,000 pounds.

**wavered** [WAY verd] *v.* moved back and forth
The bicycle <u>wavered</u> a few times until the rider found his balance.

Unit 6 Resources: Themes in the Oral Tradition
**23**

Name _____ Date _____

**"Icarus and Daedalus"** by Josephine Preston Peabody
# Vocabulary Warm-up Exercises

**Exercise A** *Fill in each blank in the paragraph below with an appropriate word from Word List A. Use each word only once.*

I caught a [1] _____ of a flash of color beating against the garage window and took a closer look. A hummingbird was [2] _____ inside. In its [3] _____ for freedom, the tiny creature flew repeatedly toward the light and into the window. I had to rescue it without a moment's [4] _____ before it broke its neck. Quickly, I [5] _____ a net out of badminton netting and two fishing poles.

My first [6] [1] _____ to catch the bird was clumsy, but then on the second try it flew right into the net. I released it outside. Although the bird was at [7] _____ to fly away, it paused in midair before my eyes. It seemed just like a monarch bestowing his [8] _____ to show his thanks.

**Exercise B** *Revise each sentence so that the underlined vocabulary word is used in a logical way.*

**Example:** As soon as his plane was <u>aloft</u> the pilot put away his flight map.
  *As soon as his plane was <u>aloft</u>, the pilot took out his flight map.*

1. The company hired an <u>architect</u> to design the new phone system.
   _____

2. The <u>imprisoned</u> man enjoyed his freedom.
   _____

3. The customer ordered eggs and bacon to <u>quench</u> his thirst.
   _____

4. Amy listened to her mom's <u>cautions</u> and always wore a straw hat when riding her bike.
   _____

5. The acrobat <u>sustained</u> three other acrobats on his shoulders thanks to his lack of strength.
   _____

6. The athlete lost the race after he <u>overtook</u> the lead runner at the last minute.
   _____

7. When the car wheels <u>wavered</u>, Michael increased the speed.
   _____

Unit 6 Resources: Themes in the Oral Tradition
© Pearson Education, Inc. All rights reserved.
**24**

**"Icarus and Daedalus"** by Josephine Preston Peabody
# Reading Warm-up A

*Read the following passage. Pay special attention to the underlined words. Then, read it again, and complete the activities. Use a separate sheet of paper for your written answers.*

Centuries before the Wright Brothers invented the airplane, humans had tried to fly. Every <u>attempt</u> failed, but that did not stop people from trying. Watching birds fly through the air gave humans a <u>glimpse</u> of unimaginable freedom. They longed for the <u>liberty</u> of flight.

Then, during the 15<sup>th</sup> century, a man with a <u>thirst</u> for invention turned his attention to flight. This man with a desire to create new things was Leonardo da Vinci. Like many before him, Leonardo focused on the wings of birds. He designed flying machines with bird-like, flapping wings. None of them ever got off the ground. His ideas were good, but the materials he needed didn't exist.

Then, after a <u>delay</u> of 500 years, Leonardo's theory finally took flight. On December 2, 2003, a man named Angelo D'Arrigo flew a model of Leonardo's flying machine, the *Piuma*, or feather. The event took place in the Italian town where Leonardo was born.

To build the machine, D'Arrigo and his team followed Leonardo's drawings in all ways but one. They <u>fashioned</u> the model out of aluminum tubes and a synthetic fiber. These modern materials made the model about 170 pounds lighter than in Leonardo's original design.

The *Piuma* was tested in a wind tunnel. "At [almost 22 miles] per hour, I took off and flew," said D'Arrigo. "The weight of my body was totally carried by the *Piuma*." The test flight lasted for two hours.

The event won the <u>favor</u> of scholars who studied the works of Leonardo. "The idea of his great dream finally coming true really touched me," said one who expressed his approval.

Leonardo dared to think beyond the limits of his age. Unfortunately, his ideas were <u>captive</u>, held prisoners of time. Finally, one of his most daring ideas has been set free.

1. Circle the word that tells what happened to every <u>attempt</u> to fly. Rewrite the sentence, using a synonym for *attempt*.

2. Circle the words that tell what birds gave people a <u>glimpse</u> of. Write the meaning of *glimpse*.

3. Underline the word that is a synonym for <u>liberty</u>. Use the word *liberty* in a sentence.

4. Circle the word that is a synonym for <u>thirst</u>. Use the synonym to write about something you *thirst* for.

5. Underline the words that tell how long the <u>delay</u> was before Leonardo's theory took flight. What does *delay* mean?

6. Underline the names of the materials from which the model was <u>fashioned</u>. Give a synonym for *fashioned*.

7. Circle the word that is a synonym of <u>favor</u>. Use the word *favor* in a sentence.

8. Circle the phrase that means the opposite of <u>captive</u>. Give an example of when a person might be *captive*.

Name _____ Date _____

**"Icarus and Daedalus"** by Josephine Preston Peabody
# Reading Warm-up B

*Read the following passage. Pay special attention to the underlined words. Then, read it again, and complete the activities. Use a separate sheet of paper for your written answers.*

Once the plane had soared <u>aloft</u>—up, up, and up—and leveled out, Beckman released his grip on the arms of his seat. Oh, how he hated flying. Feeling <u>imprisoned</u> in a cramped airplane cabin while traveling thousands of feet above the earth was *not* his idea of a good time. Each time he needed to travel cross-country, his choice of transportation <u>wavered</u> between flying and taking the train. To save time, he always ended up flying and he loathed every minute of it.

"Is this your first flight?" the flight attendant asked sweetly.

"Oh no, I fly all the time," Beckman replied, looking decidedly green around the eyes. "Could you bring me some sparkling water? I need to <u>quench</u> my thirst."

"Certainly!" The attendant knew he meant "to settle my stomach," but she just smiled and trotted off.

It was embarrassing. A grown man, an <u>architect</u> who designed billion-dollar buildings, afraid of flying. He knew his fears were groundless—no pun intended! People flew every day. The pilots know their stuff. He would be okay.

He had watched the safety announcement before take-off. A man smiled from the TV screen and reviewed the emergency procedures. "In the event of wind turbulence, please remain seated with your seat belt buckled. Locate the emergency exit nearest to your seat, . . ."

Beckman took the man's <u>cautions</u> to heart. He checked his seat belt: buckled. He checked the emergency exit: three rows back. The flight attendant arrived with his sparkling water. Beckman opened a magazine, settled back, and tried to read. As he looked out the window, he wondered how the air <u>sustained</u> the weight of the plane. Soon, sleep <u>overtook</u> him. He was still sleeping when the plane landed.

"Well," he thought when he awoke, "that wasn't so bad, after all!"

1. Circle the words that hint at the meaning of <u>aloft</u>. Give an example of something other than a plane that goes *aloft*.

2. Underline the words that tell where Beckman felt <u>imprisoned</u>. Write about a place where you have felt *imprisoned*.

3. Underline the words that describe how Beckman's choices <u>wavered</u>. Write a phrase that means the same thing as *wavered*.

4. Circle the words that tell what Beckman requested to <u>quench</u> his thirst. Write the meaning of *quench*.

5. Underline the words that tell what Beckman did as an <u>architect</u>. Write a sentence using the word *architect*.

6. Underline the words that tell how Beckman took the man's <u>cautions</u> to heart. Write about some *cautions* you take seriously.

7. Circle the word that tells what <u>sustained</u> the weight of the plane. Give a synonym for *sustained*.

8. Circle the word that tells what <u>overtook</u> Beckman. Write the meaning for *overtook*.

Name _____ Date _____

# Writing About the Big Question

## Community or individual: Which is more important?

**Big Question Vocabulary**

| | | | | |
|---|---|---|---|---|
| common | community | culture | custom | diversity |
| duty | environment | ethnicity | family | group |
| individual | team | tradition | unify | unique |

**A.** *Use one or more words from the list above to complete each sentence.*

1. I used a lot of paper printing drafts of a _____ research project.

2. My teammate was concerned about the impact on the _____ .

3. We decided it was our _____ to recycle.

4. That way we could balance our _____ needs with those of the earth.

**B.** *Follow the directions in responding to each of the items below.*

1. Describe a time when you became so focused on getting what you wanted that you failed to consider the consequences of your actions.

   _____

   _____

2. Write two sentences explaining how the preceding experience affected those around you, such as friends or family. Use at least two of the Big Question vocabulary words.

   _____

   _____

   _____

**C.** *Complete the sentence below. Then, write a short paragraph in which you connect this experience to the big question.*

When an individual becomes too focused on his or her own desires, _____

   _____

   _____

   _____

   _____

**27**

Name _____ Date _____

*"Icarus and Daedalus"* by Josephine Preston Peabody
# Reading: Ask Questions to Analyze Cause-and-Effect Relationships

A **cause** is an event, an action, or a feeling that produces an **effect,** or result. In some literary works, multiple causes result in one single effect. In other works, a single cause results in multiple effects. Effects can also become causes for events that follow. The linking of causes and effects propels the action forward.

As you read, **ask questions** such as "What happened?" and "What will happen as a result of this?" **to analyze cause-and-effect relationships.**

**DIRECTIONS:** *Use the following graphic organizer to analyze some of the cause-and-effect relationships in "Icarus and Daedalus." The first response has been filled in as an example. Where there is no box in which to write the question you would ask yourself, ask the question mentally, and then write the effect in the next box.*

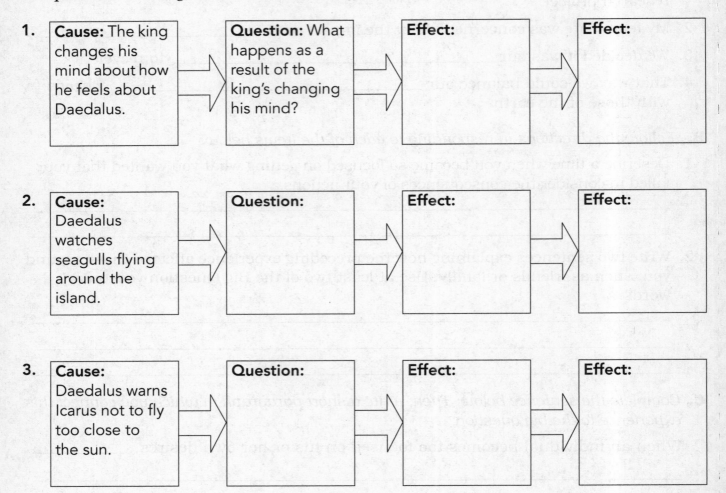

1. **Cause:** The king changes his mind about how he feels about Daedalus.    **Question:** What happens as a result of the king's changing his mind?    **Effect:**    **Effect:**

2. **Cause:** Daedalus watches seagulls flying around the island.    **Question:**    **Effect:**    **Effect:**

3. **Cause:** Daedalus warns Icarus not to fly too close to the sun.    **Question:**    **Effect:**    **Effect:**

Name _____ Date _____

"Icarus and Daedalus" by Josephine Preston Peabody
# Literary Analysis: Myth

Since time began, people have tried to understand the world around them. Ancient peoples created **myths**—stories that explain natural occurrences and express beliefs about right and wrong. Every culture has its own collection of myths, or *mythology*. In many myths, gods and goddesses have human traits, and human heroes have superhuman traits. Myths explore universal themes and explain the world in human terms.

Most myths perform some of the following functions:

• explain natural occurrences
• express beliefs about right and wrong
• show gods or goddesses with human traits
• show human heroes with superhuman traits
• explore universal themes

Not all myths perform all of those functions, however. "Icarus and Daedalus" illustrates only a few of them.

**DIRECTIONS:** *Read each excerpt from "Icarus and Daedalus" that follows, and answer the question about the functions of a myth that the excerpt illustrates.*

Among all those mortals who grew so wise that they learned the secrets of the gods, none was more cunning than Daedalus.

1. Which function of a myth does the excerpt illustrate? How can you tell?

_____
_____

"Remember," said the father, "never to fly very low or very high."

2. Which function of a myth does the excerpt illustrate? How can you tell?

_____
_____

The nearest island he named Icaria, in memory of the child; but he, in heavy grief, went to the temple of Apollo in Sicily, and there hung up his wings as an offering. Never again did he attempt to fly.

3. Which function of a myth does the excerpt illustrate? How can you tell?

_____
_____

Name _____  Date _____

**"Icarus and Daedalus"** by Josephine Preston Peabody
# Vocabulary Builder

**Word List**

aloft    captivity    liberty    reel    sustained    vacancy

**A. DIRECTIONS:** *Write the letter of the word that means the same or about the same as the word from the Word List.*

____ 1. vacancy
   A. property
   B. appointment
   C. emptiness
   D. discount

____ 2. sustained
   A. supported
   B. starved
   C. deprived
   D. competed

____ 3. liberty
   A. dependence
   B. freedom
   C. history
   D. agreement

____ 4. aloft
   A. in the air
   B. still
   C. trapped
   D. on the ground

____ 5. reel
   A. punch
   B. sing
   C. unravel
   D. stagger

____ 6. captivity
   A. exterior
   B. prison
   C. resort
   D. arrangement

**B. WORD STUDY:** *The Latin root -vac- means "empty." Answer each of the following questions using one of these words containing -vac-: vacancy, vacuous, vacuum.*

1. Why would you look for a *vacancy* sign if you needed to rent a room?

   _____

2. What has been done to a jar that is *vacuum* packed?

   _____

3. Why would a *vacuous* TV show not be worth watching?

   _____

**"Icarus and Daedalus"** by Josephine Preston Peabody

# Enrichment: Greek Gods and Modern English

The names of many of the Greek gods have entered the English language. For example, Gaea was the goddess of the earth, and we use her name in *geography, geology,* and *geometry,* words that describe basic ways of investigating and mapping the earth. All of those words contain the Greek root *-ge-,* meaning "earth." Study this list of names from Greek mythology:

| Name | Identification |
|------|----------------|
| Chaos | Time of confusion and formlessness, from which Gaea was created |
| Titans | Group of giant gods |
| Atlas | Titan who was forced to support the world on his shoulders |
| Cronus | Titan who was the god of time |
| Hercules | Half-mortal god known for his immense strength |
| Pluto | God of the underworld |

**A. DIRECTIONS:** *Use a word from the box to complete each sentence.*

> Titanic   chronological   atlas   plutonium   Herculean   chaotic

1. A book of maps is called a(n) _____.

2. Someone who is very strong is said to have _____ strength.

3. The _____, a ship launched in 1912, was the largest vessel of its time.

4. Events placed in the order in which they happened are in _____ order.

5. A confused, disorganized situation may be described as _____.

6. The element named for the planet farthest from the sun is _____.

**B. DIRECTIONS:** *Use the six words from the box in sentences of your own. Try to use* Titanic *and* atlas *in one sentence,* chronological *and* chaotic *in a second sentence, and* plutonium *and* Herculean *in a third. Consult a dictionary if you are unsure of a word's meaning.*

_____

_____

_____

_____

_____

Name _____ Date _____

"**Icarus and Daedalus**" by Josephine Preston Peabody
# Open-Book Test

**Short Answer** *Write your responses to the questions in this section on the lines provided.*

1. In the first paragraph of "Icarus and Daedalus," the author provides background that sets up the rest of the story. How do you know that Daedalus is not one of the gods? Use a detail from the paragraph to explain your answer.

   _____

   _____

2. At the beginning of "Icarus and Daedalus," Daedalus falls out of favor with King Minos. Why does the King imprison Daedalus? Use information from the second paragraph of the myth to help you answer.

   _____

   _____

3. At the beginning of "Icarus and Daedalus," Daedalus becomes inspired to create an escape plan for himself and his son. How does he gain inspiration? Use details from the beginning of "Icarus and Daedalus" to support your response.

   _____

   _____

4. Think about the effects of Daedalus making wings. Explain what the immediate effect is and what the long-term effect is. Use details from the myth in your response.

   _____

   _____

5. Why did Daedalus feel that he needed to warn Icarus about how to use his new wings? Use information from the middle of the story to support your answer.

   _____

   _____

6. In the middle of "Icarus and Daedalus," how does the author give the reader a hint that a problem may present itself? Use details from the middle of the story to support your answer.

   _____

   _____

7. In the middle of "Icarus and Daedalus," people on the ground see Daedalus and Icarus flying above them. How does their reaction show that this story is a myth? Explain your answer, using details from the middle of the story.

_____

_____

8. When the father and son start to fly in "Icarus and Daedalus," they experience the vacancy of the air around them. Why does this experience make them a little uncomfortable at first? Use your understanding of the word *vacancy* to explain your answer.

_____

_____

_____

9. Trace the events that lead to Icarus' fall in "Icarus and Daedalus." Use the graphic organizer to show the events that end in his disaster. Then, on the line, tell the main cause of Icarus' death.

**Icarus' Fall**

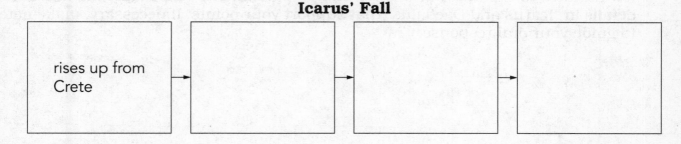

_____

10. Toward the end of "Icarus and Daedalus," Icarus feels that his body is sustained by the wind. How is his experience like that of a bird? Use your understanding of the word *sustained* to help you answer.

_____

_____

**Essay**

*Write an extended response to the question of your choice or to the question or questions your teacher assigns you.*

11. Which character is more at fault in "Icarus and Daedalus"? In a brief essay, explore the character that seems to carry the greater responsibility for Icarus' disaster. Think of the role that Daedalus plays as the father who plans the escape. Think of the role that Icarus plays as a son who longs to be free. Use details from the myth to strengthen your opinion.

12. How is Icarus responsible for his own death? In a brief essay, describe how he led himself to his doom. Include in your answer an opinion about whether he had had enough experience with the wings before he flew to his escape. Use details from the myth for support.

13. In "Icarus and Daedalus," Daedalus' escape plan is based on constructing wings for himself and his son. Given the circumstances of his plight and the time period in which he lived, does this seem to be a reasonable idea? Write an essay that offers your opinion. Use details from the myth to support your points.

14. **Thinking About the Big Question: Community or Individual: Which is more important?** How does the larger community portrayed in "Icarus and Daedalus" have an impact on the fate of the two main characters? Write an essay in which you analyze the community in which they live and discuss its importance to them. Include in your answer an understanding of both communities of which they are a part—the community of the gods and the community of mortals.

**Oral Response**

15. Go back to question 4, 6, or 9 or to the question your teacher assigns you. Take a few minutes to expand your answer and prepare an oral response. Find additional details in "Icarus and Daedalus" that support your points. If necessary, make notes to guide your oral response.

**"Icarus and Daedalus"** by Josephine Preston Peabody
# Selection Test A

**Critical Reading** *Identify the letter of the choice that best answers the question.*

_____ 1. In "Icarus and Daedalus," what event has caused Daedalus to be locked in the tower?
   A. He is being punished for trapping the king in his Labyrinth.
   B. The king changed his attitude and no longer favors him.
   C. He is being punished for playing tricks on the royal court.
   D. The king grew angry with him for not working fast enough.

_____ 2. Daedalus is described in "Icarus and Daedalus" as cunning (resourceful). Given that information, what can the reader predict he will do after being imprisoned on the island?
   A. plan a way to escape
   B. grow to like the island
   C. seek advice from his son
   D. write a poem criticizing the king

_____ 3. In "Icarus and Daedalus," why does Daedalus associate sea-gulls with liberty?
   A. A sea-gull guards him in his prison cell.
   B. Sea-gulls can fly freely to and from the island.
   C. He thinks that all sea creatures are free.
   D. Sea-gulls carry messages from him to Icarus.

_____ 4. In "Icarus and Daedalus," what is the relationship between the two main characters?
   A. They are cousins.
   B. They are king and subject.
   C. They are friends.
   D. They are father and son.

_____ 5. According to Daedalus in "Icarus and Daedalus," what will be the effect if Icarus flies too low?
   A. The sun's heat will melt his wings.
   B. The earth's fog will weigh him down.
   C. The tower guards will capture him.
   D. His wings will hit the tops of buildings.

____ 6. In "Icarus and Daedalus," what is the reason Icarus flies toward "the highest heavens"?

A. He is cold and wants to feel warmer.

B. He does not believe Daedalus' warnings.

C. He trusts that Daedalus' invention will not fail him.

D. He wants to escape the feeling of being held in captivity.

____ 7. According to "Icarus and Daedalus," why does Icarus fall into the sea?

A. The wings are not big enough to support his weight.

B. The wings melt when he flies too close to the sun.

C. He loses his way when he flies too far from Daedalus.

D. He is blinded when he flies too close to the sun.

____ 8. In "Icarus and Daedalus," which event shows that in myths, human beings may have superhuman traits?

A. Daedalus builds a labyrinth.

B. King Minos imprisons Daedalus.

C. Daedalus and Icarus are able to fly.

D. Daedalus grieves over his son's death.

____ 9. What is one lesson taught by "Icarus and Daedalus"?

A. Tyrants like King Minos are always punished.

B. The gods help those who help themselves.

C. Children should never be allowed too much freedom.

D. One should not do more than one is capable of doing.

____ 10. In terms of a modern-day device, what are the wings that Daedalus invents in "Icarus and Daedalus" most like?

A. an airplane

B. a hydroplane

C. a hang glider

D. a helicopter

**Vocabulary and Grammar**

____ 11. Where is there most likely to be a *vacancy*?

A. in a crowded city

B. in a wide-open area

C. in a popular restaurant

D. in a dense forest

_____ **12.** Which phrase most logically completes this sentence?

Sustained by _____, the long-distance runner won the race.

    **A.** intense headaches

    **B.** a desire to fail

    **C.** strong muscles

    **D.** a weak heart

_____ **13.** In which sentence is the colon used correctly?

    **A.** Daedalus gathered: feathers, wax, and thread to make wings.

    **B.** The king imprisoned Daedalus in the tower because: his favor shifted.

    **C.** Once he began to fly, Icarus longed for: warmth, freedom, and joy.

    **D.** Daedalus felt these emotions: grief, sadness, and loneliness.

_____ **14.** In which sentence is the colon used correctly?

    **A.** Daedalus was skilled at the following: inventing, building, and escaping.

    **B.** When Daedalus was imprisoned, the first thing he did was: escape from his cell.

    **C.** Daedalus invented wings by: watching birds and seeing how they flew.

    **D.** What happened to Icarus was: he fell into the sea and drowned.

**Essay**

**15.** "Icarus and Daedalus" contains two main characters: Daedalus and Icarus. Which character do you find more interesting? Why do you find him more interesting? Is it because you are better able to relate to him? Is it because he gives you more to think about? In an essay, tell whether you prefer Icarus or Daedalus, and explain why. Cite two details from the selection to support your opinion.

**16.** Before they set out on their flight, Daedalus warns Icarus of the dangers, yet Icarus forgets Daedalus' warnings when he tastes the joy of freedom. Do you believe that Daedalus shares in the responsibility for Icarus' death? Did he do everything possible to ensure the safety of Icarus' flight? In an essay, answer those questions. Explain your opinion, and suggest what—if anything—Daedalus might have done differently.

**17. Thinking About the Big Question: Community or individual: Which is more important?** "Icarus and Daedalus" portrays communities of both gods and mortals. In an essay, discuss how these communities affect the fate of the two main characters. Support your answer with specific examples from the selection.

**"Icarus and Daedalus"** by Josephine Preston Peabody
# Selection Test B

**Critical Reading** *Identify the letter of the choice that best completes the statement or answers the question.*

____ 1. When "Icarus and Daedalus" opens, Daedalus is watching the flight of sea-gulls. Where is he at that point?
A. He is lost in the Labyrinth that he built.
B. He is imprisoned in a cell in a tower.
C. He is on the island of Crete.
D. He is in a workroom making a pair of wings.

____ 2. Since Daedalus is described in "Icarus and Daedalus" as "cunning" (resourceful), what can the reader predict he will do?
A. admit to the king that he deserves his punishment
B. find a way to escape from the island of Crete
C. bribe the guards to let him out of his prison cell
D. imprison the king in the wonderful Labyrinth

____ 3. In "Icarus and Daedalus," what inspires Daedalus to build the device that will allow him to leave Crete?
A. the Labyrinth he built for King Minos
B. the tower in which he was imprisoned
C. the wax from the candles in his cell
D. the sea-gulls he sees in the sky

____ 4. In "Icarus and Daedalus," to what does Daedalus compare the experience of flying?
A. dying
B. gliding
C. soaring
D. swimming

____ 5. In "Icarus and Daedalus," about what two things does Daedalus warn Icarus when they are about to take flight?
A. the labyrinth and the king
B. the fog and the sun's heat
C. the island and the prison guards
D. the tower and the wind currents

____ 6. Which of these sentences from "Icarus and Daedalus" helps you predict that Icarus will not listen to Daedalus' warnings?
I. For Icarus, these cautions went in at one ear and out by the other.
II. Who could remember to be careful when he was to fly for the first time?
III. And not an idea remained in the boy's head but the one joy of escape.
IV. At first there was a terror in the joy. The wide vacancy of the air dazed them.
A. I, II, IV
B. II, III, IV
C. I, III, IV
D. I, II, III

Unit 6 Resources: Themes in the Oral Tradition

_____ 7. Why do Daedalus and Icarus not fly hand in hand?
   A. Daedalus is heavier than Icarus.
   B. Their wings would get in each other's way.
   C. Daedalus must fly ahead to plot the route.
   D. Icarus is impatient and wants to be on his own.

_____ 8. What do people think when they see Daedalus and Icarus in the sky?
   A. They are birds.        C. They are prisoners.
   B. They are gods.         D. They are airplanes.

_____ 9. As Icarus flies closer to the sun, what is the cause of the disaster that befalls him?
   A. The light of the sun blinds him.
   B. The heat of the sun burns him.
   C. The height of his flight exhausts him.
   D. The heat of the sun melts his wings.

_____ 10. What is another way to express the message in this passage from "Icarus and Daedalus"?

   Remember . . . never to fly very low or very high.

   A. Never fly too far from me.        C. Never disobey the king.
   B. Never let anyone imprison you.    D. Never go to extremes.

_____ 11. How does Daedalus memorialize Icarus, according to "Icarus and Daedalus"?
   A. He hangs up his wings.       C. He names a nearby island Icaria.
   B. He defies Apollo's wishes.   D. He dedicates himself to Minos.

_____ 12. What element in "Icarus and Daedalus" suggests that the story is a myth?
   A. Daedalus builds a confusing Labyrinth.
   B. Daedalus falls out of favor with the king.
   C. Daedalus possesses superhuman traits.
   D. Daedalus grieves for Icarus' death.

_____ 13. Why might a parent tell the story of "Icarus and Daedalus" to a child?
   A. It shows Daedalus as a strong father figure.
   B. It shows that fathers and sons should stick together.
   C. It shows that disobedient children get what they deserve.
   D. It shows that children should obey their parents.

_____ 14. What universal theme is implied in "Icarus and Daedalus"?
   A. Mortals should not try to be like the gods.
   B. Fathers should forbid their sons to do dangerous things.
   C. Kings should not imprison innocent people.
   D. Children should never try to do dangerous things.

## Vocabulary and Grammar

_____ 15. In which sentence is the meaning of the word *vacancy* best expressed?
   A. Escape by sea seemed impossible, for every ship was well guarded.
   B. Over time, Daedalus collected a great many large and small feathers.
   C. The wide emptiness of the air dazed them and made their brains reel.
   D. The heat from the sun had melted the wax on Icarus' wings.

Unit 6 Resources: Themes in the Oral Tradition

____ 16. Which sentence shows the meaning of the word *sustained*?
   A. At last came a day on which there was a strong wind.
   B. Daedalus and Icarus felt terror as well as joy.
   C. They were thrilled to leave the hateful island of Crete behind.
   D. Icarus felt himself supported by a great wind that filled his wings.

____ 17. In which sentence is the colon used correctly?
   A. The names of some of the Greek gods are: Zeus, Hera, and Apollo.
   B. Myths do the following: explain occurrences, express beliefs, explore themes.
   C. To make his wings, Daedalus gathers feathers: wax: and thread.
   D. Icarus longs for: warmth, freedom, and joy.

____ 18. In which sentence is the colon used correctly?
   A. Daedalus escaped from his cell: and he hoped to escape from Crete.
   B. The ships that sailed to and from the island: they were guarded.
   C. Daedalus felt these emotions: grief, sadness, and loneliness.
   D. People looked up and thought they saw: Apollo and Cupid.

**Essay**

19. In ancient Greece, a well-known proverb warned, "Nothing to excess." In other words, use moderation—do neither too much nor too little. In an essay, explain how this philosophy is reflected in "Icarus and Daedalus." Consider how moderation would have helped Icarus escape the island. Support your answer with two references to the selection.

20. Do you think that Daedalus and Icarus should have remained prisoners on Crete instead of attempting a dangerous escape? If you believe they should have attempted an escape, do you believe that Daedalus' warnings to Icarus were sufficient? In other words, does Daedalus share in the responsibility for Icarus' death? Did Daedalus do everything possible to ensure the safety of Icarus' flight? In an essay, answer those questions. Explain your opinion, and suggest what—if anything—Daedalus might have done differently.

21. In "Icarus and Daedalus," we learn that Daedalus is a cunning mortal who has learned the secrets of the gods. *Cunning* has both negative and positive meanings. In the negative sense, a cunning person uses cleverness for dishonest purposes. In the positive sense, a cunning person is skillful and resourceful. In an essay, tell what you think Daedalus is like. Is there any dishonesty in him? Is he wrong to attempt something that no human has done before? Is he instead simply a skilled inventor? What else do you learn about him? Cite at least two details from the selection to support your opinion of Daedalus.

22. **Thinking About the Big Question: Community or individual: Which is more important?** How does the larger community portrayed in "Icarus and Daedalus" have an impact on the fate of the two main characters? Write an essay in which you analyze the community in which they live and discuss its importance to them. Include in your answer an understanding of both communities of which they are a part—the community of the gods and the community of mortals.

# Vocabulary Warm-up Word Lists

*Study these words from "Demeter and Persephone." Then, complete the activities that follow.*

## Word List A

**descend** [dee SEND] *v.* to climb down
John had to <u>descend</u> into the basement to fix the water heater.

**fertile** [FER tuhl] *adj.* good for growing crops; fruitful
Ann spread manure on the soil to make it <u>fertile</u>.

**goddess** [GAHD is] *n.* female supernatural being
Early Romans worshiped Venus, the <u>goddess</u> of love.

**grim** [GRIM] *adj.* gloomy, stern, and unpleasant
The old house looked <u>grim</u> and uninviting.

**harvest** [HAHR vist] *n.* the gathering in of crops
Lisa helped her family bring in the apple <u>harvest</u>.

**innocent** [IN uh suhnt] *adj.* not guilty of a crime
They released the prisoner because he was proved <u>innocent</u>.

**joyful** [JOY fuhl] *adj.* very happy
The couple's 50th anniversary was a <u>joyful</u> occasion.

**toiled** [TOYLD] *v.* worked hard at something
The bricklayer <u>toiled</u> all week to build the fireplace.

## Word List B

**chariot** [CHAR ee uht] *n.* ancient horse-drawn vehicle
The gladiator rode his <u>chariot</u> into the Coliseum.

**defies** [dee FYZ] *v.* challenges authority
A person who <u>defies</u> the rules frequently lands in trouble.

**fragrance** [FRAY gruhns] *n.* a pleasant smell
The expensive perfume had a flowery <u>fragrance</u>.

**mightily** [MYT i lee] *adv.* with great force
The four-wheel drive pushed <u>mightily</u> up the trail.

**pangs** [PANGZ] *n.* sudden, strong, unpleasant feelings
The letter from his mom gave Tony <u>pangs</u> of homesickness.

**realm** [RELM] *n.* a kingdom
In the fairy tale, Cinderella lives in the <u>realm</u> of Prince Charming.

**thistles** [THIS uhlz] *n.* wild, prickly plants
The <u>thistles</u> growing in the field stuck to our clothes.

**veins** [VAYNZ] *n.* tubes through which blood flows in the body
Blood flows easily through clear <u>veins</u>.

**"Demeter and Persephone"** by Anne Terry White
# Vocabulary Warm-up Exercises

**Exercise A** *Fill in each blank in the paragraph below with an appropriate word from Word List A. Use each word only once.*

The [1] _____ soil had produced several healthy crops this year.

The farmhands had [2] _____ long and hard to bring in the

[3] _____ before the weather changed. Now the crops were in and the

festival had begun. This was always a [4] _____ celebration. The guests

laughed and joked as they began to [5] _____ the steps into the dining

hall. There, stood a statue of Demeter, the Greek [6] _____ of the

Harvest. Demeter's daughter, Persephone, looking young and [7] _____,

stood beside her. A cheerful fire roared in the fireplace and the table was set for the

feast. The mood was cheery, far from the [8] _____ days of winter that lay

ahead.

**Exercise B** *Answer the questions with complete explanations.*

**Example:** If Jane has healthy <u>veins</u>, will her blood flow normally?
*Yes, her blood should flow normally through healthy <u>veins</u>.*

1. Should parents reward a child who <u>defies</u> them?

   _____

2. If you suffer <u>pangs</u> of regret, would you call a doctor?

   _____

3. To walk through a field of <u>thistles</u>, would you wear boots or sandals?

   _____

4. If a man owns a <u>chariot</u>, does he need hay?

   _____

5. If you wear a heavy <u>fragrance</u>, will it keep you warm?

   _____

6. When a train moves forward <u>mightily</u>, is it easy to jump on board?

   _____

7. If you go into another <u>realm</u>, is it likely you are at home?

   _____

**"Demeter and Persephone"** by Anne Terry White
# Reading Warm-up A

*Read the following passage. Pay special attention to the underlined words. Then, read it again, and complete the activities. Use a separate sheet of paper for your written answers.*

Of all the Greek gods and <u>goddesses</u> who ruled over humankind, Hades was the least liked. He was not a cheerful fellow. In fact, he was downright <u>grim</u> compared with his brothers, Zeus and Poseidon. Hades lived in darkness. His favorite color was black. He possessed the riches in the earth but not the <u>fertile</u>, life-giving soil. Nor did the autumn <u>harvest</u> that fed humankind belong to him. His treasures were gems and metals, the nonliving things of the earth. Hades ruled the barren Underworld: the Land of the Dead.

According to the early Greeks, when people died, they would <u>descend</u> into the land of Hades. A ferryman, called Charon, rowed them across the River Styx. On the other side of this river, they met the three-headed dog Cerberus. Cerberus guarded the gates into the Underworld and allowed only the dead to pass through. Any living person who wanted to visit a departed loved-one was out of luck!

The early Greeks believed everyone went to the land of Hades after they died—the <u>innocent</u> as well as the guilty. Soldiers who protected the land and farmers who <u>toiled</u> in the fields all went to Hades. If they had lived a good life, however, their time in the Underworld could be pleasant.

Later, Romans adopted the Greek gods and changed their names. *Zeus* became *Jupiter*, *Poseidon* became *Neptune*, and *Hades* became *Pluto*.

Today people no longer believe in the Greek and Roman gods. Many do not even know who Hades/Pluto was. Nevertheless, he is still with us—in name only. *Pluto* is the name of the ninth and darkest planet in our solar system. The rare metal plutonium is also named after Pluto—and so is the <u>joyful</u>, happy-go-lucky companion of Mickey Mouse, Pluto the dog. What a switch!

1. Underline words that tell what gods and <u>goddesses</u> did. Name some *goddesses* you know about.

2. Circle the word that means the opposite of <u>grim</u>. Rewrite the sentence using a synonym for *grim*.

3. Circle the word that means the opposite of <u>fertile</u>. Write the meaning of *fertile* soil.

4. Underline the words that tell what the <u>harvest</u> did. Use the word *harvest* in a sentence.

5. Underline the words that tell where people would <u>descend</u>. Write a sentence using the word *descend*.

6. Circle the word that means the opposite of <u>innocent</u>. Write the meaning of *innocent*.

7. Underline the words that tell where farmers <u>toiled</u>. Write about something over which you have *toiled*.

8. Circle the words that describe <u>joyful</u>. Describe something you think of as *joyful*.

**"Demeter and Persephone"** by Anne Terry White
# Reading Warm-up B

*Read the following passage. Pay special attention to the underlined words. Then, read it again, and complete the activities. Use a separate sheet of paper for your written answers.*

"Curtain in five minutes, everyone!" called the stage manager. "Five minutes!"

Turner fussed with his costume while trying to remember his opening lines, "Who dares to enter the <u>realm</u> of Pluto? Speak, whoever dares to trespass into my kingdom!"

Someone behind him giggled. "Hey, Pluto, your toga is on backward."

Turner spun around and saw that Julia was teasing him. Julia was playing the part of his unhappy bride, Persephone. Her crown of dry <u>thistles</u> sat askew on her head. He straightened it carefully so as not to catch his sleeve on the prickly plants. "You should talk," he said roughly.

Julia caught Turner's mood and realized he was suffering <u>pangs</u> of stage fright. "You're going to be great," she said encouragingly.

Turner was not convinced. Rehearsals had been tough, and the role of Pluto was bigger than life. Although he had struggled <u>mightily</u> to learn his part, he couldn't seem to get it right.

"Think!" the director had roared until the <u>veins</u> in his neck seemed about to pop. "You are a god, the mighty Pluto! How do you act when a mortal <u>defies</u> your laws, when a mere *mortal* tries to disobey your command?"

While watching the director, Turner finally understood what he had to do. He began imitating the director's behavior and immediately "got" the character. Unfortunately, he still had trouble standing upright in Pluto's <u>chariot</u> because the two-wheeled vehicle wobbled back and forth.

"One minute to curtain!" said the stage manager in a loud stage whisper.

As Turner moved toward the curtain he asked over his shoulder, "What's that <u>fragrance</u> you're wearing, Julia? It makes me feel . . . I don't know . . . happy."

"That, my friend, is the sweet smell of success," Julia answered. "Now get out there and let's have some fun!"

1. Circle the word that is a synonym for <u>realm</u>. Write a sentence using the word *realm*.

2. Underline the words that describe <u>thistles</u>. Write a sentence telling where you might find *thistles*.

3. Underline the phrase that describes Turner's <u>pangs</u>. Rewrite the phrase using a synonym for *pangs*.

4. Circle the word that tells what Turner did <u>mightily</u>. Write a sentence using an antonym for *mightily*.

5. Circle the words that tell which of the director's <u>veins</u> seemed to pop. Write the meaning of *veins*.

6. Circle the word that means the same as <u>defies</u>. Write a sentence using the word *defies*.

7. Circle the words that describe a <u>chariot</u>. Tell about another time and place where you might have found a *chariot*.

8. Circle the word that is a synonym for <u>fragrance</u>. Write a sentence describing your favorite *fragrance*.

Name _____  Date _____

**"Demeter and Persephone"** by Anne Terry White
# Writing About the Big Question
## Community or individual: Which is more important?

**Big Question Vocabulary**

| | | | | |
|---|---|---|---|---|
| common | community | culture | custom | diversity |
| duty | environment | ethnicity | family | group |
| individual | team | tradition | unify | unique |

**A.** *Use one or more words from the list above to complete each sentence.*

1. Zach and his dad had a _____ of washing their cars on Sunday.

2. However, their local _____ was experiencing a water shortage.

3. They had a _____ to consider the impact of their actions on others.

4. They decided to forgo the carwash for the _____ good of the town.

**B.** *Follow the directions in responding to each of the items below.*

1. Describe a time when you or someone you know was faced with a decision that would affect a large number of people. _____
_____

2. Write two sentences explaining the decision and how it affected those involved. Use at least two of the Big Question vocabulary words.
_____
_____

**C.** *Complete the sentence below. Then, write a short paragraph in which you connect this situation to the big question.*

When making a decision that will affect the greater community, it is one's duty to
_____
_____
_____
_____
_____
_____

Name _____  Date _____

"Demeter and Persephone" by Anne Terry White

# Reading: Ask Questions to Analyze Cause-and-Effect Relationships

A **cause** is an event, an action, or a feeling that produces an **effect,** or result. In some literary works, multiple causes result in one single effect. In other works, a single cause results in multiple effects. Effects can also become causes for events that follow. The linking of causes and effects propels the action forward.

As you read, **ask questions** such as "What happened?" and "What will happen as a result of this?" **to analyze cause-and-effect relationships.**

**DIRECTIONS:** *Use the following graphic organizer to analyze some of the cause-and-effect relationships in "Demeter and Persephone." The first response has been filled in as an example. Where there is no box in which to write the question you would ask yourself, ask the question mentally, and then write the effect in the next box.*

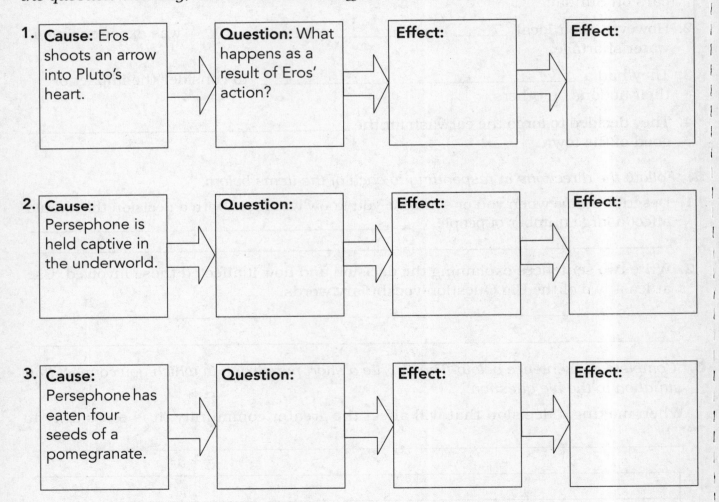

1. **Cause:** Eros shoots an arrow into Pluto's heart.  →  **Question:** What happens as a result of Eros' action?  →  **Effect:**  →  **Effect:**

2. **Cause:** Persephone is held captive in the underworld.  →  **Question:**  →  **Effect:**  →  **Effect:**

3. **Cause:** Persephone has eaten four seeds of a pomegranate.  →  **Question:**  →  **Effect:**  →  **Effect:**

Name _____ Date _____

### "Demeter and Persephone" by Anne Terry White
## Literary Analysis: Myth

Since time began, people have tried to understand the world around them. Ancient peoples created **myths**—stories that explain natural occurrences and express beliefs about right and wrong. Every culture has its own collection of myths, or *mythology*. In many myths, gods and goddesses have human traits, and human heroes have superhuman traits. Myths explore universal themes and explain the world in human terms.

Most myths perform some of the following functions:

- explain natural occurrences
- express beliefs about right and wrong
- show gods or goddesses with human traits
- show human heroes with superhuman traits
- explore universal themes

Not all myths perform all of those functions, however. "Demeter and Persephone" illustrates only a few of them.

**DIRECTIONS:** *Read each excerpt from "Demeter and Persephone" that follows, and answer the question about the function of a myth that the excerpt illustrates.*

Deep under Mt. Aetna, the gods had buried alive a number of fearful, fire-breathing giants. The monsters heaved and struggled to get free. And so mightily did they shake the earth . . .

1. Which function of a myth does the excerpt illustrate? How can you tell?

_____

_____

_____

Now an unaccustomed warmth stole through his veins. His stern eyes softened. . . . The god looked at Persephone and loved her at once.

2. Which function of a myth does the excerpt illustrate? How can you tell?

_____

_____

_____

It seemed that all mankind would die of hunger.

"This cannot go on," said mighty Zeus. "I see that I must intervene."

3. Which function of a myth does the excerpt illustrate? How can you tell?

_____

_____

_____

Name _____  Date _____

*"Demeter and Persephone"* by Anne Terry White
# Vocabulary Builder

**Word List**

   abode    defies    dominions    intervene    monarch    realm

**A. DIRECTIONS:** *Revise each sentence so that it makes sense.*

1. Zeus is pleased when a god or goddess <u>defies</u> his orders.

   _____

2. When the world is calm and at peace, Zeus is likely to <u>intervene</u>.

   _____

3. The <u>monarch</u> bowed before his subjects.

   _____

4. Pluto rules supreme outside his <u>dominions</u>.

   _____

5. Within the <u>realm</u> of fantasy, imagination is restrained.

   _____

6. With its cheerful fire and sweet scent, the Queen's <u>abode</u> gave her a sense of danger.

   _____

**B. WORD STUDY:** *The Latin root -dom- means "master" or "building." Answer each of the following questions using one of these words containing -dom-: domicile, dominant, domesticate.*

1. What do people do in a *domicile*?

   _____

2. If you are a *dominant* figure in politics, what kind of position would you hold?

   _____

3. What happens when you *domesticate* an animal?

   _____

Name _____ Date _____

"**Demeter and Persephone**" by Anne Terry White
# Enrichment: Gods and Goddesses in Greek Mythology

Much of ancient Greek culture is based on mythology. Although the gods and goddesses look and act much like men and women, they are more heroic, more beautiful, and more powerful than ordinary humans. Here is a list of the most famous Greek gods and goddesses and the realms they ruled over:

| God | Domain | Goddess | Domain |
|---|---|---|---|
| Apollo | the sun | Aphrodite | love and beauty |
| Ares | war | Artemis | the hunt and the moon |
| Nike | victory | Athena | wisdom |
| Poseidon | the seas | Demeter | earth and the harvest |
| Zeus | all the other gods and thunder | Persephone | the underworld and spring |

**A. DIRECTIONS:** *Refer to the list of gods and goddesses to complete these sentences.*

1. _____ lives part-time in the underworld and brings spring to the earth.

2. _____ is responsible for the storms that endanger the lives of sailors.

3. The day is full of light and warmth, thanks to the work of _____.

4. _____ is the goddess who is responsible for education.

5. On the battlefield, _____ and _____ are the gods to count on for support.

6. When _____ is angry, electric storms lash out at the earth.

7. _____ is often pictured wearing braids of corn.

**B. DIRECTIONS:** *Imagine that you were casting a movie about the gods and goddesses of Greek mythology. Whom might you cast to play the roles of some of the gods and goddesses described on this page? Explain your choices.*

_____

_____

_____

_____

_____

_____

_____

_____

_____

**"Icarus and Daedalus"** by Josephine Preston Peabody
**"Demeter and Persephone"** by Anne Terry White
# Integrated Language Skills: Grammar

## Punctuation: Colons

A **colon** looks like two periods, one above the other (:). Colons are used to introduce a list that follows an independent clause.

To make wings, Daedalus gathered the following materials: feathers, wax, and thread.

**A. PRACTICE:** *Each of the following sentences is missing a colon. Rewrite the sentences, and insert a colon in the correct place.*

1. All of the characters in "Demeter and Persephone" are gods or goddesses Aphrodite, Eros, Pluto, Persephone, Demeter, Zeus, and Hermes.

   _____

   _____

2. Daedalus warns Icarus not to do these things fly too low, fly too high, and fly too far from him.

   _____

   _____

**B. Writing Application:** *Write two sentences about Greek mythology. In each sentence, use a colon to introduce a list.*

_____

_____

_____

_____

_____

_____

_____

_____

_____

_____

_____

_____

_____

Name _____ Date _____

# Integrated Language Skills: Support for Writing a Myth

Use the following graphic organizer to take notes for a **myth** you will write to explain a natural phenomenon. You do not have to respond to each prompt in the chart in the order in which it appears, but you should probably decide on the phenomenon you want to explain before you decide on anything else. You might describe the problem and the resolution next and then work on the characters. Coming up with the title may be the last thing you do.

| |
|---|
| **Natural phenomenon that myth will explain:** |
| **Title of myth:** |
| **Names and traits of characters**—how they look, what they do, what they say to one another: |
| **Problem to be solved** and creative way in which it will be solved: |

Now, write the first draft of your myth.

Name _____  Date _____

**"Icarus and Daedalus"** by Josephine Preston Peabody
**"Demeter and Persephone"** by Anne Terry White

# Integrated Language Skills: Support for Extend Your Learning

**Listening and Speaking: "Icarus and Daedalus"**

Before you present your **debate,** discuss the following points with the members of your group. Then, respond to the prompts that follow.

- Daedalus shares some responsibility for what happened to Icarus.
- Icarus alone is responsible for his failure.

My group's argument: _____

Points in support of our argument: _____

_____

_____

_____

Expected arguments by opposition: _____

_____

_____

_____

Our counterarguments: _____

_____

_____

_____

**Listening and Speaking: "Demeter and Persephone"**

Before you present your **debate,** discuss the following points with the members of your group. Then, respond to the prompts that follow.

- Demeter was justified in changing the weather on Earth.
- Demeter was not justified in changing the weather on Earth.

My group's argument: _____

Points in support of our argument: _____

_____

_____

Expected arguments by opposition: _____

_____

_____

Our counterarguments: _____

_____

_____

_____

**52**

Name _____ Date _____

### "Demeter and Persephone" by Anne Terry White
# Open-Book Test

**Short Answer** *Write your responses to the questions in this section on the lines provided.*

1. In the beginning of "Demeter and Persephone," the author explains that Pluto was alarmed by the giants' activity. Why does he not want his realm "open to the light of day"? Use details from the beginning of the myth to support your answer.

_____

_____

2. In the beginning of "Demeter and Persephone," Aphrodite says that Pluto defies her power. What evidence does the myth offer to support her statement? Use your understanding of the myth to support your response.

_____

_____

_____

3. In "Demeter and Persephone," Aphrodite tells Eros to shoot an arrow into Pluto. Think about what she says as she instructs Eros. What is the reason for her action? Use information from the beginning of the myth to help you answer.

_____

_____

4. In "Demeter and Persephone," what is the immediate effect of the arrow that Eros shoots into the heart of Pluto? Use details from the myth.

_____

_____

5. In the middle of "Demeter and Persephone," extraordinary events indicate that the story is a myth. What actions does Pluto take during his kidnapping of Persephone that show he is a god? Use details from the myth to support your answer.

_____

_____

_____

6. In the middle of "Demeter and Persephone," what effect does the river nymph's action have on Demeter and on mankind? Use information from the middle of the story to support your answer.

_____

_____

_____

7. In the middle of "Demeter and Persephone," Zeus sees that he must intervene after Demeter's reaction to losing her daughter. Why does Zeus feel this way? Explain your answer, using your understanding of the word *intervene*.

_____

_____

_____

_____

8. Toward the end of "Demeter and Persephone," Zeus says Persephone may return to her mother forever under one condition. What causes her to have to return to the underworld for part of each year? Use details from the myth to support your answer.

_____

_____

_____

_____

9. Myths like "Demeter and Persephone" often show gods and goddesses as having human characteristics. List two of the gods or goddesses in the myth and their human qualities. Then, explain which of them seems most human, and why.

| God/Goddess | Human Qualities |
| --- | --- |
|  |  |
|  |  |

_____

_____

10. How does the end of "Demeter and Persephone" help the reader understand that the story is a myth? Use details from the end of the myth and your understanding of myths to explain your answer.

_____

_____

_____

_____

## Essay

*Write an extended response to the question of your choice or to the question or questions your teacher assigns you.*

11. The actions of Aphrodite and Eros start a chain of events in "Demeter and Persephone." Do you think they should be punished by Zeus for their actions? In a brief essay, explain the role Aphrodite and Eros play and give your opinion about the responsibility they should carry. Use details from the myth to support your opinion.

12. Myths often connect the gods to humans. How does the myth of "Demeter and Persephone" do this? In a brief essay, analyze this connection and tell what it says about humans' power over their own lives. Use details from the myth to support your response.

13. In "Demeter and Persephone," Persephone reacts strongly against Pluto's offer of jewels. How does her reaction emphasize the difference between the two worlds? Respond in an essay that includes your interpretation of why the author may have placed jewels in the underworld. Use details from the myth to support your points.

14. **Thinking About the Big Question: Community or Individual: Which is more important?** Which is more important in "Demeter and Persephone," the individual or the community? Write your response as a brief essay that includes details from the myth to support your opinion.

## Oral Response

15. Go back to question 3, 6, or 10 or to the question your teacher assigns you. Take a few minutes to expand your answer and prepare an oral response. Find additional details in "Demeter and Persephone" that support your points. If necessary, make notes to guide your oral response.

**"Demeter and Persephone"** by Anne Terry White
# Selection Test A

**Critical Reading** *Identify the letter of the choice that best answers the question.*

_____ 1. At the beginning of "Demeter and Persephone," what causes the earth to shake?
   A. Pluto riding across the mountains in his golden chariot
   B. fire-breathing monsters struggling to get free
   C. the arrow that Eros shoots at Pluto
   D. the sadness Demeter feels

_____ 2. In "Demeter and Persephone," what causes Pluto to fall in love with Persephone?
   A. her exceptional beauty
   B. the arrow Eros shot at him
   C. his desire to settle down
   D. Zeus' command

_____ 3. In "Demeter and Persephone," on whom or what does Demeter lay the blame for her daughter's disappearance?
   A. on Pluto
   B. on Eros
   C. on mortals
   D. on the land

_____ 4. In "Demeter and Persephone," how does Demeter show her anger at losing her daughter?
   A. She dries up the land.
   B. She vows vengeance on Eros.
   C. She travels to the underworld.
   D. She steals Pluto's horses.

_____ 5. What causes Zeus to take action in "Demeter and Persephone"?
   A. He fears that humankind will revolt against the gods.
   B. He fears that humankind will die out from lack of food.
   C. He fears that Demeter will go to war to rescue Persephone.
   D. He fears that he will never again eat fruits and vegetables.

_____ 6. According to "Demeter and Persephone," what does Persephone miss most in the underworld?
   A. flowers
   B. rain
   C. food
   D. jewels

____ 7. In "Demeter and Persephone," why is Persephone sure that Pluto will obey Zeus' command to release her?

    **A.** Pluto and Zeus are brothers.

    **B.** Zeus is the most powerful god.

    **C.** She is unhappy in the underworld.

    **D.** Demeter is more powerful than Pluto.

____ 8. According to "Demeter and Persephone," why can Persephone not remain on earth all year round?

    **A.** She has eaten four seeds of a pomegranate.

    **B.** She has offended Pluto by not accepting his gifts.

    **C.** She wants to spend some time in the underworld.

    **D.** She and her mother are not getting along.

____ 9. Which of the following pairs in "Demeter and Persephone" are parent and child?

    I.   Aphrodite and Eros

    II.  Pluto and Persephone

    III. Demeter and Persephone

    IV. Zeus and Demeter

    **A.** I and IV

    **B.** II and IV

    **C.** I and III

    **D.** II and III

____ 10. What natural occurrence is explained by "Demeter and Persephone"?

    **A.** floods                  **C.** earthquakes

    **B.** famines              **D.** seasons

____ 11. Which of the following describes a human trait expressed by a god in "Demeter and Persephone"?

    **A.** Demeter's ability to make the land barren

    **B.** Pluto's ability to fall in love with Persephone

    **C.** The gods' ability to bury giants in the earth

    **D.** Hermes' ability to fly with wings on his feet

____ 12. "Demeter and Persephone" describes the actions of gods. Therefore, what kind of work can you conclude that it is?

    **A.** a tall tale           **C.** a myth

    **B.** science fiction      **D.** a ballad

## Vocabulary and Grammar

____ 13. In which sentence is the word *defies* used correctly?

A. A god *defies* Aphrodite by refusing to fall in love.

B. Demeter *defies* Persephone by welcoming her daughter home.

C. Hermes *defies* Zeus by obeying his command.

D. Persephone *defies* Pluto by returning to him for four months.

____ 14. Which of these sentences expresses the meaning of the word *intervene*?

A. Aphrodites does not want any god to resist her power.

B. Zeus hesitates to influence either side in an argument between two gods.

C. Demeter grieves for her daughter without knowing the details of her fate.

D. Because Zeus is all-powerful, he knows where Persephone is.

____ 15. In which sentence is a colon used correctly?

A. Persephone struggled mightily: but she could not escape.

B. Zeus sent: the gods and goddesses to plead with Demeter.

C. A myth often has the following characters: gods, goddesses, and mortals.

D. Persephone ate four seeds: so she spends four months with Pluto.

## Essay

16. Think about the major characters in "Demeter and Persephone": Pluto, Demeter, and Persephone. Which character do you find most appealing? What do you like about him or her? In an essay, discuss the reasons for your choice. Cite two details from the selection to support your points.

17. By the conclusion of "Demeter and Persephone," three characters—Demeter, Pluto, and Persephone—experience a partial loss. Do you think that the loss suffered by any one of those characters is greater than that suffered by the other two? If not, explain why all three characters suffer equally. If you believe that one character's suffering is greater than that of the other two, explain your ideas. Which character suffers the most? Why? Cite two details from the selection to support your points.

18. **Thinking About the Big Question: Community or individual: Which is more important?** In "Demeter and Persephone," the actions of the gods play a major role in the events of the story. Which is more important in this myth, the individual or the community? Write your response as a brief essay that includes details from the selection to support your opinion.

**"Demeter and Persephone"** by Anne Terry White
# Selection Test B

**Critical Reading** *Identify the letter of the choice that best completes the statement or answers the question.*

_____ 1. In "Demeter and Persephone," which natural occurrence is most likely being referred to by the fire-breathing giants heaving and struggling beneath Mt. Aetna?
A. a tornado
B. an avalanche
C. an earthquake
D. a volcano

_____ 2. In "Demeter and Persephone," Eros is the god of
A. love.
B. spring.
C. the underworld.
D. the harvest.

_____ 3. When Pluto first falls in love with Persephone in "Demeter and Persephone," he
A. gives her jewels.
B. gives her flowers.
C. kidnaps her.
D. courts her.

_____ 4. In "Demeter and Persephone," who helps Demeter learn what has become of Persephone?
A. a mortal
B. Pluto
C. Eros
D. a nymph

_____ 5. What is Demeter's response to the disappearance of her daughter in "Demeter and Persephone"?
A. She travels to the underworld.
B. She punishes the innocent land.
C. She pleads with Zeus.
D. She punishes Eros.

_____ 6. In what way are Zeus and Pluto related in "Demeter and Persephone"?
A. They are father and son.
B. They are uncle and nephew.
C. They are brothers.
D. They are cousins.

____ 7. In "Demeter and Persephone," why does Zeus plead with Demeter before confronting Pluto?
   A. Zeus is uncomfortable with Pluto.
   B. Zeus and Demeter are good friends.
   C. Zeus does not want to hurt Pluto.
   D. Zeus has no sympathy for Demeter.

____ 8. In "Demeter and Persephone," why does Zeus intervene to return Persephone to her mother?
   A. He wants Demeter to stop crying.
   B. He wants Pluto to marry someone else.
   C. He wants to save the human race.
   D. He wants to punish Eros.

____ 9. In "Demeter and Persephone," why does Zeus have the power to interfere in Pluto's life?
   A. Zeus is the king of the gods.
   B. Zeus is older than Pluto.
   C. Pluto has asked Zeus' advice.
   D. Demeter has threatened Zeus.

____ 10. What action by Persephone affects her stay on earth in "Demeter and Persephone"?
   A. She has eaten food in the underworld.
   B. She has worn jewels in the underworld.
   C. She has talked about the underworld.
   D. She has defied Pluto's wishes.

____ 11. According to "Demeter and Persephone," what season do we have as a result of Persephone's actions in the underworld?
   A. winter          C. summer
   B. spring          D. fall

____ 12. When Persephone returns to earth in "Demeter and Persephone," Pluto is described as having "a heavy heart." What is meant by that description?
   A. He has heart disease.          C. He is sad.
   B. He is serious.                 D. He is ill.

____ 13. What natural occurrence is explained by Persephone's return to earth?
   A. the change of the seasons
   B. the melting of the snow
   C. the distinction between night and day
   D. the passage of time during the year

____ 14. Based on the events in "Demeter and Persephone," what can you predict Pluto will do while Persephone is away?
   A. roam the earth                    C. stop loving her
   B. cause a war among the mortals     D. wait for her to return

_____ 15. What is one message of "Demeter and Persephone"?
  A. Jewels are no substitute for flowers.
  B. Gods should not fall in love.
  C. Humans cannot affect the seasons.
  D. You cannot force someone to love you.

_____ 16. Because "Demeter and Persephone" uses gods and goddesses to explore the love between a mother and her child, what kind of work can you conclude that it is?
  A. a legend
  B. a poem
  C. a myth
  D. a play

## Vocabulary and Grammar

_____ 17. Which sentence demonstrates the meaning of the word *intervene*?
  A. Hermes eagerly carries out Zeus' orders.
  B. In the underworld, Pluto gives Persephone jewels.
  C. Demeter and Persephone are reunited at the temple.
  D. Zeus tries to persuade Demeter to stop punishing the land.

_____ 18. In which sentence is the colon used correctly?
  A. Persephone spends three seasons on earth: spring, summer, and fall.
  B. Hermes drove the black horses: straight to the temple of Demeter.
  C. Zeus knew that Persephone was: with Pluto in the underworld.
  D. When Persephone saw Hermes: her heart leaped for joy.

_____ 19. In which sentence is a colon used correctly?
  A. From Pluto, Persephone received: jewels and a pomegranate.
  B. Eros shot an arrow at Pluto: and the god fell in love.
  C. Pluto had seen many beautiful women: but they had left him cold.
  D. Among the things that died were the following: crops, cattle, weeds.

## Essay

20. Who do you think is most responsible for the damage done to the earth and human beings in "Demeter and Persephone"—Eros, Pluto, or Demeter? In an essay, explain your choice. Refer to at least two details from the selection to support your explanation.

21. How are the gods in "Demeter and Persephone" like or unlike human beings? In what ways are they similar to human beings, and in what ways are they different? In an essay, respond to these questions. Cite at least three examples from the selection to support your points.

22. **Thinking About the Big Question: Community or individual: Which is more important?** Which is more important in "Demeter and Persephone," the individual or the community? Write your response as a brief essay that includes details from the myth to support your opinion.

# Vocabulary Warm-up Word Lists

*Study these words from "Tenochtitlan: Inside the Aztec Capital." Then, complete the activities.*

## Word List A

**adobe** [uh DOH bee] *n.* sun-dried brick
The house was made of <u>adobe</u> covered with plaster.

**described** [di SKRYBD] *v.* told about in words
The excited child <u>described</u> her day at the amusement park.

**excellent** [EK suh luhnt] *adj.* extremely good; superior
May we compliment the chef on this <u>excellent</u> meal?

**fibers** [FYE berz] *n.* threads of a fabric
<u>Fibers</u> from the blanket shed all over the sofa.

**gaps** [GAPS] *n.* cracks or openings, as in a wall
The dogs got out through <u>gaps</u> in the fence.

**historical** [his TAWR i kuhl] *adj.* having happened or existed
<u>Historical</u> records prove that our families are related.

**included** [in KLOOD id] *v.* held or contained
The park <u>included</u> a lovely pond where swans floated lazily.

**prevented** [pree VENT id] *v.* kept from happening
Emma's warning <u>prevented</u> us from entering the danger zone.

## Word List B

**chimneys** [CHIM neez] *n.* tall, hollow structures that carry away smoke
The large house had six <u>chimneys</u> in all.

**compounds** [KAHM powndz] *n.* walled yards with buildings in them
People who live in <u>compounds</u> seldom get lonely.

**courtyards** [KAWRT yahrdz] *n.* open spaces surrounded by walls
After dinner, the families went to their own <u>courtyards</u> to relax.

**enchanted** [en CHANT ed] *adj.* under a magic spell
The characters in the play had been <u>enchanted</u> with magic dust.

**grandchildren** [GRAND chil dren] *n.* children of one's son or daughter
Susan sees her <u>grandchildren</u> at least once a week.

**households** [HOWS hohldz] *n.* people who live in the same home
When two <u>households</u> merge, they often have too much stuff.

**site** [SYT] *n.* the place where something is or was located
The house had been built on the <u>site</u> of an old mill.

**utensils** [yoo TEN suhlz] *n.* tools
<u>Utensils</u> we use for meals include forks, knives, and spoons.

**"Tenochtitlan: Inside the Aztec Capital"** by Jacqueline Dineen
# Vocabulary Warm-up Exercises

**Exercise A** *Fill in each blank in the paragraph below with an appropriate word from Word List A. Use each word only once.*

When he got back from his trip, Timothy [1] _____ the many wonderful things he had seen. He told Sally about the house made of [2] _____, which was surprisingly cool inside. When he had asked how that was possible, the guide had told him that all the [3] _____ between the bricks had been filled in. Also, the house was actually made of two layers of sun-dried bricks. In between the layers was another layer of straw [4] _____. This filling provided [5] _____ insulation and [6] _____ cold from getting in and heat from getting out. Timothy told Sally that the tour guide had [7] _____ all sorts of information about the area. He was happy to learn the [8] _____ importance of the place.

**Exercise B** *Answer the questions with complete explanations.*

1. What might you find on the <u>site</u> of an abandoned campground?
   _____

2. What kinds of <u>utensils</u> would you use to plant some flowers?
   _____

3. What is the usual cure for an <u>enchanted</u> princess in a fairy tale who has fallen into a deep sleep?
   _____

4. What would happen if you had fireplaces but no <u>chimneys</u> in a house?
   _____

5. Name one advantage to living in <u>compounds</u> rather than in separate dwellings.
   _____

6. If you joined <u>households</u> with your best friend, how many people would be living together?
   _____

7. What is one way <u>grandchildren</u> can show their love for grandparents?
   _____

8. Do you prefer <u>courtyards</u> or back yards? Why?
   _____

## "Tenochtitlan: Inside the Aztec Capital" by Jacqueline Dineen
# Reading Warm-up A

*Read the following passage. Pay special attention to the underlined words. Then, read it again, and complete the activities. Use a separate sheet of paper for your written answers.*

Adobe is an ancient, historical building material. It is made by mixing materials such as sand, clay, water, and sometimes gravel. Often, fibers of hay or grass are added to bind the material. Once the material is mixed, it is shaped by hand into bricks. The bricks are put into molds. Then they are dried in the sun.

The biggest problem in building with adobe is the fact that the material itself is unstable. It changes depending on the amount of water in the air. The more water the bricks absorb, the weaker they become. As the water evaporates, the bricks tend to shrink. Such shrinkage can lead to gaps between the bricks. This problem cannot be prevented, but it can be solved.

Mortar can be used between the bricks to minimize the problem of the gaps. Also, the finished structure can be coated with another material. Mud plaster is one option. This is made of the same ingredients as adobe—clay, sand, water, and straw or grass. Pink or ochre pigments can be included, if desired. The mud plaster is then smoothed over the bricks.

Another coating option is whitewash. This material can be described as ground gypsum rock, water, and clay. This is brushed onto the finished adobe wall. The problem with whitewash is that it wears off and needs to be reapplied every year.

Lime plaster, which is harder than mud plaster, is another choice. It is made of lime, sand, and water. Heavy trowels or brushes are used to apply it over the adobe surface.

Since the early 1900s, cement stucco has been used to coat adobe surfaces. Cement stucco is made of cement, sand, and water. It must be applied over a wire mesh attached to the adobe. This is an excellent choice because it needs little maintenance.

1. Underline the words that mean the same as adobe. Use *adobe* in a sentence.

2. Circle the word that hints at the meaning of historical. Name a *historical* event that you wish you could have seen in person.

3. Underline the words that tell what kind of fibers were used with the mixture. What are *fibers*?

4. Circle the words that tell where the gaps might be. What does the word *gaps* mean?

5. Underline the word that tells what problem cannot be prevented. Describe a problem that you once *prevented*.

6. Circle the words that tell what can be included in the mud plaster. Use *included* in a sentence.

7. Underline the word that tells what is being described. How would you like to be *described*?

8. Circle the words that tell why cement stucco is an excellent choice. What is one *excellent* choice you made recently?

**"Tenochtitlan: Inside the Aztec Capital"** by Jacqueline Dineen
# Reading Warm-up B

*Read the following passage. Pay special attention to the underlined words. Then, read it again, and complete the activities. Use a separate sheet of paper for your written answers.*

Ever since she read about how the ancient Aztecs lived, Alicia had been <u>enchanted</u> with their way of life. It seemed like a simpler, slower time. People probably enjoyed life more, Alicia thought. She was not sure how accurate her ideas were, but she did think that modern life was too hectic.

Alicia liked the idea of individual <u>households</u> that included extended family. She enjoyed the vision of the different generations living in different wings of the home and sharing common space in the middle. Such <u>compounds</u> were not common in Alicia's time, so she could only imagine the benefits they offered.

For one thing, grandparents and their <u>grandchildren</u> could see each other every day. Thinking about her own grandparents and how little she saw them made Alicia long for a different way of life. She thought about how much easier it would be for young parents to have built-in help with their growing families.

In her imagination, Alicia designed a perfect little village. Each house was on a picturesque <u>site</u> overlooking a lake. The village was full of <u>courtyards</u> where families could gather and visit. Because each generation had a separate wing, each house would have several fireplaces and <u>chimneys</u>.

Gardens would be cultivated both for beauty and for practical reasons. They would grow flowers of all shapes, colors, and sizes. They would grow their own vegetables, like corn, tomatoes, lettuce, and onions. They would even grow their own fruit, like pears (Alicia's favorite), apples, and oranges. Even though she knew this was a fantasy, Alicia enjoyed thinking about it. Each night, as she washed the dishes, <u>utensils</u>, and glasses her family had used at dinner, she would daydream. Someday, she hoped, she could make her ideas a reality.

1. Underline the words that tell what <u>enchanted</u> Alicia. Use *enchanted* in a sentence.

2. Circle the word that describes <u>households</u>. What does the word *households* mean?

3. Underline the words that tell what the Aztec <u>compounds</u> were like. Define *compounds*.

4. Circle the words that tell what grandparents and their <u>grandchildren</u> could do. Use *grandchildren* in a sentence.

5. Underline the word that describes <u>site</u>. Describe a *site* for a home you would like to have.

6. Circle the words that tell what families could do in their <u>courtyards</u>. What does *courtyards* mean?

7. Underline the word that names things that require <u>chimneys</u>. Use *chimneys* in a sentence.

8. Circle the words that tell what Alicia washed in addition to the <u>utensils</u>. What are *utensils*?

**"Tenochtitlan: Inside the Aztec Capital"** by Jacqueline Dineen
# Writing About the Big Question

## Community or individual: Which is more important?

### Big Question Vocabulary

| | | | | |
|---|---|---|---|---|
| common | community | culture | custom | diversity |
| duty | environment | ethnicity | family | group |
| individual | team | tradition | unify | unique |

**A.** *Use one or more words from the list above to complete each sentence.*

1. Gary's volunteer _____ was made up of twenty workers.

2. Each worker contributed something _____ to the project.

3. As they worked together, they developed a strong sense of _____.

4. The work was hard, but they stayed focused on their _____ goal.

**B.** *Follow the directions in responding to each of the items below.*

1. List two different times when you worked with others on a school or community project.

_____.

_____.

2. Write two sentences explaining how your involvement in one of the preceding projects made you feel. Use at least two of the Big Question vocabulary words.

_____

_____

_____

**C.** *Complete the sentence below. Then, write a short paragraph in which you connect this situation to the big question.*

Protecting a community sometimes requires that individuals _____

_____

_____

_____

Name _____ Date _____

"**Tenochtitlan: Inside the Aztec Capital**" by Jacqueline Dineen

# Reading: Reread to Look for Connections That Indicate Cause-and-Effect Relationships

A **cause** is an event or a situation that produces an **effect,** or the result produced. In a story or an essay, each effect may eventually become a cause for the next event. This series of events results in a cause-and-effect chain, which propels the action forward.

As you read, think about the causes and effects of events. If you do not see a clear cause-and-effect relationship in a passage, **reread to look for connections** in the text. Look for words and phrases that identify cause-and-effect relationships—for example, *because, due to, for that reason, therefore,* and *as a result.*

**DIRECTIONS:** *Read the following sequences of events. Underline any words or phrases that help you identify a cause-and-effect relationship. Then, identify each event as a* cause, *an* effect, *or* both *cause and effect.*

_____ 1. The Aztecs were excellent engineers.

_____ 2. Therefore, they were able to build three causeways linking the island city to the mainland.

_____ 3. Because of their skill as engineers, they were also able to build bridges that could be removed.

_____ 4. As a result, they could prevent their enemies from reaching the city.

_____ 5. The land around Lake Texcoco was dry.

_____ 6. Because the land was dry, the Aztecs built ditches to irrigate the land.

_____ 7. As they dug, they piled up the earth from the ditches in shallow parts of the lake, thus forming swamp gardens.

_____ 8. Because they had formed swamp gardens, they had land on which to grow crops.

_____ 9. Because they had land on which to grow crops, a portion of the population was able to grow its own food.

_____ 10. Two of the lakes that fed into Lake Texcoco contained salt water.

_____ 11. For that reason, the Aztecs built an embankment to keep out the salt water.

_____ 12. The embankment also protected the city from floods.

**"Tenochtitlan: Inside the Aztec Capital"** by Jacqueline Dineen
# Literary Analysis: Legends and Facts

A **legend** is a traditional story about the past. Legends are based on facts that have grown into fiction over generations of retelling. Legends usually include these elements: a larger-than-life hero or heroine; fantastic events; roots, or a basis, in historical facts; and actions and events that reflect the culture that created the legend.

A **fact** is something that can be proved true. We uncover facts about ancient cultures by studying a variety of sources: written material, paintings, objects, and excavated ruins. When historians are unable to prove a theory about the past, they may speculate, or make a guess, based on the available evidence.

**DIRECTIONS:** *Read each excerpt from "Tenochtitlan: Inside the Aztec Capital." Then, circle whether the statement describes a* fact *or a* speculation, *and explain how you know.*

1. The Aztecs . . . built three causeways over the swamp to link the city with the mainland.

   **Fact / Speculation:** _____

   _____

2. These bridges could be removed to leave gaps, and this prevented enemies from getting to the city.

   **Fact / Speculation:** _____

   _____

3. The Spaniards' first view of Tenochtitlan was described by one of Cortés's soldiers, Bernal Diaz.

   **Fact / Speculation:** _____

   _____

4. Tenochtitlan was built in a huge valley, the Valley of Mexico.

   **Fact / Speculation:** _____

   _____

5. Archaeologists think that when Tenochtitlan was at its greatest, about one million people lived in the Valley of Mexico.

   **Fact / Speculation:** _____

   _____

6. Historians are not sure how many people in Tenochtitlan were farmers, but they think it may have been between one third and one half of the population.

   **Fact / Speculation:** _____

   _____

Name _____ Date _____

**"Tenochtitlan: Inside the Aztec Capital"** by Jacqueline Dineen
# Vocabulary Builder

**Word List**

    causeways    goblets    irrigation    nobility    outskirts    reeds

**A. DIRECTIONS:** *Read each item, and think about the meaning of the underlined word from the Word List. Then, answer each question, and explain your answer.*

1. Poorer people lived on the <u>outskirts</u> of Tenochtitlan. Did they live near the Temple Mayor?

_____

_____

2. <u>Reeds</u> were cut down in the swamps, dried, and woven into baskets. Are reeds trees?

_____

_____

3. The host passed <u>goblets</u> to his guests. Was he serving food?

_____

_____

4. People used <u>causeways</u> to travel to the mainland. Did they travel through tunnels?

_____

_____

5. The Aztecs dug <u>irrigation</u> ditches around their chinampas. Did these ditches carry water?

_____

_____

6. The <u>nobility</u> lived in homes near the city center. Would their homes be smaller than the farmers' homes?

_____

_____

**B. WORD STUDY:** *The prefix* out- *means "outside" or "more than." Answer each of the following questions using one of these words containing* out-: *outcast, outlaw, outplays.*

1. Why would you expect an *outcast* to have few friends?

_____

2. Why might an *outlaw* be wanted by the police?

_____

3. What happens when an opposing team *outplays* your team?

_____

Unit 6 Resources: Themes in the Oral Tradition

Name _____ Date _____

### "Tenochtitlan: Inside the Aztec Capital" by Jacqueline Dineen
## Enrichment: Aztec Words in English

It is believed that the majority of people living in central Mexico before the arrival of the Spanish spoke a language known as Nahuatl. Soon after the Spanish conquest, in the early 1500s, Nahuatl speakers adapted the letters of the Spanish alphabet so that their language could have a written form. As a result, we have documents from the colonial era written in Nahuatl: city records, poetry, formal addresses, and a collection of observations about pre-Conquest culture.

Nahuatl has survived. Dialects of the language are spoken today by more than one million Mexicans. Not unexpectedly, a number of Nahuatl words have entered the English language:

**English Words from Nahuatl**

| | | | | |
|---|---|---|---|---|
| avocado | chocolate | mesquite | pulque | tamale |
| chili | coyote | ocelot | shack | tomato |

**DIRECTIONS:** *Read the Nahuatl word in each numbered item. (Pronounce* tl *as "tul," hu as "w," and x as "sh.") Then, study the definition. On the line, write an English word from the box that corresponds to the Nahuatl word.*

_____ 1. **chilli:** a hot red pepper used for seasoning

_____ 2. **ocelotl:** a spotted wildcat of the southwestern United States, Mexico, and South America

_____ 3. **xacalli:** a wooden hut or thatched cabin

_____ 4. **xocolatl:** a candy or drink made from roasted, ground cacao seeds

_____ 5. **mizquitl:** a common tree or shrub of the southwestern United States and Mexico

_____ 6. **tomatl:** a juicy red or yellow fruit eaten as a vegetable

_____ 7. **ahuacatl:** a pear-shaped fruit that has a dark green or black skin and contains a single large seed

_____ 8. **poliuhqui:** a fermented drink made from the agave plant

_____ 9. **coyotl:** a small wolflike mammal of the dog family that lives in U.S. prairies and woodlands

_____ 10. **tamalli:** a dish that is made of cornmeal and meat, wrapped in corn husks, and roasted

Name _____ Date _____

## "Tenochtitlan: Inside the Aztec Capital" by Jacqueline Dineen
# Open-Book Test

**Short Answer** *Write your responses to the questions in this section on the lines provided.*

1. At what point did Tenochtitlan start to become an important city? Use details from the beginning of the selection to explain your answer.

   _____

   _____

   _____

2. Legends are based on facts that have grown into fiction. Does the information in the first few paragraphs of "Tenochtitlan" suggest that this selection is a legend or purely factual? Use information from the beginning of the selection to support your answer.

   _____

   _____

   _____

3. At the beginning of "Tenochtitlan," the construction of causeways to the city is described. What was one effect of their construction?

   _____

   _____

4. At the beginning of "Tenochtitlan," the author states that the Aztecs were "excellent engineers." Why? Use details from the beginning of the selection to help you respond.

   _____

   _____

   _____

5. In the section titled "Inside the City," the author includes Diaz's reaction to seeing Tenochtitlan. How might his description have been the inspiration of a legend? Use details from the selection.

   _____

   _____

6. The Aztecs built an embankment ten miles long to keep Tenochtitlan from flooding and for another reason. What was the other reason, and what does it tell you about the Aztecs' skill at farming?

   _____

   _____

7. In the section "Feeding the People," the author explains that an increasing amount of land around Tenochtitlan needed to be drained. What caused this need? Use details to explain your answer.

_____

_____

8. The poorer people lived on the outskirts of Tenochtitlan. Why did they live there? Use your understanding of the word *outskirts* to help you respond.

_____

_____

9. The poorer Aztecs in Tenochtitlan used reeds to build their houses. Other than the fact that they were lightweight, why were reeds used? Use your understanding of the word *reeds* to explain your answer.

_____

_____

10. Meeting the needs of the people in Tenochtitlan caused several developments in the city. List three needs that the city had and what each one caused to happen. Then, tell which cause/effect was most important to the development of the city.

| Needs (Causes) | Results (Effects) |
|---|---|
| | |
| | |
| | |

_____

_____

_____

**Essay**

*Write an extended response to the question of your choice or to the question or questions your teacher assigns you.*

11. Facts are statements that can be proved. Legends often grow out of facts that get told and retold so many times that they become fiction. Choose three facts about Tenochtitlan that would lend themselves to a legend. In a brief essay, explain how those facts could be changed over time to become part of a legend about the city.

Name _____  Date _____

12. A legend is a traditional story about the past. It is based on facts but has become fiction over time. Write a brief summary of a legend about Tenochtitlan. Use elements of a legend and details from the selection in your writing.

13. The people in Tenochtitlan probably did not think of themselves as "larger than life" in any way. If you wrote a legend about the city, how would you describe the inhabitants in ways that make them legendary? Write a brief essay to explain your answer. Use details from the selection.

14. **Thinking About the Big Question: Community or Individual: Which is more important?** "Tenochtitlan" traces the development of a major historical city. In this context, does the individual or the community seem more important? Write an essay in which you assess the importance of one or the other, according to the selection.

**Oral Response**

15. Go back to question 1, 2, or 10 or to the question your teacher assigns you. Take a few minutes to expand your answer and prepare an oral response. Find additional details in the selection that support your points. If necessary, make notes to guide your oral response.

Unit 6 Resources: Themes in the Oral Tradition
© Pearson Education, Inc. All rights reserved.
73

**"Tenochtitlan: Inside the Aztec Capital"** by Jacqueline Dineen
# Selection Test A

**Critical Reading** *Identify the letter of the choice that best answers the question.*

___ 1. "Tenochtitlan: Inside the Aztec Capital" is an essay based on fact. What is a fact?
   A. something that happened long ago
   B. something that can be proved true
   C. something that is an opinion
   D. something that is false

___ 2. According to "Tenochtitlan: Inside the Aztec Capital," what is the meaning of the city's name?
   A. Temple of the Goddess of the Corn Plant
   B. Island in the Middle of a Swampy Lake
   C. Place of the Fruit of the Prickly Pear Cactus
   D. Place of the Fruit of the Maguey Cactus

___ 3. Based on your reading of "Tenochtitlan: Inside the Aztec Capital," what can you conclude was the Aztecs' main reason for building their city on an island in a lake?
   A. to have a regular supply of cactus
   B. to defend themselves from enemies
   C. to build causeways over the swamp
   D. to build a huge temple to the emperor

___ 4. According to "Tenochtitlan: Inside the Aztec Capital," how did the residents of Tenochtitlan get fresh water?
   A. by animal transport
   B. through canals
   C. by slave labor
   D. through aqueducts

___ 5. According to "Tenochtitlan: Inside the Aztec Capital," what was the Spaniards' response when they first saw Tenochtitlan?
   A. astonishment
   B. boredom
   C. puzzlement
   D. ridicule

___ 6. According to "Tenochtitlan: Inside the Aztec Capital," what evidence suggests that corn was precious to Aztec society?

A. Only nobles could eat it.

B. Only priests could raise it.

C. Aztec manuscripts make many references to it.

D. Special gods and goddesses were in charge of it.

___ 7. According to "Tenochtitlan: Inside the Aztec Capital," how did residents of the city travel from place to place?

A. by foot

B. by wagon

C. by canoe

D. by donkey

___ 8. "Tenochtitlan: Inside the Aztec Capital" states or suggests that the Aztecs used water for which of the following purposes?

    I. crop irrigation

    II. drinking

    III. recreation

    IV. canals

A. I, II, III

B. I, III, IV

C. II, III, IV

D. I, II, IV

___ 9. Which of the following sentences about "Tenochtitlan: Inside the Aztec Capital" contains purely factual information?

A. Archaeologists estimate that as many as one million people lived in the Valley of Mexico.

B. Many residents of Tenochtitlan depended on food from outside the city.

C. Historians think that at least one third of Tenochtitlan's residents were farmers.

D. The houses of the city's poor were probably dark, smoky, and unpleasant.

___ 10. According to "Tenochtitlan: Inside the Aztec Capital," which of the following could provide food for one family?

A. a chinampa

B. a maguey cactus

C. a flock of turkeys

D. a farm outside the city

___ 11. According to "Tenochtitlan: Inside the Aztec Capital," why did the Aztecs grow the maguey cactus?

A. It thrives on arid land.

B. It has many uses.

C. It is beautiful.

D. It is fragrant.

____ 12. According to "Tenochtitlan: Inside the Aztec Capital," which of the following is a source of information about Tenochtitlan?

A. the memoirs of Acamapichtli

B. an account by Bernal Diaz

C. an account by Hernando Cortés

D. oral histories by the Aztecs

**Vocabulary and Grammar**

____ 13. In which sentence is the word *reeds* used correctly?

A. Aztecs used *reeds* to grow crops.

B. Aztecs used *reeds* to make pulque.

C. People slept on mats made of *reeds.*

D. Clothes were made of woven *reeds.*

____ 14. In which sentence is the comma or commas used correctly?

A. The maguey cactus was used for its needles, fiber, and liquid.

B. Farmers had only simple tools, the soil was extremely fertile.

C. The Aztecs constructed aqueducts, and built many causeways.

D. Houses in Tenochtitlan were built of adobe, or of wattle-and-daub.

**Essay**

15. Writers write articles for a variety of reasons. They may wish to share personal information or persuade readers to their way of thinking. They may wish to inform readers about something or amuse them. For what reason did Jacqueline Dineen write "Tenochtitlan: Inside the Aztec Capital"? In an essay, explain why you think Dineen wrote the article. Cite two details from the article to support your choice.

16. "Tenochtitlan: Inside the Aztec Capital" suggests a number of cause-and-effect relationships. For example, because there was no fresh water in the city, the Aztecs brought water to the city. In that case, the cause is the lack of fresh water. The effect is what the Aztecs did to solve the problem. In an essay, describe a cause-and-effect relationship relating to one of the following facts. In other words, tell what the Aztecs did because of one of these situations:

• Tenochtitlan was built on an island in a swampy lake.

• One swamp garden could provide food for only one family.

17. **Thinking About the Big Question: Community or Individual: Which is more important?** "Tenochtitlan" traces the development of a major historical city. Does the individual or the community seem more important in the history of this city? Express your opinion in an essay that draws on specific examples from the selection.

**"Tenochtitlan: Inside the Aztec Capital"** by Jacqueline Dineen
# Selection Test B

**Critical Reading** *Identify the letter of the choice that best completes the statement or answers the question.*

_____ 1. "Tenochtitlan: Inside the Aztec Capital" is an essay based on fact. Which definition best describes a fact?
   A. a statement in an encyclopedia
   B. a statement that can be proved true
   C. a statement made long ago
   D. a statement that predicts an event

_____ 2. According to "Tenochtitlan: Inside the Aztec Capital," to what was the name "The Place of the Fruit of the Prickly Pear Cactus" first given?
   A. a canal
   B. a chinampa
   C. a city
   D. a temple

_____ 3. According to "Tenochtitlan: Inside the Aztec Capital," what is the main reason the Aztecs built causeways?
   A. to bring fresh water to the city
   B. to prevent enemies from entering the city
   C. to connect the city to the mainland
   D. to irrigate the farmland

_____ 4. Based on your reading of "Tenochtitlan: Inside the Aztec Capital," what can you conclude was an important reason for the Aztecs' building their capital in the middle of a lake?
   A. to have access to fresh water
   B. to honor the Storm Goddess
   C. to provide a defense against enemies
   D. to practice their skill at engineering

_____ 5. According to "Tenochtitlan: Inside the Aztec Capital," what prevented enemies from getting to the city?
   A. warriors stationed along the causeways
   B. removable bridges on the causeways
   C. a moat surrounding the city
   D. an army stationed in the city

_____ 6. According to "Tenochtitlan: Inside the Aztec Capital," what was the source of the water in Lake Texcoco?
   A. rivers flowing from mountains
   B. underground springs
   C. irrigation canals
   D. the Gulf of Mexico

Name _____ Date _____

_____ 7. Speculation is a conclusion based on guesswork rather than fact. Which of the following sentences about "Tenochtitlan: Inside the Aztec Capital" is a speculation rather than a fact?
A. Archaeologists think that one million people lived in the Valley of Mexico.
B. The Aztecs rebuilt their temples on the same site every 52 years.
C. Fresh water was brought from the mainland to the city by aqueducts.
D. The Aztecs piled up the earth to make swamp gardens, called chinampas.

_____ 8. According to "Tenochtitlan: Inside the Aztec Capital," historians are not sure of the facts about which topic?
A. the location of Tenochtitlan
B. the importance of corn and maguey
C. the use of cacao to make chocolate
D. the number of farmers in Tenochtitlan

_____ 9. Based on your reading of "Tenochtitlan: Inside the Aztec Capital," what can you conclude was the reason corn was featured in the Aztec codex?
A. Corn was protected by the gods.
B. Corn was the main Aztec crop.
C. Corn was disliked by the Spanish.
D. Corn was easy to draw and paint.

_____ 10. According to "Tenochtitlan: Inside the Aztec Capital," which members of Aztec society were most like the nobles in social status?
A. the farmers                          C. the priests
B. the engineers                        D. the craftspeople

_____ 11. According to "Tenochtitlan: Inside the Aztec Capital," the grander houses were whitewashed. Because of the whitewashing, they
A. shone in the sun.                     C. were protected from bad weather.
B. were always clean.                    D. stood apart from the temples.

_____ 12. Which sentence from "Tenochtitlan: Inside the Aztec Capital" contains a word that signals a cause-and-effect relationship?
A. The twin temple stood on one side, and the king's palace on another.
B. The land around the lakes was dry because there was very little rain.
C. Most people in Tenochtitlan depended on food from outside the city.
D. The courtyards were planted with flower and vegetable gardens.

_____ 13. What is the subject of "Tenochtitlan: Inside the Aztec Capital"?
A. the Aztec people                      C. the Spanish explorers
B. contemporary archaeologists           D. contemporary Mexicans

## Vocabulary and Grammar

_____ 14. Which sentence expresses the meaning of the word *outskirts*?
A. Tenochtitlan was built on an island in Lake Texcoco.
B. Poor people lived in areas far from the heart of the city.
C. The emperor's palace was made up of several buildings.
D. Houses had no doors or windows, and they were smoky.

Name _____ Date _____

_____ 15. Which sentence refers to the use of *goblets*?
   A. Families had containers from which they drank pulque.
   B. Everyone slept on the floor on mats made of reeds.
   C. Households had stones for grinding corn into flour.
   D. Many families had beehives and kept turkeys in pens.

_____ 16. Which of the following sentences uses a comma correctly?
   A. The houses were one story high, and they had flat roofs.
   B. Tenochtitlan was by that time, the largest city in Mexico.
   C. One family, could live off the food produced on a chinampa.
   D. There were, few roads, travel was largely by canoe.

_____ 17. In which sentence is the semicolon used correctly?
   A. The embankment kept out salt water; and it protected Tenochtitlan from flooding.
   B. Tenochtitlan was built in a huge valley; called the Valley of Mexico.
   C. The city grew larger; more land was drained for farming.
   D. Farmers grew these crops; tomatoes, beans, chili peppers.

**Essay**

18. "Tenochtitlan: Inside the Aztec Capital" reveals quite a bit about Aztec society—for example, we learn that there was an emperor, or king. Who else made up the society? Were there wealthy people and poor people? What kinds of jobs did people have? In an essay, describe what you learned about Aztec society. Cite at least three details from the article to support your description.

19. The Aztecs had to solve a number of basic problems in order to build a city the size of Tenochtitlan. In an essay, describe how the Aztecs solved the problem of securing an adequate supply of food. Where did the people get the food they ate? What steps did they take to ensure that there was water to irrigate crops? Cite at least two facts from "Tenochtitlan: Inside the Aztec Capital" to support your explanation.

20. Historians discover facts about earlier cultures in a variety of ways. In an essay, describe what one of these illustrations accompanying "Tenochtitlan: Inside the Aztec Capital" tells you about the Aztecs:

   • the map of the city
   • the photograph of maguey cactus plants
   • the drawing of the emperor's palace

   Describe at least two things that the illustration—and the accompanying caption—reveal about Tenochtitlan.

21. **Thinking About the Big Question: Community or individual: Which is more important?** "Tenochtitlan" traces the development of a major historical city. In this context, does the individual or the community seem more important? Write an essay in which you assess the importance of one or the other, according to the selection.

# Vocabulary Warm-up Word Lists

*Study these words from "Popocatepetl and Ixtlaccihuatl." Then, complete the activities that follow.*

## Word List A

**behalf** [bee HAF] *n.* support
　The lawyer acted on <u>behalf</u> of the prisoner.

**capacity** [kuh PAS i tee] *n.* ability, talent, or skill
　Theresa has a great <u>capacity</u> for kindness.

**capital** [KAP i tuhl] *n.* the seat of government
　The <u>capital</u> of Italy is Rome.

**coastal** [KOHS tuhl] *adj.* of, on, or near the seashore
　Hermosa Beach is a charming <u>coastal</u> city in Southern California.

**conflict** [KAHN flikt] *n.* a struggle, fight, or battle
　The <u>conflict</u> in the Middle East has been going on for a long time.

**emperor** [EM per er] *n.* ruler over several kingdoms or countries
　The <u>emperor</u> decreed that all towns would pay more taxes.

**peril** [PER uhl] *n.* danger
　The shark presented a great <u>peril</u> to the surfers.

**siege** [SEEJ] *n.* a surrounding of a city by an enemy force
　The <u>siege</u> ended when the town surrendered.

## Word List B

**approximately** [uh PRAHK suh mit lee] *adv.* about; around
　We had <u>approximately</u> two inches of rain last night.

**bribe** [BRYB] *n.* a gift offered in exchange for a favor
　It is against the law to offer a <u>bribe</u> to a police officer.

**exhibited** [ig ZIB it ed] *v.* displayed or showed publicly
　Marla <u>exhibited</u> great courage when she made that dangerous play.

**fragments** [FRAG muhnts] *n.* parts broken off or incomplete
　Dave swept up the <u>fragments</u> of the broken mirror.

**outcome** [OWT kum] *n.* a result or conclusion
　The <u>outcome</u> of the mystery is still unknown.

**pyramid** [PEER uh mid] *n.* a square-bottomed structure with four sides shaped like triangles that meet in a point at the top
　We visited a <u>pyramid</u> in Mexico and marveled at its size.

**reign** [RAYN] *n.* the period during which a king or queen rules
　Shakespeare wrote during the <u>reign</u> of Queen Elizabeth.

**variety** [vuh RYE i tee] *n.* an absence of sameness; diversity
　The vase contains a <u>variety</u> of summer flowers.

Name _____ Date _____

### "Popocatepetl and Ixtlaccihuatl" by Julie Piggott Wood
# Vocabulary Warm-up Exercises

**Exercise A** *Fill in each blank in the paragraph below with an appropriate word from Word List A. Use each word only once.*

Nicholas wanted to grow up to be [1] _____ of fourteen countries. His mother told him that was an unusual ambition for a boy who always tried to avoid [2] _____ with others. Nicholas laughed and told her that he was not really afraid to put himself in [3] _____, if it would help him achieve his dream. "On [4] _____ of all underdogs, I declare that I will rule with great compassion," he claimed. "All [5] _____ areas will be open for surfers and swimmers. The [6] _____ of my country will be this very city! Those who object to this will be put under [7] _____ until they change their minds!" His mother reminded herself that Nicholas had a great [8] _____ for wild imagination.

**Exercise B** *Answer the questions with complete sentences or explanations.*

1. Is a <u>bribe</u> something you would be proud to take? Explain.
   _____

2. If it were your job to <u>reign</u> over a country, what would be your first act?
   _____

3. What would be the actions of a dog who <u>exhibited</u> fear?
   _____

4. If you wanted to make a <u>pyramid</u> shape out of paper, what shapes would you have to cut?
   _____

5. <u>Approximately</u> how much time do you need to get ready for school in the morning?
   _____

6. For you, what is an ideal meal that has foods from a <u>variety</u> of food groups?
   _____

7. What is the expected <u>outcome</u> of a series of swim lessons?
   _____

8. What kinds of <u>fragments</u> might you find on the site of a burned-down house?
   _____

**"Popocatepetl and Ixtlaccihuatl"** by Julie Piggott Wood

# Reading Warm-up A

*Read the following passage. Pay special attention to the underlined words. Then, read it again, and complete the activities. Use a separate sheet of paper for your written answers.*

The story of how Cortéz conquered Montezuma and the great Aztec civilization begins in 1519. The Spaniards had already set up colonies in the New World. The Spanish governor in Cuba selected Cortéz to explore the <u>coastal</u> areas of Mexico and Central America. Cortéz set sail with 11 ships, 500 men, and a <u>capacity</u> for adventure.

When he got to the island of Cozumel, he met Gerónimo de Aguilar, a Spaniard who had survived the <u>peril</u> of a shipwreck a few years before. He had learned to speak the native language. Cortéz hired him as an interpreter.

They landed near what is now the city of Veracruz. There, messengers sent on <u>behalf</u> of Montezuma met them. Although he didn't call himself an <u>emperor</u>, Montezuma was the ruler of the Aztecs. He had been told of the approach of the Spaniards. He sent gifts of precious feathers and gold necklaces. Cortéz took the messengers as prisoners. He fired cannons, forcing the messengers to watch. The terrified messengers were then sent home.

Montezuma was puzzled. He had thought that Cortéz was the god Quetzalcoatl, whose return had been predicted for that very year. Various signs had convinced him; now he was not so sure.

By the time Cortéz arrived in Tenochtitlan, the Aztec <u>capital</u>, he had gained allies. Neighboring tribes were the enemies of the Aztecs and were glad to help Cortéz. Montezuma welcomed Cortéz, not realizing the Spaniard's intentions. When it became clear that Cortéz wanted nothing less than all the gold in Mexico, it was too late for Montezuma to do anything. By then, large numbers of the population had died from smallpox, brought in by the Spaniards. The <u>siege</u> of Tenochtitlan lasted several months. By the spring of the following year, the <u>conflict</u> was over. The mighty Aztec empire had fallen to the Spaniards.

1. Underline the words that further describe the <u>coastal</u> areas Cortéz was to explore. What *coastal* area would you especially like to visit, and why?

2. Circle the words that further explain the <u>capacity</u> the men had. For what do you have a great *capacity*?

3. Underline the word that tells what <u>peril</u> Aguilar survived. Name one *peril* that you have survived.

4. Circle the word that explains on whose <u>behalf</u> the messengers came. Describe a time you acted on someone else's *behalf*.

5. Underline the word that means about the same as <u>emperor</u>. Define *emperor*.

6. Circle the word that names the Aztec <u>capital</u>. What is the *capital* of your state?

7. Underline the words that tell how long the <u>siege</u> lasted. What does *siege* mean?

8. Circle the words that tell when the <u>conflict</u> ended. Describe a *conflict* you had with someone recently.

Name _____ Date _____

## "Popocatepetl and Ixtlaccihuatl" by Julie Piggott Wood
# Reading Warm-up B

*Read the following passage. Pay special attention to the underlined words. Then, read it again, and complete the activities. Use a separate sheet of paper for your written answers.*

Donnie was so excited to have a time machine at last. He decided to go back to the time of the ancient Aztecs in Mexico. He had seen pictures of crumbling Aztec pyramids in books. He wanted to see what a <u>pyramid</u> looked like before <u>fragments</u> of it broke off.

He wanted to go back to the <u>reign</u> of the famous Montezuma, so he set the dial for 1518, one year before the arrival of Cortéz. The trip through the centuries took <u>approximately</u> five minutes in real time.

Donnie was not prepared for what he saw when he got there—the city of Tenochtitlan was beautiful! It was hard to believe that ancient people could have built such a large city without electricity or any modern machines.

He was also not prepared for what happened as soon as he was noticed by the locals. They spoke to him in words he could not understand, and they made a <u>variety</u> of hand signals that he could not interpret. When he did not answer to their satisfaction, they <u>exhibited</u> hostile behavior toward him. He was taken prisoner and brought before the great Montezuma.

He finally began to understand that he was being asked to identify himself. He remembered reading that Montezuma believed that the god Quetzalcoatl would return to Tenochtitlan in 1519. Maybe Donnie had put the wrong year into the dial of the time machine. Donnie knew, however, that he did not look at all like Quetzalcoatl. Montezuma was expecting a light-skinned man with a dark beard, one of the many identities the god was said to take. As he was taken away by the guards, Donnie wondered what would be the <u>outcome</u> of his adventure. Was it possible that a guard might accept a <u>bribe</u>?

1. Underline the word that tells what kind of <u>pyramid</u> Donnie wanted to see. Use *pyramid* in a sentence.

2. Circle the words that tell what happened to the <u>fragments</u>. Use *fragments* in a sentence.

3. Underline the word that tells whose <u>reign</u> Donnie wanted to observe. What does *reign* mean?

4. Circle the words that <u>approximately</u> describes. Define *approximately*.

5. Underline the words further explained by the word <u>variety</u>. Describe a *variety* of hand signals that you use in everyday life.

6. Circle the words that tell what the locals <u>exhibited</u> toward Donnie. Tell about a time someone *exhibited* this type of behavior toward you.

7. Underline the words that tell what <u>outcome</u> Donnie wondered about. If this story continued, what do you think might be the *outcome*?

8. Circle the word that tells who might accept a <u>bribe</u>. Use *bribe* in a sentence.

**"Popocatepetl and Ixtlaccihuatl"** by Juliet Piggott Wood
# Writing About the Big Question

## Community or individual: Which is more important?

### Big Question Vocabulary

| | | | | |
|---|---|---|---|---|
| common | community | culture | custom | diversity |
| duty | environment | ethnicity | family | group |
| individual | team | tradition | unify | unique |

**A.** *Use one or more words from the list above to complete each sentence.*

1. Cassie's coach begins each new season with a special _____.

2. She always hosts a _____ dinner the night before the first game.

3. Cassie doesn't want to go this year, but she feels it is her _____ .

4. The coach sees the dinner as a way to _____ the team.

**B.** *Follow the directions in responding to each of the items below.*

1. List two examples that show the value of tradition or community involvement.

   _____

   _____

2. Write two sentences describing one of the preceding examples and explain how it benefits those involved. Use at least two of the Big Question vocabulary words.

   _____

   _____

   _____

   _____

**C.** *Complete the sentences below. Then, write a short paragraph in which you connect this idea to the big question.*

   **Tradition** and **duty** to one's **community** should _____

   _____

   _____

   _____

   _____

   _____

Name _____ Date _____

**"Popocatepetl and Ixtlaccihuatl"** by Juliet Piggott Wood
# Reading: Reread to Look for Connections That Indicate Cause-and-Effect Relationships

A **cause** is an event or a situation that produces an **effect,** or the result produced. In a story or an essay, each effect may eventually become a cause for the next event. This series of events results in a cause-and-effect chain, which propels the action forward.

As you read, think about the causes and effects of events. If you do not see a clear cause-and-effect relationship in a passage, **reread to look for connections** in the text. Look for words and phrases that identify cause-and-effect relationships—for example, *because, due to, for that reason, therefore,* and *as a result.*

**DIRECTIONS:** *Read the following sequences of events. Underline any words or phrases that help you identify a cause-and-effect relationship. Then, identify each event as a* cause, *an* effect, *or both* cause and effect.

_____ 1. The Emperor wants Ixtla to rule the empire after he dies.

_____ 2. Therefore, Ixtla becomes more serious and more studious.

_____ 3. Ixtla also studies harder because she has fallen in love.

_____ 4. The Emperor becomes ill.

_____ 5. As a result, he rules the empire less effectively.

_____ 6. Because the empire has grown weaker, enemies are emboldened to surround it.

_____ 7. Because enemies surround the empire, the Emperor commands his warriors to defeat them.

_____ 8. Jealous warriors tell the Emperor that Popo has been killed in battle.

_____ 9. The Emperor tells Ixtla that Popo has died.

_____ 10. Because she is heartbroken and does not want to marry anyone but Popo, Ixtla grows sick and dies.

_____ 11. When Popo learns the circumstances of Ixtla's death, he kills the warriors who lied to the Emperor.

_____ 12. Popo grieves for Ixtla.

_____ 13. Therefore, Popo instructs the warriors to build two pyramids.

_____ 14. Popo stands atop the second pyramid, holding a burning torch.

_____ 15. Over time, the pyramids became mountains.

Unit 6 Resources: Themes in the Oral Tradition

"**Popocatepetl and Ixtlaccihuatl**" by Juliet Piggott Wood
# Literary Analysis: Legends and Facts

A **legend** is a traditional story about the past. A legend generally starts out as a story based on **fact**—something that can be proved true. Over the course of many generations, however, the story is retold and transformed into fiction. It becomes a legend.

Every culture has its own legends to immortalize real people who were famous in their time. Most legends include these elements:

- a larger-than-life hero or heroine
- fantastic events
- roots, or a basis, in historical facts
- actions and events that reflect the culture that created the legend

A powerful Aztec emperor wants to pass his kingdom on to his daughter, Ixtlaccihuatl, or Ixtla. Ixtla studies hard so that she will be worthy of this role. She loves Popocatepetl, or Popo, a brave and strong warrior in the service of the emperor. The emperor, Ixtla, and Popo are three larger-than-life characters who will form the basis of the legend.

**DIRECTIONS:** *Read each excerpt from "Popocatepetl and Ixtlaccihuatl." On the line, identify the element or elements of a legend that the passage reflects, and briefly explain how you recognized the element.*

1. The pass through which the Spaniards came to the ancient Tenochtitlan is still there, as are the volcanoes on each side of that pass. Their names have not been changed. The one to the north is Ixtlaccihuatl and the one on the south of the pass is Popocatepetl.

    **Element of legend:** _____

    **Explanation:** _____

2. There was once an Aztec Emperor in Tenochtitlan. He was very powerful. Some thought he was wise as well, whilst others doubted his wisdom.

    **Element of legend:** _____

    **Explanation:** _____

3. As time went on natural leaders emerged and, of these, undoubtedly Popo was the best. Finally it was he, brandishing his club and shield, who led the great charge of running warriors across the valley, with their enemies fleeing before them.

    **Element of legend:** _____

    **Explanation:** _____

4. So Popocatepetl stood there, holding the torch in memory of Ixtlaccihuatl, for the rest of his days.

    The snows came and, as the years went by, the pyramids of stone became high white-capped mountains.

    **Element of legend:** _____

    **Explanation:** _____

Name _____ Date _____

### "Popocatepetl and Ixtlaccihuatl" by Juliet Piggott Wood
# Vocabulary Builder

**Word List**

decreed    feebleness    relish    routed    shortsightedness    unanimous

**A. DIRECTIONS:** *Answer each question after thinking about the meaning of the underlined word from the Word List. Then, explain your answer.*

1. When the Emperor <u>decreed</u> that the triumphant warrior would marry his daughter, did he ask a question?

_____

2. Would the story have ended happily if the warriors' support for Popo had been <u>unanimous</u>?

_____

3. Would the Emperor have shown <u>shortsightedness</u> by considering the needs of his kingdom after his death?

_____

4. When the warriors <u>routed</u> the enemy, did the battles continue?

_____

5. Did the Emperor's <u>feebleness</u> inspire him to lead his warriors into battle?

_____

6. Did Ixtla <u>relish</u> the idea of marrying Popo?

_____

**B. WORD STUDY:** *The Latin prefix* uni- *means "having or consisting of only one." Answer each of the following questions using one of these words containing* uni-*: unicycle, unicorn, unite.*

1. Why would it be challenging to balance on a *unicycle*?

_____

2. What is a *unicorn* said to have on its forehead?

_____

3. If two separate groups *unite*, what do they form?

_____

Name _____ Date _____

**"Popocatepetl and Ixtlaccihuatl"** by Juliet Piggott Wood
# Enrichment: Volcanoes

A **volcano** is a place in the earth's surface through which molten rock and other materials reach the surface. Deep within the earth, under tremendous pressure and at extreme temperatures, rock exists in the form of hot liquid. That liquid is called **magma.** Magma is constantly moving, and some magma eventually works its way to the surface of the earth. In some places, it works its way through cracks in solid rock. In other places, it reaches the surface by melting the solid rock that lies in its path. When magma reaches the earth's surface, it is **lava.**

Not all volcanic eruptions are alike, and different types of eruptions create different types of volcanoes. There are four major types of volcanoes: cinder cone, composite, shield, and lava dome.

**DIRECTIONS:** *Do research on the Internet or in a library to find out about the four major kinds of volcanoes. In the second column of the following chart, briefly describe how the volcano forms and what it is made of. In the next column, describe the size and shape of a typical volcano of this type. In the last column, cite the name and location of a famous volcano of the type you have described.*

| Types of Volcano | Formation and Composition | Typical Shape and Size | Name and Location of Famous Volcano |
|---|---|---|---|
| Cinder cone | | | |
| Composite | | | |
| Shield | | | |
| Lava dome | | | |

Unit 6 Resources: Themes in the Oral Tradition

Name _____ Date _____

# Integrated Language Skills: Grammar

## Commas and Semicolons

A **comma** (,) is used in the following ways:

| Function | Example |
|---|---|
| to separate two independent clauses that are joined by a conjunction | One mountain is called Popocatepetl, and the other one is called Ixtlaccihuatl. |
| to separate three or more words, phrases, or clauses in a series | There were goblets for pulque and other drinks, graters for grinding chilis, and storage pots of various designs. |
| after an introductory word, phrase, or clause | Unfortunately, some warriors were jealous of Popo. On an island in a swampy lake, the Aztecs built a city. As the city grew, more and more land was drained. |

The **semicolon** (;) looks like a period above a comma. It has two main uses:

| Function | Example |
|---|---|
| to join independent clauses that are not joined by a conjunction | One mountain is called Popocatepetl; the other one is called Ixtlaccihuatl. |
| to separate items in a series when one or more of the items itself contains a comma | The three main characters in the legend are the Emperor; his daughter, Ixtla; and Popo, a warrior. |

**A. PRACTICE:** *Each sentence is missing one or more commas or semicolons. Rewrite each sentence with the correct punctuation.*

1. The family consisted of a couple their married children and their grandchildren.

_____

2. Aztec houses were very plain everyone slept on mats of reeds.

_____

**B. WRITING APPLICATION:** *Write two sentences about the Aztecs. In one, use one or more semicolons, and in the other, use one or more commas.*

_____

_____

_____

**"Tenochtitlan: Inside the Aztec Capital"** by Jacqueline Dineen
**"Popocatepetl and Ixtlaccihuatl"** by Juliet Piggott Wood
## Integrated Language Skills: Support for Writing a Description

Use this chart to take notes as you prepare to write a **description** of Tenochtitlan or Ixtla. Write down as many details as you can to describe the various aspects of the city or of Ixtla's character. Include verbs and adjectives that appeal to the five senses: sight, touch, taste, smell, and hearing.

| |
|---|
| Background information about Tenochtitlan (When was it built? Where was it located?) or about Ixtla (Who is she? What is she like? What is expected of her?): |
| Physical description of Tenochtitlan or Ixtla: |
| Activities in which Ixtla or the residents of Tenochtitlan take part: |

Now, use your notes to write a draft of a description of the city of Tenochtitlan or the character of Ixtla. Be sure to use vivid verbs and adjectives that will make your description interesting to your readers. Use words that appeal to the senses of sight, touch, taste, smell, and hearing.

**"Tenochtitlan: Inside the Aztec Capital"** by Jacqueline Dineen
**"Popocatepetl and Ixtlaccihuatl"** by Juliet Piggott Wood

# Integrated Language Skills: Support for Extend Your Learning

**Listening and Speaking: "Tenochtitlan: Inside the Aztec Capital"**

Respond to the following prompts as you prepare a **persuasive speech** aimed at convincing authorities that building a city in the middle of a lake is a good idea.

Explanation of position: _____

_____

Main points in support of position (facts, statistics, and quotations by authorities):

_____

_____

_____

_____

Phrases that will remind me of my points: _____

_____

_____

Once you have organized your material, transfer your notes to cards that you can refer to as you deliver your speech.

**Listening and Speaking: "Popocatepetl and Ixtlaccihuatl"**

Respond to the following prompts as you prepare a **persuasive speech** aimed at convincing the Emperor that Popo and Ixtla should be allowed to marry.

Explanation of position: _____

_____

Main points in support of position (solid evidence that will appeal to Emperor's emotions and sense of reason): _____

_____

_____

_____

_____

Phrases that will remind me of my points: _____

_____

_____

Once you have organized your material, transfer your notes to cards that you can refer to as you deliver your speech.

Name _____  Date _____

**"Popocatepetl and Ixtlaccihuatl"** by Juliet Piggott Wood
# Open-Book Test

**Short Answer** *Write your responses to the questions in this section on the lines provided.*

1. Parts of "Popocatepetl and Ixtlaccihuatl" are fact. List two facts from the selection and tell how you know they are facts.

   _____

   _____

2. At what point does "Popocatepetl and Ixtlaccihuatl" turn into a legend? Explain how you know, using details from the selection.

   _____

   _____

3. The Emperor in "Popocatepetl and Ixtlaccihuatl" is considered both wise and unwise. Why do his people differ in their opinions of him? Use details from the middle of the selection.

   _____

   _____

4. The Princess Ixtlaccihuatl is the only child of the Emperor and Empress. Fill in the web with words that describe the Princess. Then, draw a conclusion about the Princess as a daughter.

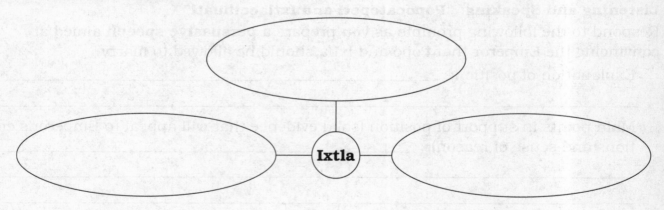

   _____

5. Popocatepetl seems to be an excellent match for Ixtlaccihuatl. Explain why. Base your answer on details from the middle of the selection.

   _____

   _____

   _____

Unit 6 Resources: Themes in the Oral Tradition

6. What effect does the Emperor's continued stubbornness have on Popocatepetl and Ixtlaccihuatl? Use information from the middle of the selection to support your answer.

_____

_____

7. The Emperor delays sending Popocatepetl and the other warriors to defend the city. What effect does this delay have on the war? Use details from the selection to explain.

_____

_____

_____

8. The Emperor's warriors make a unanimous decision that Popocatepetl was mainly responsible for their victory. Is the support of Popo as the new Emperor also unanimous among the men? Use your understanding of the word *unanimous* to help you explain your answer.

_____

_____

_____

9. In "Popocatepetl and Ixtlaccihuatl," the warriors arrive to tell the Emperor that his enemies have been routed. What action on the part of the warriors conveys the meaning of the word *routed*? Explain your answer, using information from the end of the selection.

_____

_____

10. In the final paragraphs of "Popocatepetl and Ixtlaccihuatl," elements of both fact and legend are included. Give one example of a fact that could be proved about the mountains, and give one example of a legendary element that is specific to this selection.

_____

_____

## Essay

*Write an extended response to the question of your choice or to the question or questions your teacher assigns you.*

11. Legends often contain a human hero who is larger than life. Think about Popocatepetl. In a brief essay, explain why he is a good hero for a legend. Use details from the selection.

12. In "Popocatepetl and Ixtlaccihuatl," the jealous warriors take action against Popocatepetl. The results are disastrous for everyone. In a brief essay, explain how the warriors miscalculated the results of their lies to the Emperor. Analyze the ways in which they did not fully think through their initial plans.

13. The Emperor in "Popocatepetl and Ixtlaccihuatl" has some good qualities, but his failings bring about tragic results. In an essay, analyze at least two negative results of his lack of wisdom.

14. **Thinking About the Big Question: Community or Individual: Which is more important?** How do you think Ixtlaccihuatl would answer the Big Question? Explain your answer in a brief essay. Consider how she lived and why she died. Use details from the selection to support your opinion.

**Oral Response**

15. Go back to question 4, 5, or 10 or to the question your teacher assigns you. Take a few minutes to expand your answer and prepare an oral response. Find additional details in the selection that support your points. If necessary, make notes to guide your oral response.

**"Popocatepetl and Ixtlaccihuatl"** by Juliet Piggott Wood
## Selection Test A

**Critical Reading** *Identify the letter of the choice that best answers the question.*

____ 1. What people does the legend "Popocatepetl and Ixtlaccihuatl" tell about?
  A. the Mexicans
  B. the Spaniards
  C. the Texcocoan
  D. the Aztec

____ 2. According to "Popocatepetl and Ixtlaccihuatl," why is Ixtlaccihuatl called The White Woman?
  A. The peak of the volcano is in the clouds.
  B. The peak of the volcano is covered with snow.
  C. The peak of the volcano has white flowers on it.
  D. The peak of the volcano has white sheep grazing on it.

____ 3. Which of the following sentences from "Popocatepetl and Ixtlaccihuatl" uses a word or phrase that signals a cause-and-effect relationship?
  A. It is not known for how many years the Emperor ruled in Tenochtitlan.
  B. She was a dutiful daughter and learned all she could from her father.
  C. She had a pleasant disposition, and, as a result, she had many friends.
  D. An emperor, they felt, who was not truly wise could not also be truly great.

____ 4. In "Popocatepetl and Ixtlaccihuatl," which of these events causes Ixtla to become more studious and serious?
  I.   She realizes her great responsibilities.
  II.  She discovers that parties are boring.
  III. She realizes that her father is not wise.
  IV.  She falls in love with Popocatepetl.
  A. I and III
  B. II and IV
  C. I and IV
  D. II and III

____ 5. According to "Popocatepetl and Ixtlaccihuatl," why does the Emperor at first refuse to let Ixtlaccihuatl marry Popocatepetl?
  A. He does not like or trust Popo.
  B. He wants Ixtla to marry someone else.
  C. He wants Popo to lead the army.
  D. He wants Ixtla to remain single.

_____ 6. According to "Popocatepetl and Ixtlaccihuatl," why is Ixtla fearful when she hears of her father's bribe?

A. She knows he is near death.

B. She wants to marry only Popo.

C. She does not want to be Empress.

D. She has disguised herself as a warrior.

_____ 7. Which emotion causes Popo to act as he does at the end of "Popocatepetl and Ixtlaccihuatl"?

A. confusion

B. wisdom

C. joy

D. grief

_____ 8. Which element of a legend do the characters Popo and Ixtla most obviously represent?

A. larger-than-life human beings

B. a fantastic, unrealistic occurrence

C. a historical fact

D. Aztec culture

_____ 9. Which of the following adjectives best describes the Emperor in "Popocatepetl and Ixtlaccihuatl?"

A. selfish

B. courageous

C. loving

D. wise

_____ 10. At the end of "Popocatepetl and Ixtlaccihuatl," two pyramids turn into volcanic mountains. Which element of a legend does the transformation most clearly represent?

A. larger-than-life human beings

B. a fantastic, unrealistic occurrence

C. a historical fact

D. Aztec culture

_____ 11. Which statement best reflects the conclusion of "Popocatepetl and Ixtlaccihuatl"?

A. Revenge leads to death.

B. Soldiers are ambitious.

C. True love lasts long after death.

D. Wars do not bring lasting peace.

## Vocabulary and Grammar

___ **12.** Which sentence demonstrates the meaning of the word *unanimous*?
   **A.** The Emperor demanded that Popo's body be brought home.
   **B.** All the warriors agreed that Popo had led them to victory.
   **C.** Ixtla felt so much sorrow that she became ill and died.
   **D.** Popo honored Ixtla by holding a torch in her memory.

___ **13.** In which sentence is the comma or commas used correctly?
   **A.** Ixtla was beautiful, dutiful, and serious.
   **B.** Ixtla, honored her father, but wanted to marry Popo.
   **C.** Popo was a great warrior, he led the Aztecs to victory.
   **D.** Popo built a pyramid, to honor Ixtla.

___ **14.** In which sentence is the semicolon used correctly?
   **A.** The Emperor was powerful; but he was not wise.
   **B.** The Emperor was powerful; he won many battles.
   **C.** Popo and Ixtla live forever; and the volcanoes bear their names.
   **D.** These are the names of the volcanoes; Popocatepetl and Ixtlaccihuatl.

## Essay

**15.** In "Popocatepetl and Ixtlaccihuatl," Ixtla and Popo fall in love. Are they well suited to each other? In an essay, describe each character. Tell what does or does not make him or her a good match for the other. Cite one detail about each character to support your opinion.

**16.** In "Popocatepetl and Ixtlaccihuatl," Popo becomes angry with the warriors who lied to the Emperor and thereby cause Ixtla's death. He responds by challenging them to combat, and he kills each one. What do you think of Popo's response? Were the warriors responsible for Ixtla's death? How else might Popo have behaved? In an essay, describe your reaction to Popo's behavior. If you believe it was just, explain why. If you believe it was unjust, explain why, and suggest a response that would have been more appropriate.

**17. Thinking About the Big Question: Community or individual: Which is more important?** In "Popocatepetl and Ixtlaccihuatl," Ixtlaccihuatl is torn between her loyalty to her family and her feelings for her beloved. How do you think she would answer the Big Question? Explain your answer in a brief essay. Consider how she lived and why she died. Use details from the selection to support your opinion.

**"Popocatepetl and Ixtlaccihuatl"** by Juliet Piggott Wood
# Selection Test B

**Critical Reading** *Identify the letter of the choice that best completes the statement or answers the question.*

____ 1. What people does the legend "Popocatepetl and Ixtlaccihuatl" tell about?
   A. the Aztecs living before the Spanish conquest
   B. the Aztecs living after the Spanish conquest
   C. the Spanish at the time of the conquest
   D. the residents of Mexico City today

____ 2. In "Popocatepetl and Ixtlaccihuatl," about what did the Aztec people disagree?
   A. whether the Emperor was brave
   B. whether the Emperor was powerful
   C. whether the Emperor was wise
   D. whether the Emperor was handsome

____ 3. According to "Popocatepetl and Ixtlaccihuatl," Ixtla studies hard in order to succeed her father. That information suggests that Ixtla is
   A. dutiful.
   B. reluctant.
   C. friendly.
   D. romantic.

____ 4. In "Popocatepetl and Ixtlaccihuatl," what characteristic does the Emperor show when he refuses to let Ixtla marry Popo?
   A. thoughtfulness
   B. selfishness
   C. sincerity
   D. reluctance

____ 5. According to "Popocatepetl and Ixtlaccihuatl," an Emperor who is not wise cannot be
   A. elected.
   B. defeated.
   C. happy.
   D. great.

____ 6. "Popocatepetl and Ixtlaccihuatl" tells how the Emperor falls ill. What happens as a result?
   A. Popo and Ixtla get married.
   B. The Empress begins to rule.
   C. The warriors leave the kingdom.
   D. Enemies surround the capital.

____ 7. According to "Popocatepetl and Ixtlaccihuatl," what causes the warriors to lie about Popo's death?
   A. ignorance                                    C. pride
   B. jealousy                                     D. fear

____ 8. Based on "Popocatepetl and Ixtlaccihuatl," what can you conclude about the Emperor when he believes the warriors' lies about Popo?
   A. He does not want Ixtla to marry Popo.
   B. He is naive and too quick to trust.
   C. He is too sorrowful to think sensibly.
   D. He does not want Ixtla to marry at all.

____ 9. According to "Popocatepetl and Ixtlaccihuatl," Ixtla dies of a broken heart. What is another way to describe the cause of her death?
   A. the flu
   B. a heart attack
   C. severe grief
   D. a stroke

____ 10. At the end of "Popocatepetl and Ixtlaccihuatl," what do the two volcanoes symbolize?
   A. temples
   B. lovers
   C. burial mounds
   D. buried cities

____ 11. Which statement best reflects the conclusion of "Popocatepetl and Ixtlaccihuatl"?
   A. There can be no revenge.
   B. Ambition is its own reward.
   C. True love outlasts death.
   D. War breeds only war.

____ 12. Why might the volcanoes Popocatepetl and Ixtlaccihuatl have been the subject of an Aztec legend?
   A. They erupted constantly.
   B. They appeared suddenly.
   C. They were part of the landscape.
   D. They attracted wealthy tourists.

____ 13. Which element of "Popocatepetl and Ixtlaccihuatl" is most obviously based on fact?
   A. the volcanoes                                C. Popo and Ixtla
   B. the Emperor                                  D. the warriors

____ 14. In what way is "Popocatepetl and Ixtlaccihuatl" characteristic of a legend?
   A. It is a fantastic narrative about someone's ancestors.
   B. It is a narrative about larger-than-life human beings.
   C. It is a narrative featuring animal characters.
   D. It is a factual narrative about the past.

## Vocabulary and Grammar

____ 15. Which sentence expresses the meaning of the word *decreed*?
   A. The Aztec warriors marched on their enemies.
   B. Ixtla studied hard to learn to be a good ruler.
   C. The Emperor ordered that Popo's body be brought back.
   D. For the rest of his life, Popo stood on a pyramid holding a torch.

____ 16. Which sentence expresses the meaning of the word *refute*?
   A. The liars knew that the other men would prove them wrong.
   B. The tribes outside Tenochtitlan began to surround the city.
   C. Ixtla decided that she would rather die than live without Popo.
   D. The Emperor said that the winning warrior might marry Ixtla.

____ 17. In which sentence is the comma used correctly?
   A. The warriors defeated the Aztec enemies, the Emperor was happy.
   B. When the Emperor was in his middle years, his daughter was born.
   C. Popo had two pyramids built, one was for him and one was for Ixtla.
   D. Popo and Ixtla fell in love, the Emperor refused to allow them to marry.

____ 18. In which sentence is the semicolon used correctly?
   A. Popo challenged the liars to fight him; no one tried to stop him.
   B. The enemies of the Aztecs surrounded the city; and they waited for dawn to break.
   C. Popo and Ixtla continued to see each other; but they were not permitted to marry.
   D. The Emperor showed that he was unwise; not letting Popo and Ixtla marry.

## Essay

19. Based on "Popocatepetl and Ixtlaccihuatl," what can you conclude about the place of women in Aztec society? In an essay, tell what you know about women in Aztec society. Cite three details from the selection to support your statements.

20. Based on your reading of "Popocatepetl and Ixtlaccihuatl," what can you conclude about the traits the Aztecs admired? Consider the Emperor, Ixtla, Popo, and the warriors who lied. Which of their characteristics were held in high esteem? Which were not? In an essay, describe the characteristics the Aztecs seem to have found most worthy. Cite at least three examples from the selection.

21. "Popocatepetl and Ixtlaccihuatl" contains many references to Aztec history, culture, and traditions. However, the legend also has universal appeal. In an essay, discuss the aspects of the legend that might appeal to people in any culture at any time. Cite three examples from the selection to support your points.

22. **Thinking About the Big Question: Community or individual: Which is more important?** How do you think Ixtlaccihuatl would answer the Big Question? Explain your answer in a brief essay. Consider how she lived and why she died. Use details from the selection to support your opinion.

**"To the Top of Everest"** by Samantha Larson
**"The Voyage from Tales from the Odyssey"** by Mary Pope Osborne
# Vocabulary Warm-up Word Lists
*Study these words from the selections. Then, complete the activities.*

## Word List A

**destination** [des ti NAY shun] *n.* the place to which someone or something is headed
   The squirrel ran down the tree and across the grass to reach its <u>destination</u>, a pile of acorns under a bush.

**devour** [dee VOW er] *v.* eat hungrily and fast; swallow something whole
   Our dog can <u>devour</u> his food in a few seconds.

**embers** [EM berz] *n.* glowing bits of wood or coal that remain after a fire dies down
   The orange <u>embers</u> of the fire glowed among the ashes.

**enchanted** [en CHANT ed] *adj.* magical
   The story was about a wizard who turned a prince into an <u>enchanted</u> frog.

**outline** [OWT lyn] *n.* a line around the edges of a thing that shows its shape
   I put my hand on a piece of paper and traced around it with a pencil to make an <u>outline</u>.

**previously** [PREE vee us lee] *adv.* earlier; before
   Max enjoyed the movie even though he had seen it <u>previously</u> a few times.

**scenic** [SEEN ik] *adj.* offering views of a landscape that is beautiful and interesting
   The train traveled through a <u>scenic</u> valley, where snow-covered mountains rose up from green forests on both sides of the track.

**solar** [SO luhr] *adj.* using energy of the sun
   Mary's class is building a car that runs on <u>solar</u> power instead of gas.

## Word List B

**ashore** [uh SHOR] *adv.* on or to the land or shore
   After riding in the boat all day, she is ready to go <u>ashore</u> to eat dinner at home.

**consciousness** [KAHN shis nis] *n.* awareness of feelings and happenings around you
   When he returned to <u>consciousness</u>, he heard everyone cheering around him.

**correspondents** [KOR uh SPAHN dents] *n.* journalists who report the news from far away; people who exchange information with others.
   Our newspaper pays <u>correspondents</u> to send in news from distant places.

**mob** [mahb] *n.* any crowd; often used to mean a crowd that is not orderly
   He pressed through the <u>mob</u> of people to find his sister.

**overboard** [OH ver BORD] *adv.* over the side of a ship, usually into the water
   Enjoy your boat ride, but please do not litter by tossing trash <u>overboard</u> into the sea.

**possess** [puh ZES] *v.* to own a thing, or to have a quality or characteristic
   She does <u>possess</u> a talent for cooking because everything she makes tastes just great.

**recover** [ree CUH ver] *v.* to return to health; to get something back that was lost
   A policeman helped Jack recover his stolen bike.

**restless** [REST les] adj. unable to stop being active and relax
   After the race, I felt restless and could not sit down, so I walked around for a long time.

Name _____ Date _____

### "To the Top of Everest" by Samantha Larson
### "The Voyage from Tales from the Odyssey" by Mary Pope Osborne
## Vocabulary Warm-up Exercises

**Exercise A**   *Fill in the blanks, using each word from Word List A only once.*

Tom designed a [1] _____ powered car and entered it in a race. The [2] _____ of the race was a college a hundred miles away. The route went past [3] _____ villages and lakes. Tom had entered this race once [4] _____ and had come in last. That was the time his car seemed to have a mind of its own. It stopped and started without a key so many times during the race that Tom thought it might be [5] _____ . The problem turned out to be something simple, a faulty wire.  This time, things went more smoothly. The car could not travel at great speeds, but it did not break down. After a few hours, Tom saw the [6] _____ of the main college hall in the distance. His car came in fifth place out of forty-six cars. To celebrate, he and his friends went out for dinner. All of them seemed to be in the mood to [7] _____ a few tasty pizzas. They walked into an old-fashioned pizza parlor with a wood-fired oven. Tom watched the cook pull his pizza from an oven full of glowing [8] _____. All in all, he thought as they sat talking and laughing, it had been a good day.

**Exercise B**   *Answer the questions with complete explanations.*

1. If you were on a boat, and a man fell <u>overboard</u>, would you offer him a chair?
   _____

2. Would you know who was standing over you if you lost <u>consciousness</u>?
   _____

3. If a person looks impatient and cannot seem to keep still, would you say he is <u>restless</u>?
   _____

4. If Sarah mails her drawing to her friend, does Sarah still <u>possess</u> the drawing?
   _____

5. If you were tired after driving all day in a car, would you suggest that it was time to go <u>ashore</u>?
   _____

6. If you were in a <u>mob</u> of people, would you be alone?
   _____

7. If Alex sends a letter to Chris, who lives in Peru, are they <u>correspondents</u>?
   _____

8. Could I <u>recover</u> the ring on my finger?
   _____

Name _____ Date _____

"**To the Top of Everest**" by Samantha Larson
"**The Voyage from Tales from the Odyssey**" by Mary Pope Osborne
## Reading Warm-up A

*Read the following passage. Pay special attention to the underlined words. Then, read it again, and complete the activities. Use a separate sheet of paper for your written answers.*

When Jerome glimpsed the lake from the car window, he knew his family was about three miles from its destination, Cousin Isabel's cottage. He remembered exactly where to turn off the road, too. Isabel's driveway lay across from a funny old barn with a giant smiley face painted on one side.

There it was—the smiley face, still smiling. The car turned down the long, dirt driveway. It ran through a grassy meadow. From there it was easy to see the outline of Isabel's cottage against the sky. Jerome thought the edges of its roof looked different from the time when he had visited there previously. Sure enough, as they neared the cottage he saw a row of rectangular solar panels mounted on each side of the roof.

Isabel came out to greet them. She saw Jerome looking at the panels and said they had just been installed. The panels absorbed enough energy from the sun to supply all the power needed to run her water heater.

Jerome and his sister, Ella, spent the afternoon at the lake with Isabel. Their mother rested after the long drive. She sat on the deck at the cottage watching the scenic view of the lake and the mountains rising behind it.

After dinner, Isabel lit a fire in her outdoor fireplace. Everyone was ready to devour roasted marshmallows. Jerome quickly ate three in a row with graham crackers and chocolate. The fire burned until the flames died out. Only embers were left, glowing in the dark. It was time to walk up the driveway to the meadow to watch stars.

Away from the lights of the city where they lived, the stars were brighter. There appeared to be a lot more of them, too. Suddenly, two stars seemed to come magically alive. These enchanted stars shot across the sky, trailing long white tails. Isabel explained that they were not stars at all. They were pieces of dust from a comet that caught on fire as they entered Earth's atmosphere. Jerome was impressed that she knew this, but he preferred his own, less scientific explanation: the stars had come alive to celebrate the beauty of the night sky.

1. Underline the words that describe Jerome's destination. Use *destination* in a sentence.

2. Circle the word in a nearby sentence that has a meaning similar to outline. Use *outline* in a sentence.

3. Underline words that are clues to the meaning of previously. Use *previously* in a sentence.

4. Underline the phrase that tells what the solar panels did. Describe a place you know of where you think *solar* panels could be useful.

5. Underline the words that tell what made the view scenic. Write a sentence about a *scenic* place you have visited in a city or in the country.

6. What did Jerome devour? Circle the words. Then, write a sentence using *devour*.

7. Circle the words that give a clue to the meaning of embers. Use *embers* in a sentence.

8. Circle words in a nearby sentence that have a meaning similar to enchanted. Use *enchanted* in a sentence.

"To the Top of Everest" by Samantha Larson
"The Voyage from Tales from the Odyssey" by Mary Pope Osborne
# Reading Warm-up B

*Read the following passage. Pay special attention to the underlined words. Then, read it again, and complete the activities. Use a separate sheet of paper for your written answers.*

The English Channel is a 21-mile-wide stretch of chilly ocean between France and England. Swimming across it is considered one of the hardest things in the world to do. Gertrude Ederle (1905–2003) became famous in 1926 for being the first woman ever to conquer it.

During her lifetime, Ederle set 29 records and won three Olympic medals in swimming. Her first attempt to cross the channel in 1925 failed. Her coach thought she might have swallowed too much salt water or lost consciousness and was no longer aware of what she was doing. He grabbed her arm to pull her out, which disqualified her. Ederle said she had just been resting. She soon hired a new coach, because she felt restless to try again.

At about 7 a.m. on August 6, 1926, she set out from the coast of France accompanied by two boats. In the first one rode her coach, family, and supporters. They helped keep her spirits up and, when she was hungry, passed food to her overboard, over the side of the boat. Journalists followed in the second boat; people all over the world awaited reports from these correspondents about Ederle's condition and progress.

Fourteen hours and thirty-one minutes later, Ederle swam ashore in England, setting a new record. Only five others had swum the Channel, all men, and she had done it the fastest.

Instantly a hero, she was invited to the White House by President Calvin Coolidge, who called her "America's best girl." New York City threw her a parade, and a mob of two million people lined the streets to shower her with ticker-tape.

The long hours in cold water damaged Ederle's hearing, which never did fully recover; she became partly deaf. Ederle turned this setback into something useful by giving swimming lessons to deaf children. It is clear that certain people possess a very strong will to achieve a goal, and Ederle had that quality. Late in her life she told an interviewer, "When somebody tells me I cannot do something, that's when I do it."

1. Circle the nearby words that have a meaning similar to consciousness. Use *consciousness* in a sentence.

2. Underline the phrase that gives a clue to the meaning of restless. Give a synonym for *restless*.

3. Circle the words that define overboard. Use *overboard* in a sentence.

4. Circle the word with a meaning similar to correspondents. Where could you read or hear reports from *correspondents*?

5. Underline the word that tells where Ederle swam ashore. Use *ashore* in a sentence.

6. Circle the words that give a clue to the meaning of mob. What is another situation in which you might find a *mob*?

7. Underline the word that tells what Ederle did not fully recover. Use the word *recover* in a sentence.

8. Underline the words that are a clue to the meaning of possess. Write an antonym for *possess*.

Unit 6 Resources: Themes in the Oral Tradition

Name _____ Date _____

**"To the Top of Everest"** by Samantha Larson
**"The Voyage from Tales from the Odyssey"** by Mary Pope Osborne
# Writing About the Big Question

## Community or individual: Which is more important?

### Big Question Vocabulary

| | | | | |
|---|---|---|---|---|
| common | community | culture | custom | diversity |
| duty | environment | ethnicity | family | group |
| individual | team | tradition | unify | unique |

**A.** *Use one or more words from the list above to complete each sentence.*

1. The _____ of rock climbers prepared for their journey.

2. They had a _____ goal of reaching the summit.

3. They were awed by the _____ of flora and fauna around them.

4. They felt fortunate to be in such a beautiful _____ .

**B.** *Follow the directions in responding to each of the items below.*

1. List two times when you traveled to a new place. _____ .
_____

2. Write two sentences describing one of the preceding experiences, and explain how it affected your view of the world. Use at least two of the Big Question vocabulary words.
_____
_____

**C.** *Complete the sentence below. Then, write a short paragraph in which you connect this idea to the big question.*

Travel enriches an individual's view of the world. A community of travelers
_____
_____
_____
_____
_____
_____

Name _____ Date _____

### "To the Top of Everest" by Samantha Larson
### "The Voyage from Tales from the Odyssey" by Mary Pope Osborne
# Literary Analysis: Comparing Universal Themes

A universal theme is a message about life that is expressed regularly in many different cultures and time periods. Universal themes include the importance of courage, the power of love, and the danger of greed. Universal themes are often found in epics, or stories or long poems about the adventures of a larger-than-life hero. Epic tales usually focus on the hero's bravery, strength, and success in battle or adventure. In addition to telling the story of a hero, an epic is a portrait of the culture that produced it. The following **epic conventions** are traditional characteristics of this form of literature:

- An epic involves a dangerous journey, or *quest*, that the hero must take.
- Gods or powerful characters help the hero.
- The setting of an epic is broad, covering several nations or even the universe.
- The style is serious and formal.

Because epics have become an important part of the literature of different cultures, they often inspire the works of later generations. For example, it is not unusual to find an allusion, or reference, to the ancient Greek epic the *Odyssey* in a contemporary adventure story. As you read "To the Top of Everest" and "The Voyage from Tales from the Odyssey," look for the use of epic conventions in the stories.

**DIRECTIONS:** *Use the following chart to compare "To the Top of Everest" and "The Voyage from Tales of the Odyssey." If the information to answer a question does not appear in the selection, write* information not mentioned.

| Questions | "To the Top of Everest" | "The Voyage from Tales from the Odyssey" |
|---|---|---|
| 1. What is the setting? | | |
| 2. What dangerous journey is undertaken? | | |
| 3. Who helps along the journey? | | |
| 4. What is the character's attitude? | | |
| 5. What obstacles must be overcome? | | |
| 6. What is the outcome? | | |

Name _____ Date _____

**"To the Top of Everest"** by Samantha Larson
**"The Voyage from Tales from the Odyssey"** by Mary Pope Osborne
# Vocabulary Builder

**Word List**

designated    impervious    inflicted    saturation

**A. DIRECTIONS:** *Think about the meaning of each italicized word from the Word List. Then, explain whether the sentence makes sense. If it does not make sense, write a new sentence. In the new sentence, use the italicized word correctly.*

1. Jenna *inflicted* comfort with her gentle touch.

   **Explanation:** _____

   **New sentence:** _____

2. The leaky bottle resulted in the *saturation* of Emma's cotton bib.

   **Explanation:** _____

   **New sentence:** _____

3. We *designated* our star player as our choice for team captain.

   **Explanation:** _____

   **New sentence:** _____

4. Her proud smile suggested she was *impervious* to our compliments.

   **Explanation:** _____

   **New sentence:** _____

**B. DIRECTIONS:** *Write the letter of the word that means* the same or about the same *as the word from the Word List.*

____ 1. designated
    A. designed                  C. described
    B. arranged                D. marked

____ 2. impervious
    A. unaffected              C. lazy
    B. angry                   D. bored

____ 3. inflicted
    A. stopped               C. caused
    B. soothed               D. increased

Name _____ Date _____

"To the Top of Everest" by Samantha Larson
"The Voyage from Tales from the Odyssey" by Mary Pope Osborne
# Support for Writing to Compare Universal Themes

Use this graphic organizer to take notes for an **essay** in which you compare and contrast the themes of "To the Top of Everest" and "The Voyage from Tales from the Odyssey."

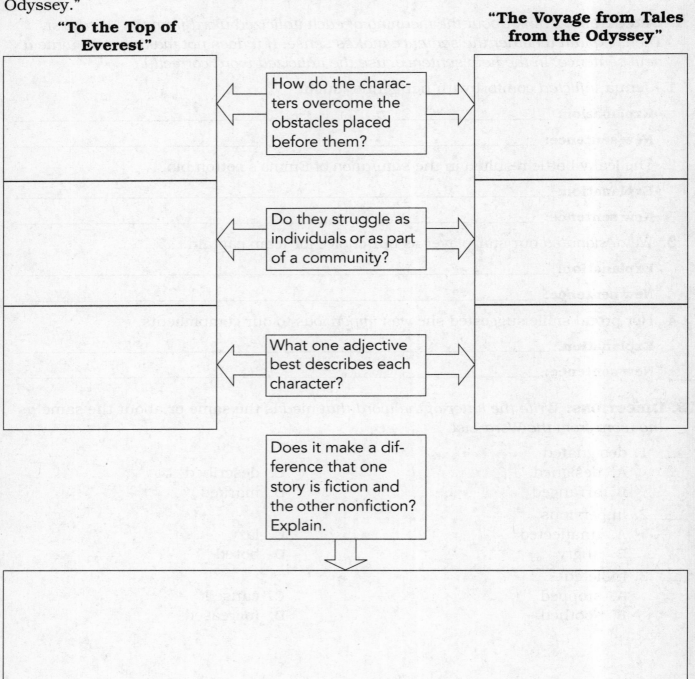

**"To the Top of Everest"**

**"The Voyage from Tales from the Odyssey"**

How do the characters overcome the obstacles placed before them?

Do they struggle as individuals or as part of a community?

What one adjective best describes each character?

Does it make a difference that one story is fiction and the other nonfiction? Explain.

Now, use your notes to write an essay comparing and contrasting the themes of "To the Top of Everest" and "The Voyage from Tales from the Odyssey."

Name _____  Date _____

## "To the Top of the World" by Samantha Larson
## "The Voyage" from Tales from the Odyssey by Mary Pope Osborne
## Open-Book Test

**Short Answer** *Write your responses to the questions in this section on the lines provided.*

1. In "To the Top of the World," Larson writes on April 28 that an area had been designated "safe." Would you want to be in a place that has been designated safe? Explain your answer based on the definition of *designated*.

   _____

2. In the May 17 entry in "To the Top of the World," Larson does not express her feelings about reaching the summit of Mount Everest. Why might her entry for that day be especially brief? Cite a detail from the blog to support your answer.

   _____

   _____

3. In "To the Top of the World," the mountain climbers do not go directly to the third camp. Instead, they make stops at the first two camps. What is the reason for their slow progress?

   _____

   _____

4. In "The Voyage," Ino seems to be impervious to the great storm. Would you want to be impervious to a dangerous storm? Explain your answer based on the definition of *impervious*.

   _____

5. Complete this character web for Odysseus in "The Voyage." Then, on the line below, tell why Odysseus is able to survive the difficult things that happen to him.

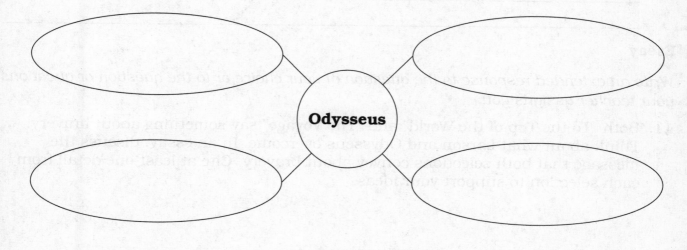

   _____

6. In "The Voyage," Athena is unable to protect Odysseus fully from Poseidon's anger. Why is Athena unable to protect Odysseus fully? Use details from the story to support your answer.

_____

_____

7. Both Larson in "To the Top of the World" and Odysseus in "The Voyage" are brave. What does Larson do to show that she is brave? What does Odysseus do to show that he is brave?

_____

_____

_____

8. In what way are the experiences of Larson in "To the Top of the World" and the experiences of Odysseus in "The Voyage" alike?

_____

_____

_____

9. In "To the Top of the World," Larson battles the environment to climb Mount Everest. In "The Voyage," Odysseus battles the environment to reach the shore. In what way do their experiences differ?

_____

_____

10. Consider Larson's reason for climbing Mount Everest in "To the Top of the World" and Odysseus's reason for battling the great storm in "The Voyage." How are their reasons different?

_____

_____

## Essay

*Write an extended response to the question of your choice or to the question or questions your teacher assigns you.*

11. Both "To the Top of the World" and "The Voyage" say something about bravery. Think about what Larson and Odysseus overcome. In an essay, discuss the message that both selections convey about bravery. Cite at least one detail from each selection to support your ideas.

12. A hero is a character whose actions are inspiring or noble. Often heroes struggle to overcome the obstacles that stand in their way. In an essay, discuss who better lives up to the definition of a hero—Larson in "To the Top of the World" or Odysseus in "The Voyage." Cite at least one detail from each selection to support your ideas.

13. "To the Top of the World" is a blog, and "The Voyage" is the retelling of an epic. In an essay, discuss how the two genres influence your view of Larson and Odysseus and their adventures. Use at least one detail from each selection to support your ideas.

14. **Thinking About the Big Question: Community or Individual: Which is more important?** In an essay, discuss the kinds of efforts that are described in "To the Top of the World" and "The Voyage." Do they involve an entire community or a single individual? Cite at least one detail from each selection to support your points.

## Oral Response

15. Go back to question 2, 8, or 10 or to the question your teacher assigns you. Take a few minutes to expand your answer and prepare an oral response. Find additional details in "To the Top of the World" and "The Voyage" that support your points. If necessary, make notes to guide your oral response.

**"To the Top of Everest"** by Samantha Larson
**"The Voyage from Tales from the Odyssey"** by Mary Pope Osborne
## Selection Test A

**Critical Reading** *Identify the letter of the choice that best answers the question.*

____ 1. In "To the Top of Everest," what helps Samantha train for her climb?
A. weight lifting
B. running, swimming, and dancing
C. music and French lessons
D. martial arts classes

____ 2. After Base Camp, how many more camps does Samantha's group make on their way to the summit?
A. two
B. one
C. four
D. three

____ 3. What event takes Samantha by surprise?
A. an unexpected break in the icefall
B. an avalanche
C. a sharp drop in temperature
D. a sprained ankle

____ 4. What does Samantha worry about in the final days before she reaches the summit?
A. running out of food
B. another avalanche
C. competition from other climbers
D. staying in shape

____ 5. What does Poseidon use to create danger for Odysseus?
A. whirlpools
B. strong winds
C. heavy rains
D. lightning

_____ 6. What happens to Odysseus' raft?
   A. The wind blows it away.
   B. The White Goddess takes it from him.
   C. A wave smashes it into pieces.
   D. Odysseus pulls it ashore.

_____ 7. Why does Ino give Odysseus her veil?
   A. so he will remember her
   B. to protect him from Poseidon
   C. so he can ride the waves
   D. to lull him to sleep

_____ 8. How does Athena help Odysseus?
   A. Her presence calms him and gives him hope.
   B. She overpowers the White Goddess.
   C. She overpowers Poseidon.
   D. She sings him to sleep.

_____ 9. How might you express the theme of "To the Top of Everest"?
   A. the triumph of bravery over strength and power
   B. the survival of the fittest
   C. the rewards of patience and hard work
   D. the treacherousness of nature

_____ 10. How might you express the theme of "The Voyage"?
   A. the triumph of bravery over strength and power
   B. the survival of the fittest
   C. the rewards of patience and hard work
   D. the treacherousness of nature

_____ 11. Which epic convention does "To the Top of Everest" *not* include?
   A. a dangerous journey or quest
   B. a far-ranging setting
   C. a serious style
   D. gods who help the hero

_____ 12. How does the style of "The Voyage" compare with the style of " To the Top of Everest"?
   A. "The Voyage" is more formal.
   B. "The Voyage" is more humorous.
   C. "To the Top of Everest" is more serious.
   D. "To the Top of Everest" is less informal.

## Vocabulary

____ 13. How would you describe a person who is *impervious*?
   A. snobbish
   B. sad
   C. angry
   D. unaffected

____ 14. What is something that can be *inflicted*?
   A. pain
   B. joy
   C. anger
   D. humor

____ 15. How might an object reach *saturation*?
   A. being left in the sun
   B. being left in the rain
   C. being left in the theater
   D. being left in the car

## Essay

16. Two very different characters are presented in "To the Top of Everest" and "The Voyage." In an essay, compare and contrast the challenges each character faces. What does Samantha do? How is she successful? What does Odysseus do? How is he successful? Is one character more "heroic" than the other? Explain your answer.

17. Choose either "To the Top of Everest" or "The Voyage" and explain how the work reflects some or all of the following characteristics of an epic: a dangerous journey or quest; a hero who receives help from gods or powerful characters; a far-ranging setting; a serious, formal style. Use examples to support your answer.

18. **Thinking About the Big Question: Community or individual: Which is more important?** Both selections in this section—"To the Top of the World" and "The Voyage"—describe heroic efforts by people to conquer nature. Do they involve an entire community or a single individual? Explain your answer in an essay that cites details from each selection.

"**To the Top of Everest**" by Samantha Larson
"**The Voyage from Tales from the Odyssey**" by Mary Pope Osborne
## Selection Test B

**Critical Reading** *Identify the letter of the choice that best completes the statement or answers the question.*

____ 1. According to "To the Top of Everest," how did Samantha train for her climb?
   A. She competed in back-to-back triathlons.
   B. She ran, swam, took dance classes, and rock climbed.
   C. She took music lessons, French, and photography.
   D. She biked, took martial arts classes, and lifted weights.

____ 2. Why is Samantha unnerved by the unexpected break in the icefall?
   A. She didn't think such a large area could break so easily.
   B. Icefalls, in general, made her nervous.
   C. Her team had thought it would be a safe place to take a rest.
   D. She didn't like to think about anything going wrong during their climb.

____ 3. Why does it take Samantha's group nearly two months to complete the climb?
   A. They must attempt the climb in stages so that their bodies can adjust to changes in temperature and altitude.
   B. They didn't realize how long it would take to climb almost 30,000 feet.
   C. They suffered injuries during their first few days and had to allow time for recovery.
   D. Fog and unexpected snowfalls kept them trapped in their tents for weeks.

____ 4. In the final days before their ascent to the summit, what was the group's most pressing concern?
   A. They needed to maintain their fitness level.
   B. They worried they might run out of food.
   C. They heard there was the possibility of an avalanche.
   D. They worried another team might reach the summit before they did.

____ 5. How does Poseidon complicate Odysseus' journey?
   A. He creates whirlpools that throw Odysseus off course.
   B. He sends the White Goddess to taunt him.
   C. He sends heavy rains in an attempt to drown him.
   D. He sends strong winds that create dangerous waves.

____ 6. Why does Ino give Odysseus her veil?
   A. It will help protect him from Poseidon.
   B. She wants to give him something to remember her by.
   C. It will allow him to control the waves.
   D. It will lull him into a deep sleep.

____ 7. Why does Odysseus welcome the presence of Athena?
   A. He believes Athena is more powerful than the White Goddess.
   B. He believes Athena is more powerful than Poseidon.
   C. He knows Athena will not let him die.
   D. Athena's presence is calming and gives him hope.

Name _____ Date _____

____ 8. A universal theme is a message about life that
A. focuses on the origins of the universe.
B. is expressed in a specific culture or time period.
C. is expressed in many cultures or time periods.
D. comments on good versus evil.

____ 9. The theme of "To the Top of Everest" might be expressed as
A. the rewards of patience and hard work.
B. the triumph of bravery over strength and power.
C. the survival of the fittest.
D. the treacherousness of nature.

____ 10. The theme of "The Voyage" might be expressed as
A. the rewards of patience and hard work.
B. the triumph of bravery over strength and power.
C. the survival of the fittest.
D. the treacherousness of nature.

____ 11. Unlike "The Voyage," "To the Top of Everest" does *not* include which epic convention?
A. a dangerous journey or quest
B. a far-ranging setting
C. a serious style
D. gods who help the hero

____ 12. How does the outcome of "The Voyage" differ from the outcome of "To the Top of Everest"?
A. Samantha is excited by her accomplishment; Odysseus is exhausted by his.
B. Odysseus overcomes his obstacles; Samantha fails to overcome hers.
C. Samantha overcomes her obstacles; Odysseus fails to overcome his.
D. Odysseus makes it home in the end; Samantha's journey continues.

____ 13. Compared with the style of "The Voyage," the style of "To the Top of Everest" is more
A. formal.
B. informal.
C. serious.
D. humorous.

**Vocabulary**

____ 14. In which sentence does *inflicted* make sense?
A. The teacher's praise inflicted pride in the students.
B. The patients were inflicted with a virus.
C. Tara inflicted pain with her cruel comments.
D. Wash out your wound before it becomes inflicted.

_____ 15. Which sentence describes someone who is *impervious*?
 A. A movie director shrugs off his bad reviews.
 B. An actor smiles brightly when approached by fans.
 C. A boy trembles when approached by a bully.
 D. A student beams with pride over the "A" on her test.

_____ 16. Which sentence best expresses the meaning of *designated*?
 A. The players were exhausted after the game.
 B. Lani covered her book jacket with creative designs.
 C. The young hoodlums vandalized the theater.
 D. The friends chose the Pizza Barn as their meeting spot.

_____ 17. In which sentence has the object reached *saturation*?
 A. My damp jacket hung in the mudroom.
 B. I folded the warm blanket into a neat square.
 C. I placed my dripping socks by the fireplace.
 D. My laundry basket overflowed with clothes.

**Essay**

18. Both "The Voyage" and "To the Top of Everest" present a character that can be perceived as a "hero." In an essay, compare and contrast Odysseus and Samantha. Name at least one way in which they are alike and at least two ways in which they are different. Then, tell whether you found one of the characters more "heroic." Cite at least one detail from one of the selections to support your point.

19. An epic is a story or long poem about the adventures of a larger-than-life hero. An epic may be distinguished by these traditional characteristics:

 • It involves a dangerous journey, or quest.
 • The hero receives help from gods or powerful characters.
 • The events unfold in at least several nations.
 • The story is told in a serious, formal style.

In an essay, discuss those characteristics in terms of "The Voyage" and "To the Top of Everest." To what extent are they present in "The Voyage"? To what extent are they present in "To the Top of Everest"? Conclude your essay by stating whether you think "To the Top of Everest" may be considered an epic tale. Cite at least one reason to support your opinion.

20. **Thinking About the Big Question: Community or individual: Which is more important?** In an essay, discuss the kinds of efforts that are described in "To the Top of the World" and "The Voyage." Do they involve an entire community or a single individual? Cite at least one detail from each selection to support your points.

Name _____ Date _____

# Letter: Business Letter

## Prewriting: Gathering Details

Complete the following chart to keep track of the information for your letter.

| Purpose for Writing | Your Contact Information | Your Recipient's Information | Details to Support Your Request |
|---|---|---|---|
|  |  |  |  |

## Drafting: Providing Elaboration

Use the following graphic organizer to develop the body of your business letter by filling in the appropriate information on the right.

| Introduction | → |  |
| Supporting Detail 1 | → |  |
| Supporting Detail 2 | → |  |
| Supporting Detail 3 | → |  |
| Closing/Thank You | → |  |

**Writing Workshop—Unit 6, Part 1**
# Business Letter: Integrating Grammar Skills

## Revising Incorrect Use of Commas

A **comma** signals a brief pause. You should use a comma in these situations:

| | |
|---|---|
| before a conjunction that separates two independent clauses in a compound sentence | Our library is full of books, but it also has many other materials. |
| between items in a series | The library offers pages, tapes, and DVDs. |
| between adjectives of equal rank that modify the same noun or pronoun (If the word *and* can replace the comma, the adjectives are of equal rank) | The old library was a large, ugly building. |
| to set off introductory words, phrases, or clauses | Entering the library, you turn left for fiction. |
| to set off words, phrases, and clauses that interrupt a sentence | Mrs. Lee, the librarian, is very helpful. |

## Identifying Correct Use of Commas

**A. DIRECTIONS:** *Circle the letter of the sentence that uses commas correctly.*

1. A. The library offers separate sections for fiction, nonfiction, and reference.
   B. The library offers separate sections for fiction, nonfiction and reference.

2. A. In addition, there are separate sections for children and young adults.
   B. In addition there are separate sections for children, and young adults.

3. A. When Mr. Van my neighbor, visits the library he researches his family tree.
   B. When Mr. Van, my neighbor, visits the library, he researches his family tree.

## Fixing Incorrect Use of Commas

**B. DIRECTIONS:** *Rewrite this paragraph with commas inserted or removed wherever necessary.*

After the federal government cut money to the states most state county and local governments had budget problems. Many libraries, and other local services had to be cut back. Hoping to help a group of people began Bookworms an organization that is raising funds for the local library. One of the first things Bookworms organized, was an art show. Many creative, talented, artists donated their works and the money from the sales went to the library.

## Unit 6: Themes in the Oral Tradition
# Benchmark Test 11

## MULTIPLE CHOICE

### Reading Skill: Cause and Effect

1. Which of the following is an event or action that makes something else happen?
   A. a cause
   B. an effect
   C. a result
   D. a cause-and-effect relationship

2. Which statement best describes a story arranged in a cause-and-effect order?
   A. A single important event in the story is the cause of many events.
   B. Many events in the story are all causes of a single important event.
   C. A story event causes another event, which causes another event, and so on.
   D. Events that are causes are completely unrelated to events that are effects.

3. Which of the following words or phrases signals an effect?
   A. because
   B. since
   C. due to
   D. as a result

*Read this brief selection. Then, answer the questions about it.*

This winter there were snowstorms late in the season. Because the temperatures remained cold, snow piled high on the ground. Then, due to a sudden warm spell, the snow in our yard melted all at once. There was no place for the water to go except our basement. For this reason, we had more flooding than usual.

4. Which question would best help you identify the cause-and-effect relationships in this selection?
   A. What causes snowstorms late in the season?
   B. At what temperature does water turn to ice?
   C. What happened as a result of the sudden warm spell?
   D. What effects can flooding have on people's homes?

5. Which word or phrase in the selection signals an effect?
   A. because
   B. due to
   C. all at once
   D. for this reason

6. Based on the selection, what caused the snow to pile high on the ground?
   A. a sudden warm spell
   B. cold temperatures
   C. snow plows and shovels
   D. water in the basement

7. Based on the selection, what was the effect of the snow melting all at once?
   A. a sudden warm spell
   B. cold temperatures
   C. snow piles on the ground
   D. water in the basement

## Reading Skill: Analyze Cause-and-Effect Text Structure

*Read the selection. Then, answer the questions that follow.*

By the 1830s, the frontier had crossed the Mississippi River into a dry and treeless area called the Great Plains. Settlers in this region had to design houses that did not require wood. The log cabins in which many had lived back East were just not possible. Instead, they built houses of sod, layers of earth containing grass with its roots. These houses had both advantages and disadvantages. Because soil is a natural insulator, a sod house was cool in the summer and easy to heat in the winter. However, thick walls made the house hard to ventilate, and heavy rains caused even the sturdiest sod roofs to leak. In addition, dust falling from the roof and rising from the floor made it difficult to keep the house clean.

8. What caused settlers to refrain from building log cabins on the Great Plains?
   A. The roofs of log cabins leaked during heavy rains.
   B. The area was treeless.
   C. Wood turned out not to be a good insulator.
   D. They wanted a change from their life back East.

9. Why was a sod house cool in the summer and easy to heat in the winter?
   A. The thick walls aided ventilation.
   B. The weather in the Great Plains was moderate.
   C. The soil in the sod insulated the house.
   D. The house had many windows and a large fireplace.

10. Why were sod houses so difficult to keep clean?
    A. Dust came from both the top and bottom of the house.
    B. The settlers did not have good cleaning tools.
    C. The settlers tracked dirt into the house from outside.
    D. There was no good way to clean a dirt floor.

## Literary Analysis: Myths and Legends

11. Why were myths created?
    A. to create a body of literature that would stand the test of time
    B. to explain natural occurrences and express beliefs about right and wrong
    C. to show that gods and goddesses are just like human beings
    D. to give enduring fame to heroes and heroines who contributed to the society

12. What is the term used for writing that can be proved true or false?
    A. a myth
    B. a legend
    C. fiction
    D. a fact

13. What is an important difference between a myth and a legend?
    A. Most myths were created centuries ago, while most legends are modern creations.
    B. Myths were passed down orally, while legends were written literature from the start.
    C. Most myths try to explain a natural occurrence, while legends try to record history.
    D. Myths rarely have human characters, while legends feature only human characters.

**14.** What do most legends and epics have in common?

    **A.** They are both told in an informal, everyday language.

    **B.** They usually have a single, narrow setting.

    **C.** They both usually feature a dangerous journey or quest.

    **D.** They both reflect the values of the culture that produced them.

*Read the selection. Then, answer the questions that follow.*

Narcissus, the son of the river god Cephissus, was very handsome. One day he saw his own reflection in a pool of water. Thinking the lovely creature he saw was a water nymph, he fell in love with his own reflection. He kept trying to touch the beautiful creature, but each time he reached into the water, the creature seemed to move away. He finally died in despair and was turned into the flower which bears his name.

**15.** What does the myth of Narcissus show about gods and goddesses?

    **A.** They often display human qualities.

    **B.** They are all very athletic and handsome.

    **C.** They rarely display strong emotion.

    **D.** They are protected by all-powerful gods.

**16.** What main lesson does the myth of Narcissus teach?

    **A.** People should not waste water.

    **B.** Good-looking people are often unaware of their appearance.

    **C.** Too much self-love can be self-destructive.

    **D.** It is impossible for a human being to understand beauty.

**17.** What does the myth of Narcissus explain?

    **A.** the origin of river gods

    **B.** the cause of reflections in water

    **C.** the love of water

    **D.** the origin of a flower

*Read this short legend. Then, answer the questions about it.*

As a baby, John Henry reached for a hammer. It showed that he would grow up to be a mighty man. Sure enough, when he grew up, John Henry became a steel driver, hammering steel spikes to help build the railroads. He was amazingly strong and quick, driving steel so hard that lightning sometimes came out of his hammer. One day, when he and his fellow workers were building the C&O railroad tunnel in West Virginia, his boss brought a steam drill to the job. Insisting that he was better than any machine, John Henry agreed to race against the steam drill. He beat the steam drill by four feet, but he worked so hard that he died. Millions of admirers came from all over America to attend his funeral.

**18.** Which of the following details is most likely a fact on which the legend of John Henry is based?

A. Baby John Henry reached for a hammer to show that he would become a mighty man.

B. John Henry was a steel driver who helped build the C&O railroad tunnel in West Virginia.

C. John Henry was so strong and quick that lightning sometimes came out of his hammer.

D. Millions of people came from all over America to attend John Henry's funeral.

**19.** What makes John Henry a larger-than-life hero?

A. He is proud of his job.

B. He works on the railroad.

C. He is amazingly strong and quick.

D. He is helped by gods and goddesses.

**20.** Based on the details in the selection, what can you conclude about the culture that produced the legend of John Henry?

A. It was a culture that valued strength and hard work.

B. It was a culture that loved new inventions.

C. It was a culture that produced strong babies.

D. It was a culture in which funerals were small, private family affairs.

**Literary Analysis: Epics** *Read this summary of a famous epic. Then, answer the questions about it.*

Beowulf was the nephew of the king of the Geats, a people who lived in what is now Sweden. As a young man he won fame for his courage and strength in battle; he was also a fine swimmer and sailor. One day he sailed to nearby Denmark to help the Danes destroy a terrible monster named Grendel, who made nightly raids in which he grabbed Danish people to eat. After killing Grendel, Beowulf had to face Grendel's angry mother, whom he also killed. The Danish king rewarded Beowulf with riches. Beowulf then sailed back to Geatland, where he eventually became king. Many years later, when Beowulf was an old man, he died while battling a fire-breathing dragon who threatened his people.

**21.** Which part of the epic of Beowulf involves a quest?

A. Beowulf's skill and strength in battle

B. Beowolf's trip to Denmark to help the Danes

C. Beowulf's eventually becoming king

D. Beowulf's battle with the fire-breathing dragon

**22.** In which of the following ways is Beowulf typical of an epic hero?

A. He is a high-born hero who becomes a king.

B. He is an ordinary, everyday person.

C. He is a talented swimmer and sailor.

D. He is the son of a god and goddess.

**23.** Based on the selection, what can you conclude about the culture that produced it?

A. It was a land-bound culture with little knowledge of the sea and sailing.

B. It was a culture that admired courage and strength in battle.

C. It was a culture that saw the nearby Danes as enemies.

D. It was a culture that did not have the respect for motherhood that we have today.

Name _____  Date _____

## Vocabulary: Prefixes and Roots

24. Based on your knowledge of the prefix *uni-*, what do you do when you show *unity* with others?
    A. You act as one.
    B. You keep your distance.
    C. You show kindness.
    D. You go your separate ways.

25. Using your knowledge of the prefix *out-*, what does the word *outlying* mean in the following sentence?

    Factories are being built in the outlying suburbs.

    A. quiet and peaceful
    B. unlived in
    C. close to the center
    D. lying outside the limits

26. Based on the meaning of the prefix *out-*, what does it mean when you *outspend* someone?
    A. You spend the same as that person.
    B. You spend more than that person.
    C. You spend less than that person.
    D. You do not know what that person has spent.

27. How does the meaning of the word *domicile* reflect a meaning of the root *-dom-*?
    A. A domicile is a place where a person goes to rest.
    B. A domicile is a welcoming place.
    C. A domicile is the building in which one lives.
    D. A domicile is often made of wood.

28. Using your knowledge of the root *-dom-*, what does the word *dominant* mean in the following sentence?

    Male wolves in the pack will often fight with one another to determine which one is dominant.

    A. having the most control
    B. showing age the most
    C. acting the meanest
    D. being the most skillful

29. How does the meaning of the word *vacate* reflect the meaning of the root *-vac-*?
    A. When you vacate a place, someone else moves in.
    B. When you vacate a place, you take your things with you.
    C. When you vacate a place, you leave it empty.
    D. When you vacate a place, you go somewhere else.

## Grammar

30. Which sentence below is punctuated correctly?
    A. In the office were: an old metal desk, a large swivel chair, a new computer, and a filing cabinet.
    B. The secretary sent in an order for: pens, pencils, printer ribbons, and reams of papers.
    C. Supply the following information, your name, your address, and your phone number.
    D. Office hours are at these times: Mondays at two, Wednesdays at three, and Fridays at one.

31. Which sentence below is punctuated correctly?

   A. This year we flew to Albuquerque; we then drove from there to Santa Fe.

   B. We also visited Las Vegas, New Mexico, it is nothing like Las Vegas, Nevada.

   C. The trip lasted seven days we spent two days with Aunt Mia in Taos.

   D. We have also visited Dodge City, Kansas, Denver, Colorado, and Salt Lake City, Utah.

32. Where should you add a comma in this sentence?

   Alicia Carlos and Gabriel rehearsed for weeks and gave fine performances.

   A. after *Alicia, Carlos,* and *Gabriel*

   B. after *Alicia* and *Carlos* only

   C. after *Alicia* and *Gabriel* only

   D. after *Alicia, Carlos,* and *weeks*

33. Which sentence below is punctuated correctly?

   A. The new movie theater opens at noon, and closes at midnight on weekends.

   B. It is a modern, air-conditioned, building with four different theaters.

   C. My sister Anita, mistakenly went to the theater at noon on a Wednesday.

   D. The theater opens at five but still closes at midnight on weekdays.

34. Where should you use a colon in a business letter?

   A. after the heading

   B. after the inside address

   C. after the greeting

   D. after the closing

35. Which of the following choices is an appropriate closing for a business letter?

   A. *To Whom It May Concern* followed by a colon

   B. *Dear Madam* followed by a comma

   C. *Sincerely* followed by a colon

   D. *Respectfully* followed by a comma

## ESSAY

### Writing

36. Imagine that you lived long ago and had little understanding of science. Create a myth to explain one of nature's mysteries. On a separate sheet of paper, jot down your ideas for a myth explaining why the sky is blue on a sunny day or why it gets dark at night.

37. Legends often are set in distant times and unusual places. On a separate sheet of paper, write a description of a place you have encountered in a legend or a place in which you might set a legend of your own creation.

38. Imagine that you have ordered an item online or over the phone and, when it arrived, there was something wrong with it. You are now writing a business letter to complain to the company that sent the item. The company is Bruffduff & Son, 2100 Michigan Avenue, Chicago, IL 60601. Write your business letter on a separate sheet of paper. Be sure to use proper business-letter form.

Name _____ Starting Date _____ Ending Date _____

# Unit 6: Themes in Oral Tradition  Skills Concept Map—2

## Community or individual: Which is more important?

**Literary Analysis:**
Oral Tradition

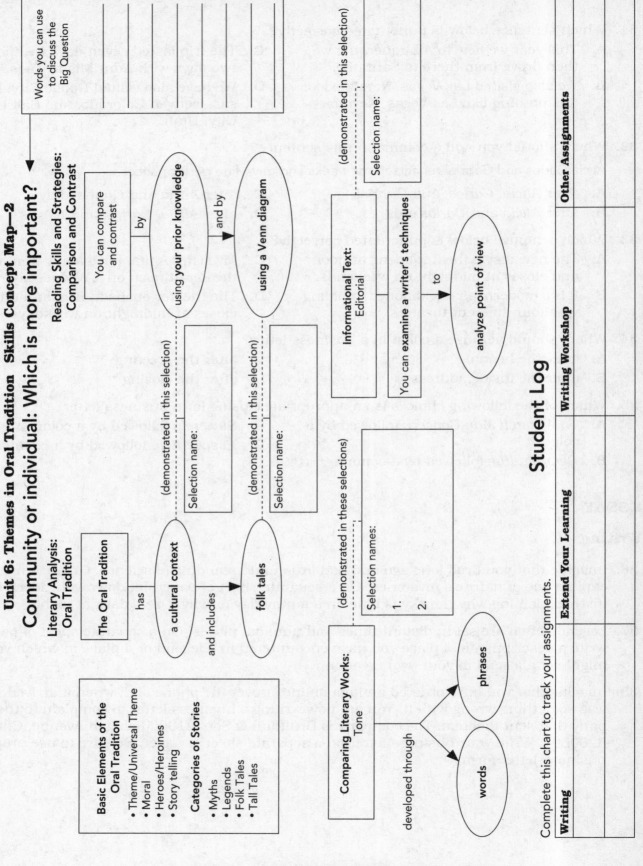

The Oral Tradition — has → a cultural context — and includes → folk tales

(demonstrated in this selection)
Selection name: _____

(demonstrated in this selection)
Selection name: _____

**Basic Elements of the Oral Tradition**
- Theme/Universal Theme
- Moral
- Heroes/Heroines
- Story telling

**Categories of Stories**
- Myths
- Legends
- Folk Tales
- Tall Tales

**Reading Skills and Strategies:**
Comparison and Contrast

You can compare and contrast — by → using your prior knowledge — and by → using a Venn diagram

**Informational Text:**
Editorial

You can examine a writer's techniques — to → analyze point of view

(demonstrated in this selection)
Selection name: _____

**Comparing Literary Works:**
Tone — developed through → phrases / words

(demonstrated in these selections)
Selection names:
1. _____
2. _____

Words you can use to discuss the Big Question

## Student Log

Complete this chart to track your assignments.

| Writing | Extend Your Learning | Writing Workshop | Other Assignments |
|---|---|---|---|
| | | | |
| | | | |

# Vocabulary Warm-up Word Lists

*Study these words from "Sun and Moon in a Box." Then, complete the activities that follow.*

# Word List A

**burden** [BER den] *n.* a load that is carried
   Barbara found carrying the suitcase to be a <u>burden</u>.

**cunning** [KUHN ing] *adj.* clever, sly
   The <u>cunning</u> thief knew how to avoid being caught.

**eagle** [EE guhl] *n.* a large bird of the hawk family
   The <u>eagle</u> built its nest high on a cliff.

**lag** [LAG] *v.* to fall behind
   Roger will <u>lag</u> in the race if he does not practice.

**relented** [ri LENT id] *v.* became less stubborn or set in one's ways
   Mary's sister <u>relented</u> and allowed Mary to borrow her earrings.

**reliable** [ri LYE uh buhl] *adj.* dependable or trustworthy
   The <u>reliable</u> clock kept very good time.

**talons** [TAL uhnz] *n.* sharp claws
   The hawk's sharp <u>talons</u> clutched its prey.

**wooded** [WOOD id] *adj.* covered with woods or trees
   The cottage was located in a heavily <u>wooded</u> area.

# Word List B

**betray** [bee TRAY] *v.* to break faith or trust
   Paul told Ben that he would not <u>betray</u> Ben's trust.

**embarrassed** [em BAR uhst] *v.* caused to feel self-conscious
   The praise she received <u>embarrassed</u> her and made her blush.

**grasshoppers** [GRAS hahp erz] *n.* leaping, plant-eating insects with powerful hind legs
   The <u>grasshoppers</u> jumped a long distance in the garden.

**objected** [uhb JEKT id] *v.* opposed
   Sally's father <u>objected</u> to the late hour she said she would return home.

**outer** [OWT er] *adj.* located farther out than another spot or place
   You must peel the <u>outer</u> part of an orange before eating it.

**pestering** [PES ter ing] *v.* bothering or annoying endlessly
   The puppy would not stop <u>pestering</u> Amy for a treat.

**regretted** [ri GRET id] *v.* felt sorry about something that happened
   Tom <u>regretted</u> that he did not have a chance to say good-bye to his friend.

**rely** [ri LY] *v.* to count on, to depend
   Can I <u>rely</u> on you to pick me up at the train station tonight?

**"Sun and Moon in a Box"** by Richard Erdoes and Alfonso Ortiz
# Vocabulary Warm-up Exercises

**Exercise A** *Fill in each blank in the paragraph below with an appropriate word from Word List A. Use each word only once.*

Mike wanted to be a(n) [1] _____ for the costume ball. He loved these powerful, [2] _____ birds of prey. At first, Mike's mom said no because she didn't know how she'd make such a costume. At last, however, good, old [3] _____ Mom [4] _____ and said yes. She made him a great costume complete with giant feathers and big [5] _____ to wear as claws on his feet. On the night of the ball, Mike had a great time swooping around his [6] _____ yard, as he pretended to fly. The only problem was dancing at the ball. Then, the feathers and claws became a heavy [7] _____ to move around in. Mike began to [8] _____ behind the others in the conga line. Once he took them off, however, he felt as light as a feather!

**Exercise B** *Revise each sentence so that the underlined vocabulary word is used in a logical way. Be sure to keep the vocabulary word in your revision.*

**Example:** After Barry became <u>embarrassed</u>, he felt very confident.
*After Barry became <u>embarrassed</u>, he felt very self-conscious.*

1. The <u>grasshoppers</u> could not jump very far with their powerful hind legs.
   _____

2. If we lie and <u>betray</u> our friends, they will learn they can <u>rely</u> on us.
   _____

3. It is very pleasant when someone is continuously <u>pestering</u> us.
   _____

4. The <u>outer</u> layer of clothing is the hardest one to remove if you are too warm.
   _____

5. The majority of voters <u>objected</u> to the proposed law, so it easily passed.
   _____

6. Because Tom <u>regretted</u> his rudeness, he decided not to apologize.
   _____

Name _____   Date _____

**"Sun and Moon in a Box"** by Richard Erdoes and Alfonso Ortiz
# Reading Warm-up A

*Read the following passage. Pay special attention to the underlined words. Then, read it again, and complete the activities. Use a separate sheet of paper for your written answers.*

July 21

Dear Cousin Wayne,

I'm writing to you from the great nature camp I'm attending this summer! As you know, I love learning about animals, so Mom and Dad finally <u>relented</u>, after a lot of pleading on my part. They are letting me spend the summer here.

The camp is located in a <u>wooded</u> area. It is near the cliffs that overlook the river. It is an excellent spot for observing an <u>eagle</u> that lives atop the cliffs. Every day, I study the habits of this powerful bird. Like its cousin, the hawk, the eagle is a <u>cunning</u> predator. It hunts rabbits, mice, and other birds. Those are just a few of the animals it likes to eat.

I have watched the eagle as it circles a flock of mourning doves that eat on the ground near our cabin. As they realize that the eagle is descending upon them, most of the doves take flight. Often, though, one of them may <u>lag</u> behind. The eagle will swoop at the slower bird. Often the dove becomes flustered and might hit against one of the windows of the cabin. The eagle quickly grasps the prey in its sharp <u>talons</u> and flies away with it. It all seems to happen in one smooth motion.

The eagle's wingspan is wide. It beats its wings powerfully as it flies away. The prey it carries in its claws is not a heavy <u>burden</u> for it.

Although I have not seen if this eagle has hatched any chicks yet, I am going to continue to watch its nest. I have read that eagles are devoted, <u>reliable</u> parents, who always bring food back to the nest for the hungry chicks.

So far, this has been a great summer! Please write back soon and let me know what you are up to.

Love, your cousin,

Ben

1. Circle the words that tell what Ben did so that his parents <u>relented</u>. Define *relented*.

2. Underline the words that tell what is located in a <u>wooded</u> area in the story. What else might be found in a *wooded* area?

3. Circle the words that describe where the <u>eagle</u> lives. What is an *eagle*?

4. Underline the word that <u>cunning</u> describes. What is a synonym for *cunning*?

5. Underline two sentences that tell what the eagle does if a bird happens to <u>lag</u> behind. Use *lag* in a sentence.

6. Circle the words that tell what the eagle grasps in its <u>talons</u>. What other animals have *talons*?

7. Circle the words that tell what is not a heavy <u>burden</u> for the eagle. Define *burden*.

8. Underline the words that tell why eagles are <u>reliable</u> parents. Use *reliable* in a sentence.

**"Sun and Moon in a Box"** by Richard Erdoes and Alfonso Ortiz
# Reading Warm-up B

*Read the following passage. Pay special attention to the underlined words. Then, read it again, and complete the activities. Use a separate sheet of paper for your written answers.*

The Zuni are a Native American people who live in what is now the southwest United States. Together with the Hopi and Acoma peoples of this desert region, the Zuni are known as Pueblos.

The apartment-like structures the Zunis traditionally lived in are known as pueblo dwellings. These were made of stone and logs and had many levels. The <u>outer</u> rooms housed the families. These apartments surrounded a central courtyard. The families were used to living together, so they were not <u>embarrassed</u> by living in such close quarters.

When Spanish soldiers invaded the area for the second time in the 1680s, the Zuni people were wary of them. The natives feared that the invaders would <u>betray</u> the Zunis' trust. The tribe decided it was safer to move to a high, flat area, away from the soldiers.

The Zunis grew crops in the desert. The men hunted, made tools, and created jewelry. The women gathered and grew the food, cared for the children, and made pottery and baskets. Both men and women built and took care of the houses. If children wanted to join in the work, no one <u>objected</u>. The children's questions were not seen as <u>pestering</u> the adults. The children were welcomed, for that was how the Zunis could <u>rely</u> on being able to pass traditional skills on to the younger generation.

During the years, unfortunately, some traditional skills and cultural activities faded away, as European practices took their place. Many Zuni people <u>regretted</u> this state of affairs. They have since worked very hard to revive their native culture. Jewelry, pottery, and sculptures are some of the art forms created by the Zuni. The sculptures are carved from stones and minerals and represent <u>grasshoppers</u>, bears, skunks, and other animals.

Traditional beliefs, dances, and rituals are also practiced by some of today's Zuni, as they strive to keep their culture alive.

1. Underline the words that tell how the <u>outer</u> rooms of the pueblo were used. Define *outer*.

2. Circle the words that tell why the people were not <u>embarrassed</u>. What is a synonym for *embarrassed*?

3. Circle the word that tells who the Zunis thought might <u>betray</u> them. Use *betray* in a sentence.

4. Underline the words that tell to what situation no one <u>objected</u>. To what have you ever *objected*?

5. Underline the words that tell what the adults did not view as <u>pestering</u> them. What is a synonym for *pestering*?

6. Circle the words that tell upon what the Zunis could <u>rely</u>. Use *rely* in a sentence.

7. Underline the sentence that explains the state of affairs that the Zunis <u>regretted</u>. What have you ever *regretted*?

8. Underline the words that tell from what the sculptures of <u>grasshoppers</u> are made. What are *grasshoppers*?

Name _____ Date _____

# Writing About the Big Question

## Community or individual: Which is more important?

### Big Question Vocabulary

| | | | | |
|---|---|---|---|---|
| common | community | culture | custom | diversity |
| duty | environment | ethnicity | family | group |
| individual | team | tradition | unify | unique |

**A.** *Use one or more words from the list above to complete each sentence.*

1. Jesse and his friends joined a local fundraising _____.

2. The money raised would help protect the _____ and local wildlife.

3. The friends enjoyed working together toward a _____ goal.

4. They decided to make it an annual _____ .

**B.** *Follow the directions in responding to each of the items below.*

1. List two different times when you worked with others as part of a team.

   _____

   _____

2. Write two or three sentences describing one of the preceding experiences and explaining how it affected those involved. Use at least two of the Big Question vocabulary words. _____

   _____

   _____

   _____

**C.** *Complete the sentence below. Then, write a short paragraph in which you connect this idea to the big question.*

In order for people to work together as part of a team, they must _____

_____

_____

_____

_____

_____

_____

_____

_____

Name _____ Date _____

"Sun and Moon in a Box" by Richard Erdoes and Alfonso Ortiz
# Reading: Use Prior Knowledge to Compare and Contrast

A **comparison** tells how two or more things are alike. A **contrast** tells how two or more things are different. When you **compare and contrast,** you recognize similarities and differences. You can often understand an unfamiliar concept by **using your prior knowledge to compare and contrast.** For example, you may understand an ancient culture better if you look for ways in which it is similar to and different from your own culture. You also might find similarities and differences between a story told long ago and one that is popular today. To compare and contrast stories, ask questions such as "What does this event bring to mind?" or "Does this character make me think of someone I know or have read about?"

**DIRECTIONS:** *Read each passage from "Sun and Moon in a Box." In the second column of the chart, write a question that will help you compare or contrast the passage to something else you have read or to something or someone you know or know about. In the third column, write the answer to your question. The first item has been completed as an example.*

| Passage from "Sun and Moon in a Box" | Question Based on My Prior Knowledge | Comparison or Contrast |
|---|---|---|
| 1. Coyote and Eagle were hunting. Eagle caught rabbits. Coyote caught nothing but grasshoppers. Coyote said, "Friend Eagle, my chief, we make a great hunting pair." | How are these characters like Wile E. Coyote and Road Runner in the cartoons I used to watch? | Road Runner is a bird, but not an eagle, and Wile E. Coyote tries to catch him. Here, the coyote and the eagle seem to be friends. |
| 2. Whenever [the Kachinas] wanted light they opened the lid and let the sun peek out. Then, it was day. When they wanted less light, they opened the box just a little for the moon to look out. | | |
| 3. After a while Coyote called Eagle, "My chief, let me have the box. I am ashamed to let you do all the carrying." "No," said Eagle, "You are not reliable. You might be curious and open the box." | | |
| 4. [Coyote] sat down and opened the box. In a flash, . . . icy winds made all living things shiver. Then, before Coyote could put the lid back, . . . snow fell down from heaven and covered the plains and the mountains. | | |

Name _____  Date _____

"Sun and Moon in a Box" by Richard Erdoes and Alfonso Ortiz
# Literary Analysis: Cultural Context

Stories such as fables, folk tales, and myths are influenced by cultural context. **Cultural context** is the background, customs, and beliefs of the people who originally told them. Knowing the cultural context of a work will help you understand and appreciate it. You can keep track of the cultural context of a work by considering these elements: the *title* of the selection, the *time* in which it takes place, the *place* in which it takes place, the *customs* of the characters, the *beliefs* that are expressed or suggested.

Consider this passage from "Sun and Moon in a Box":

Now, at this time, the earth was still soft and new. There was as yet no sun and no moon.

The passage tells you that the folk tale is set in the distant past, before Earth looked as it does today and before there was a sun and a moon. From the cultural context, you can infer that the people who told the tale believed there was a time when Earth existed, but the sun and the moon as yet did not.

**DIRECTIONS:** *Read each passage from "Sun and Moon in a Box." In the second column of the chart, indicate which element of the cultural context—*time, place, customs, *or* beliefs—*the passage illustrates. Then, explain your choice. Tell why you think the example shows the element you have chosen.*

| Passage from "Sun and Moon in a Box" | Element of Cultural Context and Explanation |
|---|---|
| **1.** [Eagle and Coyote] went toward the west. They came to a deep canyon. | |
| **2.** Whenever [the Kachinas] wanted light they opened the lid and let the sun peek out. . . . When they wanted less light, they opened the box just a little for the moon to look out. | |
| **3.** "Let us steal the box," said Coyote. "No, that would be wrong," said Eagle. "Let us just borrow it." | |
| **4.** Eagle grabbed the box and . . . Coyote ran after him on the ground. After a while Coyote called Eagle: "My chief, let me have the box. I am ashamed to let you do all the carrying." | |

Unit 6 Resources: Themes in the Oral Tradition
© Pearson Education, Inc. All rights reserved.
**133**

Name _____ Date _____

# Vocabulary Builder

## Word List

cunning     curiosity     pestering     regretted     relented     reliable

**A. DIRECTIONS:** *Circle* T *if the statement is* true *or* F *if it is* false. *Then, explain your answer.*

1. A car that starts only half the time is *reliable*.

   T / F _____

   _____

2. A teacher who refuses her students' pleas to make a test easier has *relented*.

   T / F _____

   _____

3. Someone who always gets caught cheating is *cunning*.

   T / F _____

   _____

4. A man who thoroughly disliked a movie, probably *regretted* going to see it.

   T / F _____

   _____

5. Parents would be charmed by a child who is *pestering* them.

   T / F _____

   _____

6. A gossipy neighbor's *curiosity* naturally leads him to mind his own business.

   T / F _____

   _____

**B. WORD STUDY:** *The Latin suffix* -ity *means "state, quality, or condition of." Answer each of the following questions using one of these words containing* -ity: *elasticity, sincerity, predictability.*

1. How might you test an object's *elasticity*?

   _____

2. What might lead you to question a person's *sincerity*?

   _____

3. Why might you appreciate a coworker's *predictability*?

   _____

Name _____ Date _____

**"Sun and Moon in a Box"** by Richard Erdoes and Alfonso Ortiz

# Enrichment: Coyote, the Character With Many Roles

"Sun and Moon in a Box" is not the only story in which Coyote plays a part. Coyote characters are extremely common in Native American tales and myths. In those stories, Coyote plays many roles.

Sometimes, Coyote is a hero. Then, he is part human, or he helps humans. In one tale, Coyote helps defeat a monster that is eating all the other animals.

At other times, Coyote is a trickster. As a trickster, Coyote fools humans and other animals. As a trickster, Coyote likes to steal things and make trouble. The key to the trickster character is survival. Whatever people or other animals do to him, Coyote survives and comes out on top. As a trickster, Coyote is somewhat like the real-life coyote of today. Many ranchers do not like coyotes because they prey on the ranchers' livestock. Consider the situation from the coyote's point of view, however: The animal is only trying to survive.

Coyote can also play the fool. Like any fool, Coyote lacks judgment. He does stupid things.

No matter what his role, the Coyote of myth and folklore often teaches a moral lesson.

**Directions:** *Answer the following questions. Support your responses with evidence from the preceding passage, your reading of "Sun and Moon in a Box," and anything else you know about the role of Coyote in folklore.*

1. Does Coyote play the role of a hero in "Sun and Moon in a Box"? How can you tell?

   _____

   _____

2. Does Coyote play the role of a trickster and/or a survivor in "Sun and Moon in a Box"? How can you tell?

   _____

   _____

   _____

3. Does Coyote play the role of a fool in "Sun and Moon in a Box"? How can you tell?

   _____

   _____

4. Does Coyote teach a moral lesson in "Sun and Moon in a Box"? Defend your answer. If he does teach a lesson, explain what it is.

   _____

   _____

   _____

**"Sun and Moon in a Box"** by Alfonso Ortiz and Richard Erdoes
# Open-Book Test

**Short Answer** *Write your responses to the questions in this section on the lines provided.*

1. The first few paragraphs of "Sun and Moon in a Box" describe the abilities of Eagle and Coyote as hunters. Which character seems more impressive? Use details from the selection to explain.

   _____
   _____
   _____

2. Near the beginning of "Sun and Moon in a Box," it becomes clear that Eagle is sorry to have Coyote as a traveling companion. Why is Eagle displeased? Use details to support your answer.

   _____
   _____
   _____

3. How does the setting of "Sun and Moon in a Box" show the cultural context of the story? Think about when and where the story takes place. Use details from the story to explain.

   _____
   _____
   _____

4. What belief about the sun and the moon is shared by both the Kachinas and Eagle in "Sun and Moon in a Box"? Use details from the middle of the story to support your answer.

   _____
   _____
   _____

5. In the middle of "Sun and Moon in a Box," Eagle says that Coyote is not reliable. On what actions or qualities does Eagle base this opinion of his companion? Use your understanding of the word *reliable* to respond.

   _____
   _____
   _____

6. In the middle of "Sun and Moon in a Box," why does Coyote say he is ashamed to have Eagle carry the box? Consider what Coyote really wants. Use details from the story to answer.

   _____
   _____
   _____

7. In "Sun and Moon in a Box," Coyote calls Eagle his "chief." How does this suggest the cultural context of the story? Explain your answer, using details from the story.

_____

_____

_____

8. In the middle of "Sun and Moon in a Box," Coyote asks several times to hold the box, and Eagle repeatedly refuses. How do Eagle's refusals reveal his opinions of both Coyote and himself? Use details from the middle of the selection to support your response.

_____

_____

_____

9. Toward the end of "Sun and Moon in a Box," Eagle relented to Coyote's many requests to carry the box. Does *relented* give the idea that Eagle is happy about giving Coyote the box? Explain, using the definition of *relented*.

_____

_____

10. The Zuni people used stories like "Sun and Moon in a Box" to show their beliefs. Use the chart to compare the Zuni to our modern culture. Read the quotation from the story. Then, write a question based on your prior knowledge. Write a comparison or contrast that shows how we are similar to or different from the Zuni.

| Quotation | Question | Comparison/Contrast |
|---|---|---|
| "Let us steal the box," said Coyote. "No, that would be wrong," said Eagle. "Let us just borrow it." | | |

_____

## Essay

*Write an extended response to the question of your choice or to the question or questions your teacher assigns you.*

11. Think about the relationship between Eagle and Coyote in "Sun and Moon in a Box." Eagle is the leader, and Coyote is the follower. In a brief essay, identify the ways in which each character demonstrates his position as leader or follower. Use information from the story as support for your answer.

12. In "Sun and Moon in a Box," which character—Eagle or Coyote—do you find more admirable? In a brief essay, compare their good and bad qualities. Include in your answer an opinion about which character turns out to be more of a disappointment. Use details from the selection for support.

13. In "Sun and Moon in a Box," Eagle makes a distinction between stealing the box and borrowing it. In an essay, explain whether what he does is really borrowing the box. Is his action at all justifiable? Use details from the story to support your opinion.

14. **Thinking About the Big Question: Community or Individual: Which is more important?** "Sun and Moon in a Box" describes how a community's cultural beliefs affect the individuals living in the community. Write an essay in which you explore whether the individual or the community is more important, or valued more highly, in this story. In your answer, include a discussion about the Kachinas' sense of community responsibility.

## Oral Response

15. Go back to question 1, 3, or 8 or to the question your teacher assigns you. Take a few minutes to expand your answer and prepare an oral response. Find additional details in the selection that support your points. If necessary, make notes to guide your oral response.

**"Sun and Moon in a Box"** by Richard Erdoes and Alfonso Ortiz
# Selection Test A

**Critical Reading** *Identify the letter of the choice that best answers the question.*

_____ 1. Where does "Sun and Moon in a Box" take place?
 A. in the West
 B. in a city
 C. in outer space
 D. on a mountaintop

_____ 2. Who are the main characters in "Sun and Moon in a Box"?
 A. the Kachinas
 B. the Sun and the Moon
 C. Eagle and Coyote
 D. summer and winter

_____ 3. In "Sun and Moon in a Box," the narrator says,
 Eagle regretted to have Coyote for a companion.
 Why does he say that?
 A. Eagle realizes that Coyote is a thief.
 B. Eagle has to do all the hunting to feed the two of them.
 C. Eagle must carry Coyote across the canyons and rivers.
 D. Eagle does not want to share the sun and the moon with Coyote.

_____ 4. According to "Sun and Moon in a Box," for what do the Kachinas use the sun and the moon?
 A. to create the seasons
 B. to create day and night
 C. to light their homes
 D. to light their dances

_____ 5. In "Sun and Moon in a Box," how are Eagle and Coyote alike?
 A. They are Kachina dancers.
 B. They want to steal the box.
 C. They are creatures who hunt.
 D. They are humans in disguise.

____ 6. In "Sun and Moon in a Box," which statements describe ways in which Coyote and Eagle are different?

    I. Eagle can fly, and Coyote can run.

    II. Eagle catches rabbits, and Coyote catches grasshoppers.

    III. Eagle can talk, but Coyote cannot talk.

    IV. Eagle wants to borrow the box, and Coyote wants to steal it.

    **A.** I, II, III       **B.** II, III, IV       **C.** I, II, IV       **D.** I, III, IV

____ 7. In "Sun and Moon in a Box," Eagle is afraid to let Coyote carry the box. What trait of Coyote's is he worried about?

    **A.** his intelligence

    **B.** his laziness

    **C.** his dishonesty

    **D.** his pride

____ 8. In "Sun and Moon in a Box," what is Coyote's real reason for asking Eagle to let him carry the box?

    **A.** He wants it for himself.

    **B.** He wants to share the work.

    **C.** He wants to return it.

    **D.** He wants to let the sun escape.

____ 9. In "Sun and Moon in a Box," what happens when Coyote opens the box?

    **A.** The sun blinds him forever.

    **B.** He grows a winter coat for warmth.

    **C.** The sun and moon escape, and winter comes.

    **D.** Eagle captures the sun and moon and returns them to the box.

____ 10. According to "Sun and Moon in a Box," what is the climate like before Coyote opens the box?

    **A.** It is summer all the time.

    **B.** There are two seasons, spring and fall.

    **C.** There are two seasons, summer and winter.

    **D.** There are four seasons.

____ 11. Which word *best* describes Eagle's action in giving the box to Coyote?

    **A.** mean

    **B.** cautious

    **C.** foolish

    **D.** helpful

____ 12. Based on your reading of "Sun and Moon in a Box," you can draw conclusions about the beliefs of the Zuni people, the tellers of this story. Which statements best describe their beliefs?

    I. The sun and the moon are precious.

    II. The box should be hidden in a canyon.

    III. It is important to keep one's promises.

    IV. The eagle is trustworthy; the coyote is not.

    **A.** I, II, III    **B.** I, III, IV    **C.** II, III, IV    **D.** I, II, IV

____ 13. What kind of work is "Sun and Moon in a Box"?

    **A.** a drama              **C.** a biography

    **B.** a folk tale           **D.** an essay

## Vocabulary and Grammar

____ 14. In which sentence is the meaning of the word *relented* expressed?

    **A.** Coyote begged and begged Eagle to let him carry the box.

    **B.** The Kachinas kept the sun and the moon in a box and used them wisely.

    **C.** Eagle at last gave in to Coyote and allowed him to carry the box.

    **D.** The sun and the moon flew into the sky, causing a change in the climate.

____ 15. In which sentence is the capitalization correct?

    **A.** "My chief, I cannot fly," said coyote.

    **B.** "Let us steal the box," said coyote.

    **C.** "No, I don't trust you," Eagle repeated.

    **D.** "my chief, I am really embarrassed."

## Essay

16. Several times Coyote asks Eagle to let him carry the box, and each time Eagle says no. At last, Eagle takes pity on Coyote and lets him carry it. As you were reading "Sun and Moon in a Box," did you think that Eagle should have let Coyote carry the box? Why or why not? Explain your response in an essay. Cite a detail from the story to support your point of view.

17. In what ways are Coyote and Eagle alike? In what ways are they different? In an essay, cite at least one example from "Sun and Moon in a Box" that shows the two characters' similarities and at least one example that shows their differences.

18. **Thinking About the Big Question: Community or individual: Which is more important?** "Sun and Moon in a Box" describes how a community's cultural beliefs affect the individuals living in the community. Write an essay in which you explore whether the individual or the community is more important in this story.

Name _____  Date _____

**"Sun and Moon in a Box"** by Richard Erdoes and Alfonso Ortiz
# Selection Test B

**Critical Reading** *Identify the letter of the choice that best completes the statement or answers the question.*

____ 1. What is the setting of the opening of "Sun and Moon in a Box"?
  A. the present day
  B. the distant future
  C. a time before animals roamed the earth
  D. a time before the sun and the moon were in the sky

____ 2. In "Sun and Moon in a Box," what are the Kachinas doing when Coyote and Eagle first see them?
  A. eating
  B. hunting
  C. dancing
  D. singing

____ 3. According to "Sun and Moon in a Box," for what do the Kachinas use the sun and the moon?
  A. to create day and night
  B. to heat their pueblo
  C. to search out prey to hunt
  D. to create the seasons

____ 4. Based on "Sun and Moon in a Box", what can you infer about the Kachinas?
  A. They keep all pretty things for themselves.
  B. They treat the sun and the moon as if they were precious.
  C. They keep every element of nature in a box.
  D. They want to attract the attention of Eagle and Coyote.

____ 5. The following statements are based on contrasts between Eagle and Coyote in "Sun and Moon in a Box." Which statement most likely reflects a traditional belief of the Zuni?
  A. Rabbits are superior to grasshoppers.
  B. Flying is more highly valued than running.
  C. Flying is more highly valued than swimming.
  D. Borrowing is acceptable, but stealing is not.

____ 6. In "Sun and Moon in a Box," why does Eagle say that the box is "precious"?
  A. It is covered with jewels.
  B. It is made of gold.
  C. It contains the sun and the moon.
  D. It belongs to the Kachinas.

Name _____  Date _____

____ 7. Which of the following statements *best* summarizes the argument Coyote makes to persuade Eagle to let him carry the box?
A. Others will think badly of me if I let you do all the work.
B. I will share the blame with you when the Kachinas find us.
C. You took the box originally, so I should be the one to carry it.
D. I always keep my promises, so let me carry the box.

____ 8. In "Sun and Moon in a Box," why does Eagle allow Coyote to carry the box?
A. He is tired of carrying it.
B. He wants to trust Coyote.
C. He regrets having taken it.
D. He is playing a trick on Coyote.

____ 9. Toward the end of "Sun and Moon in a Box," Eagle says,
"I knew what kind of low, cunning, stupid creature you are. I should have remembered that you never keep a promise."

What can you infer from Eagle's remark?
A. Coyote and Eagle have just met.
B. Eagle has a good memory.
C. Eagle is more intelligent than Coyote.
D. Coyote has broken promises before.

____ 10. How does the setting at the beginning of "Sun and Moon in a Box" compare with the setting at the end?
A. The beginning takes place in a canyon, and the end takes place at a river.
B. The beginning takes place in summer, and the end takes place in winter.
C. The beginning takes place in the sky, and the end takes place on the ground.
D. The beginning takes place by a river, and the end takes place at Kachina Pueblo.

____ 11. Which statement describes a similarity between Eagle and Coyote in "Sun and Moon in a Box"?
A. Both are trustworthy.
B. Both are swimmers.
C. Both are hunters.
D. Both are cunning.

____ 12. Which statement describes a belief of the Zuni that is expressed in "Sun and Moon in a Box"?
A. Animals are more powerful than humans.
B. Animals are deceitful and cunning.
C. Animals have character traits.
D. Animals are trustworthy and strong.

____ 13. Based on "Sun and Moon in a Box," you can infer that the Zuni traditionally believed coyotes are
A. stupid.
B. dishonest.
C. poor hunters.
D. excellent hunters.

Unit 6 Resources: Themes in the Oral Tradition
© Pearson Education, Inc. All rights reserved.
143

_____ 14. Based on "Sun and Moon in a Box," you can infer that the Zuni traditionally valued
  A. cunning.
  B. curiosity.
  C. reliability.
  D. beauty.

## Vocabulary and Grammar

_____ 15. In which sentence is the word *relented* used correctly?
  A. Eagle *relented* and let Coyote carry the box.
  B. Coyote *relented* and refused to say he was sorry.
  C. Eagle *relented* and did not change his position.
  D. Coyote *relented* and kept making the same point.

_____ 16. In which sentence is the meaning of the word *curb* expressed?
  A. The Kachinas protected the sun and the moon.
  B. Eagle flew over the canyons, far above Coyote.
  C. Coyote was unable to control his curiosity.
  D. The sun and the moon escaped from the box.

_____ 17. In which sentence is the capitalization correct?
  A. Coyote said to Eagle, "you see, I cannot fly."
  B. Coyote said to eagle, "you see, I cannot fly."
  C. Coyote said to eagle, "You see, I cannot fly."
  D. Coyote said to Eagle, "You see, I cannot fly."

_____ 18. In which sentence is the capitalization correct?
  A. "No, I won't give you the box," Said eagle to coyote.
  B. "No, i won't give you the box," said eagle to coyote.
  C. "No, I won't give you the box," said Eagle to Coyote.
  D. "No, I won't give you the box," Said Eagle to Coyote.

## Essay

19. In your opinion, is Eagle fully responsible for the appearance of the first winter in "Sun and Moon in a Box"? Is he partly responsible? Does he bear no responsibility at all? Why or why not? In an essay, give your opinion. Cite at least two details from the selection to support your position.

20. Many cultures have traditionally used stories with animal characters to comment on human behavior. What comments about human behavior might the Zuni be making in "Sun and Moon in a Box"? In an essay, describe Coyote and Eagle as they are portrayed in the selection. Then, tell what message about human behavior the selection makes.

21. **Thinking About the Big Question: Community or individual: Which is more important?** "Sun and Moon in a Box" describes how a community's cultural beliefs affect the individuals living in the community. Write an essay in which you explore whether the individual or the community is more important, or valued more highly, in this story. In your answer, include a discussion about the Kachinas' sense of community responsibility.

# Vocabulary Warm-up Word Lists

*Study these words from "How the Snake Got Poison." Then, complete the activities that follow.*

## Word List A

**belly** [BEL ee] *n.* the stomach or underside of an animal
  The puppy's <u>belly</u> was round and full after it ate.

**claws** [KLAWZ] *n.* an animal's sharp, curved nails
  The cat used its <u>claws</u> for digging, scratching, and climbing.

**enemy** [EN uh mee] *n.* someone who wishes to hurt another
  The soldiers were trained to combat the <u>enemy</u> during battle.

**fight** [FYT] *v.* to take part in a physical struggle or battle
  The two boxers will <u>fight</u> in the boxing ring.

**poison** [POY zuhn] *n.* a substance that causes death or illness
  The skull-and-crossbones label on the paint meant it was <u>poison</u>.

**rattles** [RAT uhlz] *n.* rings on a rattlesnake's tail that make a rattling sound
  The hikers thought they heard the warning sound of <u>rattles</u> nearby.

**shakes** [SHAYKS] *v.* causes to move up and down or sideways
  The ground <u>shakes</u> with every step the giant takes.

**snakes** [SNAYKS] *n.* long, scaly reptiles without legs or feet
  At the zoo, the <u>snakes</u> slid across the floor of their cage.

## Word List B

**earth** [ERTH] *n.* the planet we live on, or this world
  Countless species of insects live on the <u>earth</u>.

**generations** [jen uh RAY shuhnz] *n.* the relatives who have come before or will come after someone
  To future <u>generations</u>, today's events will be history.

**immensity** [i MEN si tee] *n.* immeasurable largeness or vastness
  The <u>immensity</u> of space is hard to imagine.

**ornament** [AWR nuh muhnt] *v.* to decorate
  During the holidays, the pine boughs served to <u>ornament</u> the house.

**protection** [pruh TEK shuhn] *n.* a defense; something that shields one from danger
  One form of <u>protection</u> for the president is a bodyguard.

**stomped** [STAHMT] *v.* injured or killed by stamping on
  The farmer <u>stomped</u> on the biting ants that came out where he was digging.

**subject** [SUHB jekt] *n.* topic being studied or thought about
  The student council discussed the <u>subject</u> of new playground equipment.

**towards** [TAWRDZ] *prep.* in the direction of
  Each morning, we walked in the same direction <u>towards</u> the school.

Name _____ Date _____

**"How the Snake Got Poison"** by Zora Neale Hurston
# Vocabulary Warm-up Exercises

**Exercise A** *Fill in each blank in the paragraph below with an appropriate word from Word List A. Use each word only once.*

Robby loved to watch old Westerns, the type of movie with a cowboy hero who would

[1] _____ an evil [2] _____, such as a bank robber. In

some movies, the cowboy had to battle dangerous creatures of nature, such as powerful

bears with sharp [3] _____ or slithering [4] _____ of

the kind that crawls on its [5] _____. The most dangerous of these

had fangs filled with [6] _____ that could kill you with one bite.

Before striking, however, Robby knew this animal [7] _____ the

[8] _____ on its tail as a warning. Such movie scenes were always

exciting to watch!

**Exercise B** *Find a synonym for each word in the following list. Then, use each synonym in a sentence that makes its meaning clear. Refer to a thesaurus if you need help finding a synonym.*

**Example:** towards **Synonym:** *at*
*The arrow was aimed at the target.*

1. immensity **Synonym:** _____
   _____

2. earth **Synonym:** _____
   _____

3. ornament **Synonym:** _____
   _____

4. protection **Synonym:** _____
   _____

5. stomped **Synonym:** _____
   _____

6. generations **Synonym:** _____
   _____

7. subject **Synonym:** _____
   _____

"How the Snake Got Poison" by Zora Neale Hurston
# Reading Warm-up A

*Read the following passage. Pay special attention to the underlined words. Then, read it again, and complete the activities. Use a separate sheet of paper for your written answers.*

Snakes are reptiles that have no legs. A snake moves along the ground by contracting the muscles on its belly. Some snakes also use these muscles for climbing trees.

Snakes live in many places of the world. Some are born live from their mother's body. Many others are hatched from tough, leathery eggs.

Baby rattlesnakes have a special pointed egg tooth, which grows on the tip of its nose. The baby snake uses the egg tooth to poke a hole through the egg when it is ready to be hatched.

Even as babies, rattlesnakes have a deadly poison in their fangs. Because of its lethal bite, people and other animals are wary of the rattlesnake. Even such animals as mountain lions or bears, with their strong jaws and teeth and sharp, pointed claws, do not try to fight a rattlesnake.

If a rattlesnake is threatened, it first gives a warning before it strikes. It shakes the series of rings called rattles that grow on its tail. This sound means danger!

Rattlesnakes belong to a larger group of snakes called pit vipers. This kind of snake has heat-sensitive pits on either side of its head. These pits help the snake find warm-blooded prey.

Most snakes are not poisonous. They are, however, the enemy of the animals they like to eat. Such prey includes toads, lizards, mice, and birds.

The python is a snake that kills its prey by squeezing it. The unlucky animal suffocates. The snake then eats it all in one bite. Large pythons can swallow an entire pig. The snake's lower jaw unhinges, which allows its mouth to open wide.

Snakes are an interesting group of reptiles. Perhaps you will visit a zoo or visit a zoo camera site on the Internet. If so, be sure to take a firsthand look at these fascinating creatures.

1. Circle the words that tell how snakes are different from other reptiles. Name a few kinds of *snakes*.

2. Circle the words that tell why the snake contracts the muscles of its belly. Define *belly*.

3. Underline the word that describes the rattlesnake's poison. Use *poison* in a sentence.

4. Circle the words that give two examples of animals with claws. What other animals have *claws*?

5. Underline the word that tells what the mountain lions or bears try not to fight. Define *fight*.

6. Circle the words that tell what the rattlesnake shakes for a warning. Use *shakes* in a sentence.

7. Underline the words that tell where the rattles grow. What are *rattles*?

8. Underline the words that tell to which animals the snakes are an enemy. Define *enemy*.

"How the Snake Got Poison" by Zora Neale Hurston
# Reading Warm-up B

*Read the following passage. Pay special attention to the underlined words. Then, read it again, and complete the activities. Use a separate sheet of paper for your written answers.*

There are many kinds of plants and animals on our earth. No matter how large or small, each one plays an important part in the balance of nature. The balance of nature is how our planet survives. It is the chain of events that takes place between plants and animals.

For example, in the grasslands of the world, there is a partnership between the plants and animals that live there. The growing grass and the graceful antelopes may look very lovely. They serve a more serious purpose than to merely ornament the world, however. The grazing animals survive by eating the grass. They give back nutrients to the soil in their waste. That, in turn, helps more grass to grow. People also benefit from this by eating the animals that are fed by the grass.

In every habitat on the planet, partnerships take place. The immensity of the world's many habitats is an amazing subject to ponder. We need to be aware of how we affect these habitats. Unfortunately, human actions sometimes have a bad effect on the balance of nature. One example of this was the way humans hunted many kinds of whales almost to extinction. If the whales were completely wiped out, much the way a colony of termites might be stomped out by an exterminator, then future generations of whales could not exist. As a consequence, the balance of nature in the ocean would be upset. Whales would not be there to play their part.

Some people realized the negative effects of such actions. They worked towards educating others about the importance of the balance of nature. Today, scientists believe the best protection for keeping a species of animals alive is by preserving the entire habitat in which it lives. This is an important challenge to us all.

1. Underline the words that tell what there are many of on earth. Define *earth*.

2. Circle the words that tell what serves to do more than ornament the world. How would you *ornament* your room?

3. Circle the words that tell what is an immensity in the world. What is an antonym of *immensity*?

4. Underline the words that tell what is an amazing subject to ponder. What *subject* do you wonder about?

5. Underline what might be stomped out by an exterminator. What does *stomped* mean?

6. Circle the words that tell what would happen to future generations of whales. Use *generations* in a sentence.

7. Circle the words that tell what people are working towards. What are you working *towards*?

8. Underline the words that tell what scientists believe is the best protection for keeping a species alive. Use *protection* in a sentence.

Name _____ Date _____

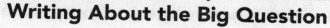
"How the Snake Got Poison" by Zora Neale Hurston

# Writing About the Big Question

## Community or individual: Which is more important?

### Big Question Vocabulary

| | | | | |
|---|---|---|---|---|
| common | community | culture | custom | diversity |
| duty | environment | ethnicity | family | group |
| individual | team | tradition | unify | unique |

**A.** *Use one or more words from the list above to complete each sentence.*

1. As an _____ , Snake had the right to protect himself.

2. However, he presented a threat to members of the larger _____.

3. They lived in an _____ of fear and anxiety.

4. For the _____ good of all involved, compromise was necessary.

**B.** *Follow the directions in responding to each of the items below.*

1. List a time when your needs or the needs of someone you know were in conflict with the needs of family, neighbors, classmates, or any larger community.

_____

_____

2. Write two sentences explaining the preceding experience and describe how the situation was resolved. Use at least two of the Big Question vocabulary words.

_____

_____

_____

**C.** *Complete the sentence below. Then, write a short paragraph in which you connect this situation to the big question.*

When the needs of the **individual** and the needs of the larger **group** are in conflict,

_____

_____

_____

_____

_____

_____

Name _____     Date _____

**"How the Snake Got Poison"** by Zora Neale Hurston
# Reading: Use Prior Knowledge to Compare and Contrast

A **comparison** tells how two or more things are alike. A **contrast** tells how two or more things are different. When you **compare and contrast,** you recognize similarities and differences. You can often understand an unfamiliar concept by **using your prior knowledge to compare and contrast.** For example, you may understand an ancient culture better if you look for ways in which it is similar to and different from your own culture. You also might find similarities and differences between a story told long ago and one that is popular today. To compare and contrast stories, ask questions such as "What does this event bring to mind?" or "Does this character make me think of someone I know or have read about?"

**DIRECTIONS:** *Read each passage from "How the Snake Got Poison." In the second column of the chart, write a question that will help you compare or contrast the passage to something else you have read or to something or someone you know or know about. In the third column, write the answer to your question. The first item has been completed as an example.*

| Passage from "How the Snake Got Poison" | Question Based on My Prior Knowledge | Comparison or Contrast |
|---|---|---|
| 1. "Ah ain't so many, God, you put me down here on my belly in de dust and everything trods upon me and kills off my generations. Ah ain't got no kind of protection at all." | How does this snake compare with Nag and Nagaina in the story "Rikki-tikki-tavi"? | Like this snake, Nag and Nagaina can talk. They also have a problem protecting themselves and their unborn children. |
| 2. "God, please do somethin' 'bout dat snake. He' layin' in de bushes there wid poison in his mouf and he's strikin' everything dat shakes de bushes. He's killin' up our generations." | | |
| 3. "Lawd, you know Ah'm down here in de dust. Ah ain't got no claws to fight wid, and Ah ain't got no feets to git me out de way. All Ah kin see is feets comin' to tromple me. Ah can't tell who my enemy is. . . ." | | |
| 4. "Well, snake, I don't want yo' generations all stomped out and I don't want you killin' everything else dat moves. Here take dis bell and tie it to yo' tail." | | |

Name _____ Date _____

"How the Snake Got Poison" by Zora Neale Hurston
# Literary Analysis: Cultural Context

Stories such as fables, folk tales, and myths are influenced by cultural context. **Cultural context** is the background, customs, and beliefs of the people who originally told them. Knowing the cultural context of a work will help you understand and appreciate it. You can keep track of the cultural context of a work by considering these elements: the *title* of the selection, the *time* in which it takes place, the *place* in which it takes place, the *customs* of the characters, the *beliefs* that are expressed or suggested.

Consider this passage from "How the Snake Got Poison":

Well, when God made de snake he put him in de bushes to ornament de ground.

The passage tells you that the folk tale is set in the distant past. From the cultural context, you can infer that the people who told the tale held beliefs about the purpose of the snake in nature.

**DIRECTIONS:** *These passages from "How the Snake Got Poison" illustrate the folk tale's cultural context by suggesting beliefs held by the people who told the tale. In the second column of the chart, tell what belief the passage illustrates.*

| Passage from "How the Snake Got Poison" | Suggested Belief |
|---|---|
| **1.** God . . . said, "Ah didn't mean for nothin' to be stompin' you snakes lak dat. You got to have some kind of a protection. Here, take dis poison and put it in yo' mouf and when they tromps on you, protect yo'self." | |
| **2.** "Snake, . . . Ah didn't mean for you to be hittin' and killin' everything dat shake de bush. I give you dat poison and tole you to protect yo'self when they tromples on you. But you killin' everything dat moves." | |
| **3.** "Here take dis bell and tie it to yo' tail. When you hear feets comin' you ring yo' bell and if it's yo' friend, he'll be keerful. If it's yo' enemy, it's you and him." | |

Name _____ Date _____

**"How the Snake Got Poison"** by Zora Neale Hurston
# Vocabulary Builder

**Word List**

immensity    ornament    suit    varmints

**A. DIRECTIONS:** *Circle* T *if the statement is* true *or* F *if it is* false. *Then, explain your answer.*

1. Colored lights and Chinese lanterns will *ornament* a backyard party.

   **T / F** _____

   _____

2. An *immensity* can easily be fenced in.

   **T / F** _____

   _____

3. A bright green dress *suits* a rosy complexion.

   **T / F** _____

   _____

4. Gardeners hope their gardens will attract *varmints*.

   **T / F** _____

   _____

**B. WORD STUDY:** *The Latin suffix* -ity *means "state, quality, or condition of." Answer each of the following questions using one of these words containing* -ity: *marketability, integrity, enmity.*

1. Why should a company consider the *marketability* of its products?

   _____

2. Why might a politician who lacks *integrity* lose an election?

   _____

3. How would you respond to someone who treats you with *enmity*?

   _____

Unit 6 Resources: Themes in the Oral Tradition
**152**

**"How the Snake Got Poison"** by Zora Neale Hurston
# Enrichment: Snakes Are Not So Bad

You may have noticed that "How the Snake Got Poison" presents the snake somewhat sympathetically. Did that surprise you? Did you think that snakes were awful? Did you think they should all be stomped on by other animals or by human beings?

Actually, snakes have gotten a lot of what could be called bad press. That is, they have a bad reputation for no good reason. Yet many people fear or hate snakes. It may be that they believe myths about snakes that are simply not true.

**Snake myth 1:** Snakes are slimy.
**Snake fact 1:** Snakes are not slimy. They have scales, which serve as their skin. The scales are dry and either smooth or bumpy.

**Snake myth 2:** Snakes lie in wait to attack human beings.
**Snake fact 2:** Only a few snakes are particularly aggressive toward humans. Most snakes avoid humans at all costs because they know that humans may hurt them. Most poisonous snakes will strike at a person only when they are cornered, captured, or harassed in some way. The fact remains, however, that poisonous snakes are poisonous, and a snake's venom can kill. Of course, the venom is primarily used on other animals. Poisonous snakes use their poison to capture their prey.

**Snake myth 3:** Snakes are of no use and should be killed.
**Snake fact 3:** As "How the Snake Got Poison" implies, snakes have a place in the natural world. Snakes feed on the huge population of rats, mice, and other animals that eat corn, rice, and other crops and foods. Snake venom is used to make painkillers and treat snakebites. Snakes also play a part in the food chain, providing meals for hawks and other large hunting birds, mongooses, and bigger snakes.

Do some research on snakes. In an encyclopedia or on the Internet, find an illustration of a colorful snake. Find out where it lives, how it reproduces, and how long it lives.

**DIRECTIONS:** *In response to each myth, write a sentence that contradicts it. Be sure the information in your sentence is accurate.*

1. Snakes are dangerous to humans.

   _____

   _____

2. Snakes are useless.

   _____

   _____

3. Snakes are slimy.

   _____

   _____

Name _____ Date _____

# Integrated Language Skills: Grammar

**Capitalization** is the use of uppercase letters (*A*, *B*, *C*, and so on). Capital letters signal the beginning of a sentence or a quotation and identify proper nouns and proper adjectives. **Proper nouns** include the names of people, geographical locations, specific events and time periods, organizations, languages, and religions. **Proper adjectives** are derived from proper nouns.

| Use of Capital Letter | Example |
|---|---|
| Sentence beginning | **T**he coyote was a bad swimmer. **H**e nearly drowned. |
| Quotation | The snake said, "**Y**ou know I'm down here in the dust." |
| Proper nouns | They traveled through the **S**outhwest. |
| Proper adjectives | Coyote might have run as far as the **M**exican border. |

**A. PRACTICE:** *Rewrite each sentence below. Use capitalization correctly.*

1. the character named coyote suggested that they steal the box.

   _____

2. the folk tale takes place in the american southwest, perhaps in present-day arizona or new mexico.

   _____

   _____

3. coyote said to eagle, "this is a wonderful thing."

   _____

4. "i do not trust you," eagle said many times. "you will open that box."

   _____

**B. Writing Application:** *Write a short episode telling what Coyote might have done after he let the sun and the moon escape from the box. Include at least one quotation, one proper noun, and one proper adjective. Use capitalization correctly.*

   _____

   _____

   _____

   _____

   _____

Name _____ Date _____

**"Sun and Moon in a Box"** by Richard Erdoes and Alfonso Ortiz
**"How the Snake Got Poison"** by Zora Neale Hurston

# Integrated Language Skills: Support for Writing a Plot Summary

Use this chart to take notes for a **plot summary** of "Sun and Moon in a Box" or "How the Snake Got Poison."

## Plot Summary

| | |
|---|---|
| **Setting:** | |
| **Major character 1:** | **Major character 2:** |

| Main event from beginning of folk tale: | Main event from middle of folk tale: | Main event from end of folk tale: |
|---|---|---|
| | | |

**Final outcome:**

Now, use your notes to write your **plot summary.** Be sure to include all the information called for on the chart.

**"Sun and Moon in a Box"** by Richard Erdoes and Alfonso Ortiz

**"How the Snake Got Poison"** by Zora Neale Hurston

# Integrated Language Skills: Support for Extend Your Learning

**Listening and Speaking: "Sun and Moon in a Box"**

Use the following prompts as you work with a partner to gather unusual facts about an animal in preparation for a **story** you will make up and present to your classmates. Remember: You will not name the animal in your presentation.

**Unusual fact 1:** _____

**Unusual fact 2:** _____

**Unusual fact 3:** _____

**Unusual fact 4:** _____

**Unusual fact 5:** _____

**Facial expressions, gestures, and movements that identify the animal:** _____

_____

_____

**Dialogue:** _____

_____

_____

_____

_____

**Listening and Speaking: "How the Snake Got Poison"**

Use the following prompts as you work with a partner to gather unusual facts about an animal in preparation for a **story** you will make up and present to your classmates. Remember: You will not name the animal in your presentation.

**Unusual fact 1:** _____

**Unusual fact 2:** _____

**Unusual fact 3:** _____

**Unusual fact 4:** _____

**Unusual fact 5:** _____

**Facial expressions, gestures, and movements that identify the animal:** _____

_____

_____

**Dialogue:** _____

_____

_____

_____

_____

Name _____ Date _____

"How the Snake Got Poison" by Zora Neale Hurston
# Open-Book Test

**Short Answer** *Write your responses to the questions in this section on the lines provided.*

1. In the first paragraph of "How the Snake Got Poison," the author says that God made the snake to ornament the ground in the bushes. In what way would a snake ornament the ground? Use your understanding of the word *ornament* to explain your answer.

   _____

   _____

2. Think about how the animals on the ground approach God in "How the Snake Got Poison." How does this help you understand a belief of the people who told the tale? Use information from the beginning of the selection to help you answer.

   _____

   _____

3. Why do you think the author has the narrator, God, and the animals all speak in the same dialect? Include examples of dialect from the selection in your answer.

   _____

   _____

4. When presented with the snake's problem in "How the Snake Got Poison," God "looked off towards immensity." Why is *immensity* a good word choice for this situation? Use your understanding of the story and the word *immensity* to explain your answer.

   _____

   _____

5. In "How the Snake Got Poison," the snake and the varmints voice their problems to God. Use the graphic organizer to compare their complaints. Then, explain what both the varmints and the snake fear most.

| Snake's Complaints | Varmints' Complaints |
|---|---|
|  |  |
|  |  |

_____

_____

_____

Unit 6 Resources: Themes in the Oral Tradition

Name _____ Date _____

6. In the middle of "How the Snake Got Poison," the varmints complain about the Snake. What, most likely, are varmints? Use details from the story in your answer.

_____

_____

_____

7. After hearing the varmints' complaints in "How the Snake Got Poison," God has a conversation with the snake. How does he seem to feel toward the snake during the conversation? Use details to explain.

_____

_____

_____

8. Toward the end of "How the Snake Got Poison," God comes up with a compromise for the snake and the varmints. Explain what the compromise is.

_____

_____

_____

9. In "How the Snake Got Poison," God purposefully gives the snake a way to defend himself. What does this tell you about how the people who originally told the tale felt about snakes?

_____

_____

_____

10. At the end of "How the Snake Got Poison," God arrives at what seems to be a fair solution to everyone's problem. How does his attitude show the cultural context of the story? Use details from the end of the story to respond.

_____

_____

_____

**Essay**

*Write an extended response to the question of your choice or to the question or questions your teacher assigns you.*

11. Think about the relationship between God and the animals he created in "How the Snake Got Poison." In a brief essay, describe the relationship. Tell whether you think God in this story is caring and helpful. Use information from the story as support for your answer.

Name _____ Date _____

12. Stories such as "How the Snake Got Poison" are influenced by the cultural context of the people who originally told them. In a brief essay, explain what beliefs and ideas the story shows about the culture of the American South in the distant past. Use details from the story to support your ideas.

13. In "How the Snake Got Poison," how is the snake at a disadvantage, compared to other animals in his world? In a brief essay, analyze the ways in which he, as an individual, has to make sure that his needs are addressed. Include in your answer a suggestion about what humans can learn from his predicament.

14. **Thinking About the Big Question: Community or Individual: Which is more important?** Write an essay in which you explore whether the individual or the community is more important in "How the Snake Got Poison." In your answer, discuss how the needs of both the community and the individual are met in this story. Use details from the story.

**Oral Response**

15. Go back to question 5, 6, or 8 or to the question your teacher assigns you. Take a few minutes to expand your answer and prepare an oral response. Find additional details in the selection that support your points. If necessary, make notes to guide your oral response.

**"How the Snake Got Poison"** by Zora Neale Hurston
# Selection Test A

**Critical Reading** *Identify the letter of the choice that best answers the question.*

____ 1. Where does most of the dialogue in "How the Snake Got Poison" take place?
A. in a desert
B. in the heavens
C. in a jungle
D. on an ark

____ 2. According to "How the Snake Got Poison," why does God put the snake in the bushes?
A. to kill all the other varmints
B. to make the ground beautiful
C. to act as God's bodyguard
D. to keep the bushes trimmed

____ 3. According to "How the Snake Got Poison," after the snake gets poison, all the other varmints complain to God. Based on your reading of the selection, what can you infer is meant by *varmints*?
A. rats and mice
B. human beings
C. other creatures
D. other snakes

____ 4. According to "How the Snake Got Poison," how are the snakes and the other varmints alike?
A. They all claim to be scared.
B. They all change their shape.
C. They all have feet.
D. They all have claws.

____ 5. In "How the Snake Got Poison," what is the complaint of the other varmints when they go to see God?
A. They are not as beautiful as the snake.
B. There are not as plentiful as the snake.
C. The snake is poisoning them.
D. The snake is hunting them.

____ 6. In "How the Snake Got Poison," what does the snake say in response to the other varmints' complaints?

    A. He cannot tell who is a friend and who is an enemy.

    B. He wants to be the most powerful varmint on earth.

    C. He wants snakes to be the only varmints on earth.

    D. He believes he is doing what God wants him to do.

____ 7. According to "How the Snake Got Poison," how did snakes change after they got poison?

    A. Before, they were being killed; afterward, they were doing the killing.

    B. Before, they lived in the bushes; afterward, they lived in the trees.

    C. Before, they had no enemies; afterward, they had many enemies.

    D. Before, they hid in the bushes; afterward, they stayed in the open.

____ 8. Who are the main characters in "How the Snake Got Poison"?

    A. the snake and the other varmints

    B. the snake and human beings

    C. God and all the varmints

    D. God and the snake

____ 9. In "How the Snake Got Poison," what is God's final gift to the snake?

    A. fangs                C. eyes

    B. skin                 D. rattles

____ 10. As he is portrayed in "How the Snake Got Poison," which word best describes God?

    A. brutal            C. reasonable

    B. vengeful         D. strict

____ 11. What cultural belief is reflected in "How the Snake Got Poison"?

    A. All creatures have a place on earth.

    B. Some creatures are superior to others.

    C. The rattlesnake is special.

    D. Rattlesnakes are untrustworthy.

____ 12. Which statement best describes a message of "How the Snake Got Poison"?

    A. The more you complain, the more likely you are to get what you want.

    B. Everyone deserves to be able to defend himself or herself.

    C. One needs a variety of tools to make it through life.

    D. There is basically an unfairness to life.

## Vocabulary and Grammar

____ 13. Which of the following sentences uses the word *ornament* correctly?
  A. Intelligent replies will *ornament* any essay question.
  B. Stained-glass windows *ornament* the old church.
  C. Words of praise *ornament* the honored guest.
  D. Ghastly shrieks *ornament* the otherwise silent night.

____ 14. In which set of sentences is the capitalization correct?
  A. "Good morning, Michael." "how are you, Amanda?"
  B. "Good morning, michael." "How are you, amanda?"
  C. "good morning, michael." "how are you, amanda?"
  D. "Good morning, Michael." "How are you, Amanda?"

____ 15. In which sentence is the capitalization correct?
  A. Zora Neale Hurston was an important figure in the harlem renaissance.
  B. Zora neale hurston grew up in the small town of eatonville, Florida.
  C. Zora Neale Hurston collected folklore in Jamaica, Haiti, and Bermuda.
  D. Zora neale hurston's writing was popular but did not earn her a living.

## Essay

16. What do you think of the snake in "How the Snake Got Poison"? Is he a sneaky character, or is he simply looking out for his own interests? Do you like him? Why or why not? In an essay, answer those questions. Mention at least one detail from the selection to support your opinion.

17. "How the Snake Got Poison" is written in dialect. It is a variation of a language in a certain region, and it has its own vocabulary, grammar, and pronunciation. In addition, the style of the writing is informal. In your opinion, do these characteristics have an overall effect on the selection? Would you have liked the selection better if it had not used dialect and an informal style? Why or why not? Express your opinion in an essay. Cite two examples from the selection to support your opinion.

18. **Thinking About the Big Question: Community or individual: Which is more important?** Think about how individuals and the community affect the outcome of the story "How the Snake Got Poison." Is the individual or the community more important in this tale? Explain your answer in an essay supported by details from the story.

Name _____ Date _____

# Selection Test B

**Critical Reading** *Identify the letter of the choice that best completes the statement or answers the question.*

_____ 1. In "How the Snake Got Poison," how does the snake reach God?
   A. by calling up to him
   B. by climbing a ladder
   C. by slithering through the bushes
   D. by stomping over other varmints

_____ 2. According to "How the Snake Got Poison," why was the snake put in the bushes?
   A. to monitor access to God
   B. to tempt human beings
   C. to make the ground beautiful
   D. to catch objectionable animals

_____ 3. Before the snake first talks to God in "How the Snake Got Poison," what is his situation?
   A. He cannot keep from being stomped to death.
   B. He cannot find enough food to eat in the bushes.
   C. He cannot move fast enough to hunt food to eat.
   D. He cannot see God from his position in the bushes.

_____ 4. How might God *best* be described in "How the Snake Got Poison"?
   A. standoffish
   B. accessible
   C. contemptuous
   D. arrogant

_____ 5. From the setting of "How the Snake Got Poison," you can make inferences about the environment of the people who told the tale. Which of the following is the most likely environment?
   A. extreme cold
   B. a temperate woodland
   C. a fishing community
   D. a vast desert

_____ 6. What kind of character is the snake in "How the Snake Got Poison"?
   A. an innocent, likable victim
   B. an especially evil creature
   C. a disrespectful, angry animal
   D. a clever being who wants to survive

_____ 7. In what way are all the creatures in "How the Snake Got Poison" alike?
   A. They all want to be powerful.
   B. They all want to be warm.
   C. They all want the snake to disappear.
   D. They all want to protect themselves.

Name _____ Date _____

_____ 8. After God gives the snake poison in "How the Snake Got Poison," but before he responds to the other creatures' complaints, what is the basic contrast between the snake and the other creatures?
   A. the place where they live
   B. their closeness to God
   C. their means of self-defense
   D. the size of their families

_____ 9. In "How the Snake Got Poison," how does the snake change after he gets poison?
   A. He goes from victim to victimizer.
   B. He moves from the trees to the bushes.
   C. He moves from the ground to the ladder.
   D. He stops slithering and begins crawling.

_____ 10. Which passage from "How the Snake Got Poison" is most clearly an example of dialect?
   A. "'God, you put me down here on my belly.'"
   B. "God looked off towards immensity."
   C. "So de snake took de poison in his mouf."
   D. "God thought it over for a while."

_____ 11. In "How the Snake Got Poison," on what does God base the second decision he makes?
   A. his annoyance with the snake
   B. his anger at human beings
   C. his fear that the animals will go to war
   D. his desire for balance in the animal world

_____ 12. What does God do in "How the Snake Got Poison" to protect the other creatures from the snake?
   A. He moves the snake to a deserted area.
   B. He takes the poison from the snake.
   C. He lectures the snake.
   D. He gives the snake rattles.

_____ 13. What cultural belief is reflected in "How the Snake Got Poison"?
   A. There is meant to be a balance in nature.
   B. Some animals are sneakier than others.
   C. Animals are smarter than human beings.
   D. Always be careful walking through bushes.

_____ 14. What can you infer about the people who told "How the Snake Got Poison"?
   A. They lived in a place with few bushes.
   B. They lived in a place with many insects.
   C. They were familiar with rattlesnakes.
   D. They were familiar with garter snakes.

_____ 15. Which statement best describes a message of "How the Snake Got Poison"?
   A. Life is fundamentally unfair.
   B. Self-protection is a key to survival.
   C. It is best to solve your problems by yourself.
   D. The more you know, the better able you are to deal with life.

## Vocabulary and Grammar

____ 16. In which sentence is the meaning of the word *ornament* expressed?
  A. The snake was being tromped on by the other creatures.
  B. The snake was put on earth to make the ground beautiful.
  C. The snake complained to God about being stomped on.
  D. God gave the snake poison with which to defend himself.

____ 17. In which sentence is the meaning of the word *immensity* expressed?
  A. The poet considered the vastness of the universe.
  B. The intensity of the storm frightened the animals.
  C. The beauty of the landscape was incomparable.
  D. The scientist analyzed the results of her experiment.

____ 18. In which sentence is the capitalization correct?
  A. In 1925, Hurston headed for new York.
  B. There, she joined the harlem renaissance.
  C. Hurston was buried in an unmarked grave in Florida.
  D. Alice walker reawakened interest in Hurston's work.

## Essay

19. In "How the Snake Got Poison," God hears the snake's plea, and then he hears the complaints of the other creatures. Finally, he hears the snake's response to those complaints. What is your opinion of all the animals' remarks? Is each argument valid? Are the animals just bickering among themselves? In an essay, state your opinion of each of the three arguments. Then, assess the solution. Might there have been a different way to solve the problem? If so, what is it?

20. In "How the Snake Got Poison," the animals call on God to resolve their dispute. In your opinion, why did they not work out their problems on their own? Why did they need the assistance of a third party? What do you think the animals' behavior says about human behavior? Respond to these questions in an essay. Cite at least two details from the selection or from your knowledge or experience to support your points.

21. How does "How the Snake Got Poison" illustrate the concept that nature must be kept in balance? At the beginning of the selection, what is out of balance? Why does God say, "You got to have some kind of protection"? How is the balance corrected? In an essay, answer these questions.

22. **Thinking About the Big Question: Community or individual: Which is more important?** Write an essay in which you explore whether the individual or the community is more important in "How the Snake Got Poison." In your answer, discuss how the needs of both the community and the individual are met in this story. Use details from the story.

# Vocabulary Warm-up Word Lists

*Study these words from "The People Could Fly." Then, apply your knowledge to the activities that follow.*

## Word List A

**babe** [BAYB] *n.* an infant or baby
   The tiny <u>babe</u> was nestled in his mother's arms.

**firelight** [FYER lyt] *n.* light from a fire
   The <u>firelight</u> cozily cast pretty shadows on the walls.

**flock** [FLAHK] *n.* a large group of animals that usually stay together
   The <u>flock</u> of geese landed on the pond.

**hip** [HIP] *adj.* located by someone's hip bone at the top of the leg
   Myra's <u>hip</u> bandage covered the stitches she had received there.

**horseback** [HAWRS bak] *adv.* used with *on*, riding on a horse
   Max thought it was fun to ride on <u>horseback</u> along the beach.

**labored** [LAY berd] *v.* worked, toiled
   The students <u>labored</u> long hours over their group history project.

**plantation** [plan TAY shuhn] *n.* a large farm or estate
   The Southern farmer grew peanuts on his <u>plantation</u>.

**soothe** [SOO*TH*] *v.* to calm or make better with gentle treatment
   The quiet music will <u>soothe</u> your frazzled nerves.

## Word List B

**African** [AF ri kuhn] *adj.* describing a person or thing from Africa
   The <u>African</u> stone sculpture shows a graceful giraffe.

**bawling** [BAWL ing] *v.* crying or shouting noisily
   When he fell, the toddler began <u>bawling</u> loudly.

**bled** [BLED] *v.* was bleeding or did bleed
   The cut on her hand <u>bled</u> for only a short time.

**clumsily** [KLUHM zuh lee] *adv.* awkwardly, ungracefully
   Anna moved <u>clumsily</u> on her skis until she took a lesson.

**misery** [MIZ uh ree] *n.* extreme unhappiness or sorrow
   The <u>misery</u> Rob felt when he had the flu could be seen on his face.

**slavery** [SLAY vuh ree] *n.* owning human beings as property
   <u>Slavery</u> in the United States ended during the Civil War.

**souls** [SOHLZ] *n.* people
   Only one hundred <u>souls</u> lived in the small village.

**sundown** [SUHN down] *n.* the time of the day when the sun sets
   At <u>sundown</u>, red and pink clouds filled the sky.

**166**

Name _____ Date _____

# Vocabulary Warm-up Exercises

**Exercise A** *Fill in each blank in the paragraph below with an appropriate word from Word List A. Use each word only once.*

Donna and her friends liked to go camping on land that used to be part of an

old cotton [1] _____. During the day, they loved to go riding on

[2] _____. At dinnertime, they [3] _____ together to cook

a good meal. Then, after dark, they would sit around the campfire, huddled close to

each other like a [4] _____ of sheep, while the [5] _____

played upon their faces. Donna would pull out a book of scary stories from the

[6] _____ pocket of her jeans. She read one story that made one of her

friends wail like a little [7] _____. To [8] _____ him, the

group decided to start toasting marshmallows!

**Exercise B** *Decide whether each statement below is true or false. Circle T or F. Then, explain your answer.*

1. One who studies <u>African</u> folk tales probably knows a lot about Africa.
   T / F _____

2. If Carol always moves <u>clumsily</u>, then she ice skates well.
   T / F _____

3. If Don cut his hand while dicing onions, he <u>bled</u>.
   T / F _____

4. The expression "<u>misery</u> loves company" means it makes people feel better when
   they know others are feeling good.
   T / F _____

5. If many <u>souls</u> attended the meeting, a lot of people were there.
   T / F _____

6. It is nice to wake up early to watch the <u>sundown</u>.
   T / F _____

7. If someone is <u>bawling</u>, he or she is not very happy.
   T / F _____

8. <u>Slavery</u> provided plantation owners with workers in the South.
   T / F _____

Name _____ Date _____

**"The People Could Fly"** by Virginia Hamilton
# Reading Warm-up A

*Read the following passage. Pay special attention to the underlined words. Then, read it again, and complete the activities. Use a separate sheet of paper for your written answers.*

My name is Rob, and my parents were slaves on a cotton <u>plantation</u> in Mississippi. I was born there, so I was a slave, too. My mama told me that when I was a <u>babe</u>, she was not given enough time to care for me. Instead, she was sent back to the fields to work. The night was her favorite time, for then we were together again. She would hold me in her arms. There in the glow and warmth of the <u>firelight</u>, she softly sang lullabies to me.

They were the bits of songs she could remember from Africa, her homeland. She couldn't sing the words loudly, for to use her native language was forbidden by the plantation owner.

When I got older, and my sister was born, I remember how my mother carried her in a sort of <u>hip</u> cloth tied to her body like a sling. Being carried that way was the only thing that could <u>soothe</u> that baby when she cried.

As a young boy, I was sent to pick cotton. The overseer rode up to our cabins on <u>horseback</u> every morning with a whip in his hand. With rough words, he told us to get moving. Like a <u>flock</u> of birds or animals, not like the people we were, we headed to the fields.

Picking cotton was hard, hot work. It cut our hands. We <u>labored</u> long hours. Sometimes we sang songs to keep our spirits alive. We disguised the words of these songs. The overseer didn't know those songs were from African music. It was our secret, and it was a way we stayed connected to the land from which we had been taken.

We had stories, too. They came from Africa, but parts of them got changed, because slaves were forbidden to practice their native culture. We were proud of our stories, though. They told of tricksters and heroes, and they were our way of keeping our roots alive.

1. Circle the word that tells the kind of <u>plantation</u> on which Rob grew up. Define *plantation*.

2. Circle the words that tell what Rob's mother told him about the time when he was a <u>babe</u>. What has a family member told you about the time when you were a *babe*?

3. Underline the words that describe the <u>firelight</u>. Use *firelight* in a sentence.

4. Circle the words that explain why Rob's mother wore a <u>hip</u> cloth tied to her body. Define *hip*.

5. Underline the words that tell what could <u>soothe</u> the boy's baby sister. What can *soothe* you?

6. Circle the words that tell who rode on <u>horseback</u>. Use *horseback* in a sentence.

7. Underline the words that tell what kind of <u>flock</u> it felt like to Rob. What is a *flock*?

8. Underline the words that tell more about how the slaves <u>labored</u> long hours. What is something at which you have *labored*?

Name _____ Date _____

"**The People Could Fly**" by Virginia Hamilton
# Reading Warm-up B

*Read the following passage. Pay special attention to the underlined words. Then, read it again, and complete the activities. Use a separate sheet of paper for your written answers.*

During the period of time from the 1500s to the 1800s, large numbers of <u>African</u> people were captured by slave traders. These unfortunate <u>souls</u> were shipped like cargo, under terrible conditions. They were taken to the West Indies and to the Americas to be sold into <u>slavery</u>.

Slave traders realized there was a great need for cheap labor in the West Indian and British colonies. They saw the taking of Africans as a way to fill this need and to profit by it.

Most of the captives came from West Africa. Some were captured in battle with other tribes and sold to the slave traders in exchange for goods. The majority of those who became slaves, however, were kidnapped from their villages by the slave traders. The traders usually chose the strongest individuals because they were more likely to survive the terrible journey. The captives' freedom and their culture were savagely stripped away from them. Imagine their <u>misery</u> as they realized they would never see another sunrise or <u>sundown</u> as a free man or woman.

The route of some slave ships ended in the American South in big cities such as New Orleans. There, the slaves were sold. Other voyages took a triangular journey. They set off from New England colonies, carrying rum to be traded in Africa. Next, slaves were taken to the West Indies and traded for sugar and molasses. This cargo, in turn, was taken to New England to be sold to the rum makers.

It is believed that one third of the captives died during the horrible crossings. They were mercilessly chained together, causing them to move <u>clumsily</u>. Those who rebelled were beaten or whipped until they <u>bled</u>. Unclean conditions and lack of food caused much illness, and the <u>bawling</u> of the suffering captives could be heard. The survivors went on to endure more hardships as slaves.

1. Underline the words that tell what happened to large numbers of <u>African</u> people. Use *African* in a sentence.

2. Circle the words that describe what happened to these unfortunate <u>souls</u>. Define *souls*.

3. Circle the sentences that explain why the slave traders wanted to capture Africans to be sold into <u>slavery</u>. Why is *slavery* wrong?

4. Underline the words that suggest why the captives felt <u>misery</u>. What is *misery*?

5. The story says that the slaves never experienced another <u>sundown</u> as free people. What does this mean?

6. Circle the words that tell why the slaves moved <u>clumsily</u>. Have you ever moved *clumsily*? Explain.

7. Underline the words that tell why some slaves <u>bled</u>. Use *bled* in a sentence.

8. Circle the words that tell why the slaves' <u>bawling</u> could be heard. Define *bawling*.

**"The People Could Fly"** by Virginia Hamilton
# Writing About the Big Question

## Community or individual: Which is more important?

### Big Question Vocabulary

| | | | | |
|---|---|---|---|---|
| common | community | culture | custom | diversity |
| duty | environment | ethnicity | family | group |
| individual | team | tradition | unify | unique |

**A.** *Use one or more words from the list above to complete each sentence.*

1. America has not always embraced the _____ of its population.

2. Some people were discriminated against because of their _____.

3. When people came together as a _____ , they made a difference.

4. There was power in their _____ that could not be denied.

**B.** *Follow the directions in responding to each of the items below.*

1. List two different groups of people who struggled against oppression.

   _____    _____

2. Write two sentences describing what helped unify one of the preceding groups in their efforts. Use at least two of the Big Question vocabulary words.

   _____

   _____

   _____

**C.** *Complete the sentence below. Then, write a short paragraph in which you connect this situation to the big question.*

In order to unify people who share a common struggle, _____

_____

_____

_____

_____

_____

_____

_____

Unit 6 Resources: Themes in the Oral Tradition

**"The People Could Fly"** by Virginia Hamilton
# Reading: Use a Venn Diagram to Compare and Contrast

When you **compare and contrast,** you recognize similarities and differences. You can compare and contrast elements in a literary work by **using a Venn diagram** to examine character traits, situations, and ideas. First, reread the text to locate the details you will compare. Then, write the details on a diagram like the ones shown below. Recording these details will help you understand the similarities and differences in a literary work.

**DIRECTIONS:** *Fill in the Venn diagrams as directed to make comparisons about elements of "The People Could Fly."*

1. Compare Toby and Sarah. Write characteristics of Toby in the left-hand oval and characteristics of Sarah in the right-hand oval. Write characteristics that they share in the overlapping part of the two ovals.

**Toby**                    **Both**                    **Sarah**

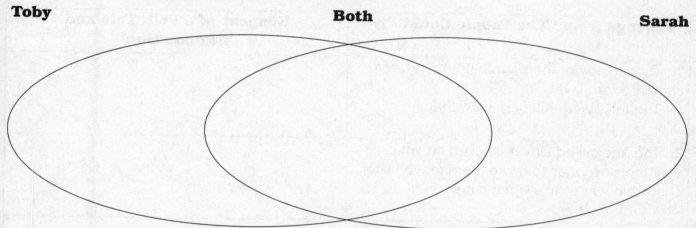

2. Compare the enslaved people with the Overseer and Driver. Write characteristics of the enslaved people in the left-hand oval and characteristics of the Overseer and Driver in the right-hand oval. Write characteristics that they share in the overlapping part of the two ovals.

**Enslaved People**              **Both**         **Overseer and Driver**

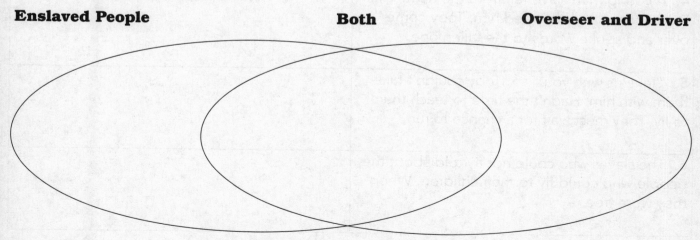

Name _____ Date _____

"The People Could Fly" by Virginia Hamilton
# Literary Analysis: Folk Tale

A **folk tale** is a story that is composed orally and then passed from person to person by word of mouth. Although folk tales originate in this **oral tradition,** many of them are eventually collected and written down. Similar folk tales are told by different cultures throughout the world. Such folk tales have common character types, plot elements, and themes. Folk tales often teach a lesson about life and present a clear separation between good and evil. Folk tales are part of the oral tradition that also includes fairy tales, legends, myths, fables, tall tales, and ghost stories.

**DIRECTIONS:** *Read each passage from "The People Could Fly." In the second column of the chart, indicate whether the passage teaches a lesson about life or whether it clearly presents good, clearly presents evil, or presents a clear distinction between the two. Then, explain your choice. Tell why you think the example shows the element you have chosen.*

| Passage from "The People Could Fly" | Element of a Folk Tale and Explanation |
|---|---|
| **1.** Then, many of the people [in Africa] were captured for Slavery. . . . <br>   The folks were full of misery, then. | |
| **2.** The one called Driver cracked his whip over the slow ones to make them move faster. That whip was a slice-open cut of pain. | |
| **3.** The . . . woman fell to the earth. <br>   The old man that was there, Toby, came and helped her to her feet. | |
| **4.** A young man slave fell from the heat. The Driver come and whipped him. Toby come over and spoke words to the fallen one. | |
| **5.** "Take us with you!" . . . Toby couldn't take them with him. Hadn't the time to teach them to fly. They must wait for a chance to run. | |
| **6.** The slaves who could not fly told about the people who could fly to their children. When they were free. | |

**172**

Name _____ Date _____

## "The People Could Fly" by Virginia Hamilton
# Vocabulary Builder

## Word List

croon    hoed    mystery    scorned    shed    shuffle

**A. DIRECTIONS:** *Write the letter of the word or group of words that means the opposite of the vocabulary word.*

___ 1. scorned
    **A.** commanded    **B.** resigned    **C.** appreciated    **D.** hired

___ 2. croon
    **A.** sing softly    **B.** speak quietly    **C.** speak haltingly    **D.** sing loudly

___ 3. shuffle
    **A.** jump    **B.** walk quickly    **C.** drag    **D.** pull into

___ 4. mystery
    **A.** ritual    **B.** secret    **C.** explanation    **D.** magic

___ 5. shed
    **A.** put on    **B.** pull down    **C.** take off    **D.** drop

___ 6. hoed
    **A.** dug    **B.** straightened    **C.** released    **D.** planted

**B. WORD STUDY:** *The Greek root -myst- means "a secret rite." Answer each of the following questions using one of these words containing -myst-: mystified, mystical, mystic.*

1. How would you reply if you were *mystified* by a friend's request?

    _____

    _____

2. When might an ancient artifact be considered a *mystical* object?

    _____

    _____

3. Why might someone seek guidance from a *mystic*?

    _____

    _____

**"The People Could Fly"** by Virginia Hamilton
# Enrichment: Oral Tradition

There is probably not a society in history that has not had an oral tradition. Before there was writing, there were stories. Those stories did not die out when the people who made them up died. Instead, people repeated their stories to an audience—perhaps their children, perhaps other people in their community. They told their stories over and over again. Eventually, the members of the audience committed the stories to memory. At last, they were able to repeat the stories to their own audiences.

You probably already have the beginnings of an oral tradition committed to memory. Have you told the same story to more than one friend? Have you heard stories from others in your family that you could repeat? How about song lyrics? How many of those have you memorized? Have you memorized any poems? Have you memorized a part for a play? Can you quote dialogue from your favorite movie or television show? All of those might be the start of your own oral tradition.

Now, think about adding a folk tale to the mix.

**DIRECTIONS:** *Follow these steps to commit a folk tale to memory.*

1. Choose a folk tale that you are particularly fond of—"The People Could Fly" or another folk tale in your textbook, or one you have read on your own. Be sure it is short—no more than two or three pages.

2. You will probably not be able to memorize the entire folk tale in one day. So, divide it into sections—for example, five sections, one for every day of a week of school.

3. Each day, work on one section. Read it over and over again. Read it to yourself, and then read it aloud. On the chart below, make some notes of key events or key phrases. The important thing, however, is to *read and repeat,* not to write.

4. Do not try to memorize every word. Concentrate on repeating the key events and the key lines of dialogue in each section.

5. After the first day, review the previous days' sections before starting on that day's section.

6. Once you become comfortable with the process, ask a classmate, friend, or family member to be your audience.

| Section 1 | Section 2 | Section 3 | Section 4 | Section 5 |
|-----------|-----------|-----------|-----------|-----------|
|           |           |           |           |           |
|           |           |           |           |           |

**"The People Could Fly"** by Virginia Hamilton
# Open-Book Test

**Short Answer** *Write your responses to the questions in this section on the lines provided.*

1. Folk tales are often written in an informal style that sounds like spoken language. The author has written "The People Could Fly" in this style. Find at least two examples in the first few paragraphs that demonstrate this style.

   _____

   _____

2. In "The People Could Fly," why were the people on boats from Africa "full of misery"? Use details from the beginning of the selection in your answer.

   _____

   _____

3. In the land of slavery, the people who could fly kept their power. Was it possible to tell them apart from the other slaves? Explain, using details from "The People Could Fly."

   _____

   _____

   _____

4. In "The People Could Fly," Sarah "trembled to be so hard worked and scorned." Why is being scorned particularly hard for Sarah to bear? Consider what is special about her.

   _____

   _____

5. In "The People Could Fly," the narrator says the slave owner is "callin himself their Master." How does this description suggest the narrator's attitude toward the Master? Use additional details that describe the Master to support your answer.

   _____

   _____

   _____

6. In the middle of "The People Could Fly," Sarah cannot croon to her baby. Why does Sarah find the act impossible? Use your understanding of the story to help you answer.

   _____

   _____

   _____

**7.** In the middle of "The People Could Fly," Sarah calls Toby "Father." Explain the relationship between the two characters. Use details from the first half of the story.

_____

_____

**8.** Use the Venn diagram to compare and contrast the personalities of Toby and Sarah. How are they similar and different? Then, tell who you think is the more important character, and why.

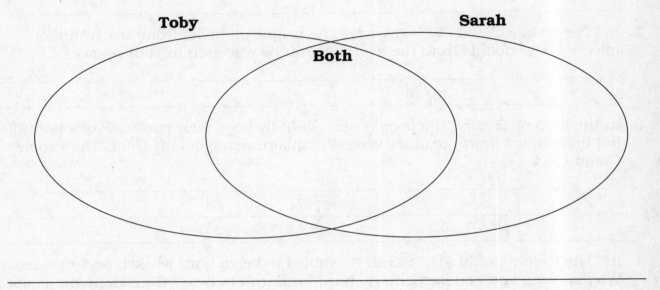

_____

_____

_____

**9.** At the end of "The People Could Fly," some of the slaves fly away. Others who cannot fly "must wait for a chance to run." What message was this part of the folk tale originally intended to convey to the listeners? Explain in your answer who the listeners probably were.

_____

_____

_____

**10.** Folk tales were often passed down by word of mouth. How does the end of "The People Could Fly" show that it is a folk tale?

_____

_____

## Essay

*Write an extended response to the question of your choice or to the question or questions your teacher assigns you.*

11. Think about the difference in the way people are labeled in "The People Could Fly." What is the author suggesting by using names for the slaves and titles for those who practice slavery? In a brief essay, analyze the choices made by the author. Use information from the story as support for your answer.

12. Several times in "The People Could Fly," the people who can fly are compared to birds. How are these people like, and unlike, birds at different points in the story? In an essay, describe how the people who can fly behave: in Africa; right after their capture; when Sarah escapes; and when the others escape with Toby. Include in your answer an analysis of when they behave most like birds.

13. In "The People Could Fly," there is an extended description of the moment when Toby helps the others rise into the sky to gain their freedom. In an essay, analyze the reason that the author may have chosen to write such a colorful description. Include in your analysis an understanding of the purpose of this folk tale. Use details from the selection to support your opinion.

14. **Thinking About the Big Question: Community or Individual: Which is more important?** In "The People Could Fly," Toby is able to save many members of his community. Write an essay in which you analyze his role. Is he or any other individual character more important than the community? In your answer, include details from the story that support your analysis.

## Oral Response

15. Go back to question 2, 8, or 9 or to the question your teacher assigns you. Take a few minutes to expand your answer and prepare an oral response. Find additional details in the selection that support your points. If necessary, make notes to guide your oral response.

"**The People Could Fly**" by Virginia Hamilton

# Selection Test A

**Critical Reading** *Identify the letter of the choice that best answers the question.*

____ 1. According to "The People Could Fly," when did the people first fly?
  A. when they lived in Africa long ago
  B. when they were on the boat from Africa
  C. when they were enslaved in America
  D. when they escaped from slavery

____ 2. According to "The People Could Fly," why did the people at one time shed their wings?
  A. They preferred sailing to flying.
  B. The slave ship had no room for wings.
  C. They no longer knew the magic.
  D. They knew they could never escape.

____ 3. In "The People Could Fly," why is the one called Master compared to a piece of coal?
  A. He works in a mine.
  B. He uses coal in his fireplace.
  C. He is hard and unyielding.
  D. He is black like his slaves.

____ 4. A folk tale may have villains and heroes. Who are the villains in "The People Could Fly"?
  I.   the one called Master
  II.  Toby
  III. the Driver
  IV.  Sarah
  V.   the Overseer
  A. I, II, IV
  B. II, IV, V
  C. II, III, IV
  D. I, III, V

____ 5. In "The People Could Fly," how are Toby and Sarah alike?
  A. They are slaves with children.
  B. They are slaves who wish to escape.
  C. They are slaves who are old.
  D. They know magic words.

6. Which character in "The People Could Fly" says the magic words?
   A. the Overseer
   B. Toby
   C. the Driver
   D. Sarah

7. Folk tales often show a clear difference between good and evil. In "The People Could Fly," which two elements or characters represent that difference?
   A. freedom and slavery
   B. Toby and Sarah
   C. the magic words and the wings
   D. the one called Master and the Driver

8. Which of these characters is most different from Toby in "The People Could Fly"?
   A. Sarah
   B. Sarah's child
   C. the Overseer
   D. the other slaves

9. In "The People Could Fly," Toby does not fly until the end of the folk tale. Which statement best explains why he does not fly away sooner?
   A. He no longer has wings.
   B. He is too old to fly far.
   C. He cannot remember the magic words.
   D. He wants to help other slaves escape.

10. In "The People Could Fly," what does flying stand for?
    A. going to market
    B. going to church
    C. escaping to freedom
    D. dreaming about birds

11. In "The People Could Fly," Toby's magic words allow slaves to fly, yet he does not say the words to everyone. What lesson is taught when Toby leaves a group of slaves waiting for a chance to run?
    A. Toby will come back for them before long.
    B. Toby is not as powerful as the Overseer.
    C. Not all the slaves can hear the magic words.
    D. People escaped from slavery in different ways.

_____ 12. How does a folk tale such as "The People Could Fly" usually come to be?
   A. It is written down by hand.
   B. It is made up by a group of people.
   C. It is passed down by word of mouth.
   D. It is published in paperback form.

_____ 13. Why would a folk tale such as "The People Could Fly" have been important to people living in slavery?
   A. It gave them hope.
   B. It showed them how to work faster.
   C. It told them how to avoid the Driver.
   D. It reminded them of Africa.

## Vocabulary and Grammar

_____ 14. In which sentence is the meaning of the word *scorned* expressed?
   A. Toby remembered the magic words.
   B. The slaves hated being looked down on.
   C. Master was a hard, unfeeling man.
   D. Sarah's baby would not stop crying.

_____ 15. What does the abbreviation stand for in this sentence?
   Virginia Hamilton held a B.A. from Antioch College.
   A. barium
   B. Buenos Aires
   C. batting average
   D. bachelor of arts

## Essay

16. In "The People Could Fly," how are Toby and the Overseer different? What is each character like? What characteristics does each one represent? In an essay, compare the two characters, showing their differences. Cite two details from the selection to support your main ideas.

17. "The People Could Fly" takes places during the time of slavery in America. In your opinion, what lesson about slavery does the folk tale teach? What lesson about freedom does it teach? State your ideas in an essay. Support your points with two references to the selection.

18. **Thinking About the Big Question: Community or individual: Which is more important?** In "The People Could Fly," Toby is able to save many members of his community. Write an essay in which you analyze his role. Is he or any other individual character more important than the community? In your answer, include details from the story that support your analysis.

**"The People Could Fly"** by Virginia Hamilton
# Selection Test B

**Critical Reading** *Identify the letter of the choice that best completes the statement or answers the question.*

____ 1. According to "The People Could Fly," what is the source of the people's ability to fly?
   A. helium
   B. wings
   C. magic
   D. dreams

____ 2. In "The People Could Fly," why do the slaves describe the so-called Master as "a hard lump of clay"?
   A. He owns a quarry.
   B. He manufactures pottery.
   C. He refuses to change.
   D. He is muscular.

____ 3. In "The People Could Fly," how are the Overseer and the Driver alike?
   I. They work for the so-called Master.
   II. They can speak the magic words.
   III. They wish to help Sarah and her baby.
   IV. They behave cruelly toward the people.

   A. I and III
   B. II and IV
   C. II and III
   D. I and IV

____ 4. According to "The People Could Fly," why does Sarah keep working even though her baby is crying?
   A. The Overseer will whip them if she stops.
   B. She does not know how to comfort the baby.
   C. She needs to earn money so she can feed the baby.
   D. The so-called Master will sell the baby if she stops.

____ 5. In "The People Could Fly," why does Sarah tell Toby that she must go soon?
   A. She and her baby are being whipped.
   B. She and her baby are hungry for lunch.
   C. She misses her homeland and family.
   D. She wants to raise her child in Africa.

____ 6. What is the most important difference between Toby and the Overseer in "The People Could Fly"?
   A. One is skilled, and one is unskilled.
   B. One is elderly, and one is young.
   C. One is white, and one is black.
   D. One is cruel, and one is kind.

____ 7. What role does Toby play in "The People Could Fly"?
   A. He encourages the people to work.
   B. He helps certain people care for their children.
   C. He helps certain people fly away.
   D. He teaches the people to accept slavery.

___ 8. What is an important distinction among the slaves in "The People Could Fly"?
   A. Some work in the fields, and some work in the house.
   B. Some still have the power to fly, and some do not.
   C. Some have children, and some do not.
   D. Some trust Toby, and some do not.

___ 9. According to "The People Could Fly," what does Toby hope will become of the slaves who do not go with him?
   A. They will persuade the so-called Master to treat them better.
   B. They will learn how to fly and escape on their own.
   C. They will gain their freedom by running away.
   D. They will plan and carry out an uprising.

___ 10. In "The People Could Fly," why does the one who calls himself Master say that the escape is a lie?
   A. He does not believe the Overseer's story about flying slaves.
   B. He is sure that all the slaves will return to work the next day.
   C. He thinks that he must have miscounted the slaves on his estate.
   D. He does not want to admit that he has been fooled by Toby.

___ 11. In "The People Could Fly," which two elements or characters represent a clear distinction between good and evil?
   A. blackbirds and eagles
   B. slavery and freedom
   C. the Master and the Overseer
   D. wings and magic

___ 12. What does Toby most likely represent in "The People Could Fly"?
   A. the people's wish to return to Africa
   B. the people's wish to live in freedom
   C. the people's wish to be treated fairly
   D. the people's wish to have a better Master

___ 13. What lesson about life is taught by "The People Could Fly"?
   A. Africans who were enslaved brought magic with them.
   B. It was possible to escape from slavery if you knew magic.
   C. Cruel people get more out of workers than do kind people.
   D. When conditions are bad, it is essential to keep hope alive.

___ 14. Which of the following topics is essential to the message of "The People Could Fly"?
   A. the importance of using magic wisely
   B. the triumph of freedom over slavery
   C. the commitment to being a good worker
   D. the importance of being a good mother

____ 15. How does a folk tale such as "The People Could Fly" originate?
   A. It begins as an oral tradition.
   B. It begins as a cave painting.
   C. It appears in a collection of folk tales.
   D. It is generated by computer software.

## Vocabulary and Grammar

____ 16. In which sentence does the word *scorned* make sense?
   A. Sarah found herself *scorned* by Toby as he said the magic words.
   B. The people were so *scorned* by the Overseer that they hated him.
   C. The people on the slave ship *scorned* one another in order to survive.
   D. Toby *scorned* the people so that they would be able to fly away.

____ 17. In which sentence is the meaning of the word *croon* expressed?
   A. The baby grew quiet when Sarah sang and hummed soothingly.
   B. The Overseer snarled at the people to make them work faster.
   C. Toby encouraged the people to believe that they could fly.
   D. The baby whimpered and fussed while Sarah worked.

____ 18. In which sentence does the word *shuffle* make sense?
   A. The people *shuffled* as they flew over the land to freedom.
   B. The Driver *shuffled* toward the people and cracked his whip.
   C. Sarah *shuffled* slowly as the Overseer criticized her work.
   D. The people *shuffled* around one another as they danced.

____ 19. Which of the following abbreviations is correct?
   A. Mr for *Mister*
   B. M.B.A. for *master of business administration*
   C. mr. for *meter*
   D. M.A. for *Massachusetts*

## Essay

20. Why might enslaved Africans have told a folk tale like "The People Could Fly"? Might it have served as a comfort? As an inspiration? Might it have served some other purpose? Express your thoughts in an essay. Cite two details from the selection to support your main ideas.

21. If Toby is an example of an African who has not forgotten about flying despite the oppression of slavery, what does Sarah represent? In an essay, contrast Toby and Sarah. Show how they are alike and how they are different.

22. **Thinking About the Big Question: Community or individual: Which is more important?** In "The People Could Fly," Toby is able to save many members of his community. Write an essay in which you analyze his role. Is he or any other individual character more important than the community? In your answer, include details from the story that support your analysis.

# Vocabulary Warm-up Word Lists

*Study these words from "All Stories Are Anansi's." Then, apply your knowledge to the activities that follow.*

## Word List A

**accepted** [ak SEPT ed] *v.* took something that was offered
> Donna graciously <u>accepted</u> the compliment.

**offering** [AWF er ing] *v.* presenting for acceptance
> Linda was <u>offering</u> the guests cake while I poured lemonade.

**opinion** [uh PIN yuhn] *n.* belief about a particular subject
> In Jeremy's <u>opinion</u>, a cell phone is a nuisance.

**protect** [pruh TEKT] *v.* to keep safe
> We must <u>protect</u> the environment.

**respect** [ri SPEKT] *n.* a feeling of admiration or consideration
> In Japan, people show great <u>respect</u> to their elders.

**therefore** [THAIR for] *adv.* for that reason
> The tiger was wounded and <u>therefore</u> more dangerous.

## Word List B

**accustomed to** [uh KUS tuhmd] *adj.* used to; in the habit of
> Americans are <u>accustomed to</u> having many choices.

**acknowledge** [ak NAHL ij] *v.* to accept that something is true
> Most people <u>acknowledge</u> that the Internet has changed our lives.

**dispute** [dis PYOOT] *n.* a serious argument or disagreement
> The worker <u>dispute</u> over wages ended in a strike.

**prisoner** [PRIZ uhn ner] *n.* someone who is taken and held by force
> The guard locked the <u>prisoner</u> in a tiny cell.

**prowling** [PROWL ing] *v.* quietly moving around on the hunt
> We heard the bear <u>prowling</u> outside the cabin, looking for food.

**warriors** [WOR ee erz] *n.* experienced and skillful soldiers
> We honor our nation's <u>warriors</u> on Veterans Day.

Name _____ Date _____

## Exercise A
*Fill in each blank in the paragraph below with an appropriate word from Word List A. Use each word only once.*

Doris [1] _____ the invitation to go to the concert, but only out of
[2] _____ for her mother who loved classical music. She knew her
mom was [3] _____ her an opportunity to enjoy "finer things," but
in Doris's [4] _____, classical music was a waste of time. To
[5] _____ her mom's feelings, Doris acted like she really loved the
performance. [6] _____, she wasn't terribly surprised when her mom
invited her to another concert the following month.

## Exercise B
*Find a synonym for each word in the following vocabulary list. Use each synonym in a sentence that makes the meaning of the word clear.*

**Example:** prowling **Synonym**: *raiding*
   *When I heard a noise in the middle of the night, I knew my brother was* raiding *the kitchen for a snack.*

1. dispute      **Synonym:** _____
_____

2. prisoner     **Synonym:** _____
_____

3. acknowledge  **Synonym:** _____
_____

4. accustomed   **Synonym:** _____
_____

5. warriors     **Synonym:** _____
_____

**"All Stories Are Anansi's"** by Harold Courlander
# Reading Warm-up A

*Read the following passage. Pay special attention to the underlined words. Then, read it again, and complete the activities. Use a separate sheet of paper for your written answers.*

Storytelling is as old as language. In times past, storytellers were the keepers of folklore. Some cultures accepted these tellers of tales as a gift from the gods. Adults, as well as children, eagerly gathered around the storyteller to hear the stories they knew by heart. Usually the storyteller had a trick or two that would take the audience by surprise, but not too often. It was the repetition of the familiar words that audiences loved. Today, many people have the opinion that storytelling is just for children. They forget the time when everyone joined the story circle.

We all have a need for stories. Our stories are everywhere: in conversations, newspapers, television, and films. Each kind of story fulfills a special need. Stories from folklore fulfill a need, too. Storyteller Tim Sheppard tells us, "Every effort to explain shared customs and values needs a tale. Every bit of wisdom is best expressed by a story." In other words, the values and wisdom of our culture are preserved in our lore. Traditional tales teach us about ourselves by offering insights into what we as a group admire and fear. For this reason, we respect our folk stories. We continue to protect and preserve them to keep them from dying out. Today, as in the past, the storyteller helps us do this.

Listening to a live storyteller is a unique experience. Like a spinning spider, the storyteller traps you in a web of words and holds you captive. The teller spins and spins, until the world of the story is fully formed. Yet, each listener imagines the world in a personal way, therefore creating a unique universe in his or her own mind.

So, look for the storytellers in your area. Enter the circle where storytelling is for all. The stories you will hear are timeless, meaningful, and meant only for listening.

1. Underline the words that tell how cultures accepted tellers of tales. Write a sentence using the word *accepted*.

2. Underline the words that give the opinion of many people. Write your *opinion* on another subject.

3. Underline the words that tell what traditional tales are offering. Rewrite the sentence using a synonym for *offering*.

4. Circle the words that tell what we respect. Write the meaning of *respect*.

5. Circle the words that tell from what we protect our folk stories. Write about something you think your community should *protect* and preserve.

6. Underline the words that tell what, therefore, creates a unique universe. Write a sentence using the word *therefore*.

Name _____  Date _____

*Read the following passage. Pay special attention to the underlined words. Then, read it again, and complete the activities. Use a separate sheet of paper for your written answers.*

If it weren't for spiders, we would all be dead. This sounds like an exaggeration, but it probably isn't. If it weren't for spiders, the insects and other small critters that carry animal diseases and destroy food crops would eventually overrun the world. Though some may <u>dispute</u> this claim, people who study these things <u>acknowledge</u> that spiders do keep the insect population in check. How do they do it? Well, spiders eat a lot, and there are a lot of them. In just one acre of meadowland, there can be as many as two million hungry spiders.

Saving the world is a big job. It requires extraordinary weapons and skills. Luckily, the W.A.S. (World Army of Spiders) has both. Spider weapons include silk, stealth, and venom. Spider skills include the ability to spin, spit, jump, pounce, mimic, dive, fish, lasso, cast nets, fly through the air, and walk on water.

You are <u>accustomed to</u> seeing spiders spin webs to trap their victims. Have you ever seen the Ogre-faced Spider cast its small flat web down upon its prey and hold it <u>prisoner</u>? You are used to seeing spiders <u>prowling</u> around in the dirt. Have you ever seen a Fishing Spider run across the surface of water? The Bolas Spider spins a line beaded with sticky droplets. It throws the line like a lasso and when the glue sticks to a victim, the spider hauls it in. The Trap Door Spider hides underground beneath a trap door lined with silk. The Water Spider hides underwater inside an air bubble made of silk. The Ant Mimic Spider fools its enemies by mimicking the ants with which it lives.

Spider <u>warriors</u> around the world are secretly watching, silently capturing, and steadily devouring the earth's smallest enemies.

Aren't you glad they are?

1. Circle the words that tell what some people may <u>dispute</u>. Rewrite the sentence using a synonym for **dispute**.

2. Underline the words that tell what some people <u>acknowledge</u>. Write the meaning of **acknowledge**.

3. Circle the words that mean the same as <u>accustomed to</u>. Write a sentence about something you are **accustomed to** seeing.

4. Underline the words that tell how the Ogre-faced Spider holds its prey <u>prisoner</u>. Give a synonym for **prisoner**.

5. Underline the words that tell where spiders are seen <u>prowling</u>. Name two places where you might find spiders **prowling**.

6. Underline the words that tell what spider <u>warriors</u> are doing. Name a famous group of **warriors** you've studied or read about.

Unit 6 Resources: Themes in the Oral Tradition
**187**

**"All Stories Are Anansi's"** by Harold Courlander
# Writing About the Big Question

## Community or individual: Which is more important?

### Big Question Vocabulary

| | | | | |
|---|---|---|---|---|
| common | community | culture | custom | diversity |
| duty | environment | ethnicity | family | group |
| individual | team | tradition | unify | unique |

**A.** *Use one or more words from the list above to complete each sentence.*

1. The two con men targeted a _____ of small-town residents.

2. They worked as a _____ to gain the residents' trust.

3. They offered a free seminar and created a friendly _____.

4. Once they had what they wanted, both _____ disappeared.

5. After that, the _____ was wary of strangers offering free advice.

**B.** *Follow the directions in responding to each of the items below.*

1. List two people you have heard or read about who exploited others for personal gain.

   _____   _____

2. Write two sentences describing one of the preceding incidents and how it affected those involved. Use at least two of the Big Question vocabulary words.

   _____

   _____

**C.** *Complete the sentence below. Then, write a short paragraph in which you connect this situation to the big question.*

When an individual exploits others for personal gain, _____

_____

_____

_____

_____

_____

Name _____  Date _____

**"All Stories Are Anansi's"** by Harold Courlander
# Reading: Use a Venn Diagram to Compare and Contrast

When you **compare and contrast,** you recognize similarities and differences. You can compare and contrast elements in a literary work by **using a Venn diagram** to examine character traits, situations, and ideas. First, reread the text to locate the details you will compare. Then, write the details on a diagram like the ones shown below. Recording these details will help you understand the similarities and differences in a literary work.

**DIRECTIONS:** *Fill in the Venn diagrams as directed to make comparisons about elements of "All Stories Are Anansi's."*

1. Compare Anansi and Onini, the great python. Write characteristics of Anansi in the left-hand oval and characteristics of Onini in the right-hand oval. Write characteristics that they share in the overlapping part of the two ovals.

**Anansi**                    **Both**                    **Onini**

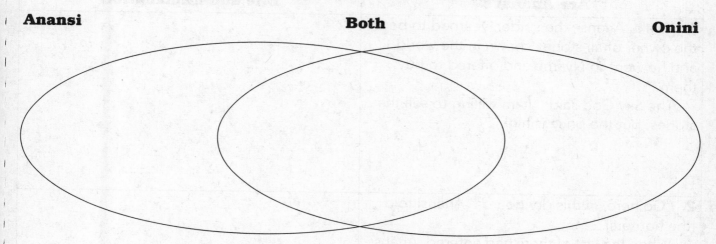

2. Compare Mmoboro, the hornets, with Osebo, the leopard. Write characteristics of the hornets in the left-hand oval and characteristics of the leopard in the right-hand oval. Write characteristics that they share in the overlapping part of the two ovals.

**Hornets**                    **Both**                    **Leopard**

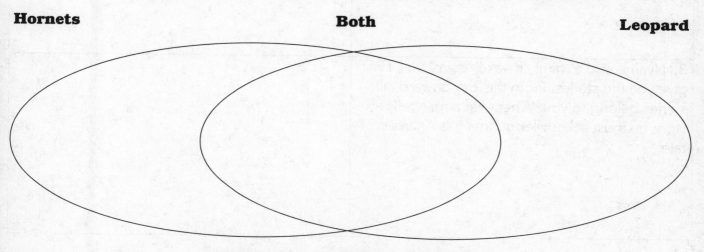

Unit 6 Resources: Themes in the Oral Tradition

Name _____ Date _____

"All Stories Are Anansi's" by Harold Courlander

# Literary Analysis: Folk Tale

A **folk tale** is a story that is composed orally and then passed from person to person by word of mouth. Although folk tales originate in this **oral tradition,** many of them are eventually collected and written down. Similar folk tales are told by different cultures throughout the world. Such folk tales have common character types, plot elements, and themes. Folk tales often teach a lesson about life and present a clear separation between good and evil. Folk tales are part of the oral tradition that also includes fairy tales, legends, myths, fables, tall tales, and ghost stories.

**DIRECTIONS:** *Read each passage from "All Stories Are Anansi's." In the second column of the chart, indicate what value or lesson about life the passage teaches. Then, explain your choice.*

| Passage from "All Stories Are Anansi's" | Value or Lesson About Life and Explanation |
|---|---|
| 1. Kwaku Anansi, the spider, yearned to be the owner of all stories known in the world, and he went to Nyame and offered to buy them.<br><br>    The Sky God said: "I am willing to sell the stories, but the price is high." | |
| 2. "Go here, in this dry gourd," Anansi told [the hornets]. . . .<br><br>    When the last of them had entered, Anansi plugged the hole with a ball of grass, saying: "Oh, yes, but you are really foolish people!" | |
| 3. Nyame said to him: "Kwaku Anansi, . . . I will give you the stories. From this day onward, all stories belong to you. Whenever a man tells a story, he must acknowledge that it is Anansi's tale." | |

Unit 6 Resources: Themes in the Oral Tradition

© Pearson Education, Inc. All rights reserved.

**190**

Name _____ Date _____

**"All Stories Are Anansi's"** by Harold Courlander
# Vocabulary Builder

## Word List

acknowledge    dispute    gourd    opinion    python    yearned

**A. DIRECTIONS:** *Write the letter of the word that means* the same or about the same as *the vocabulary word.*

____ 1. yearned
     A. rejected        B. questioned       C. desired        D. ignored

____ 2. gourd
     A. cup             B. fork             C. platter         D. knife

____ 3. acknowledge
     A. taunt          B. challenge        C. credit          D. dismiss

____ 4. python
     A. panther       B. snake          C. cougar         D. spider

____ 5. opinion
     A. statement    B. fact            C. statistic      D. belief

____ 6. dispute
     A. argument     B. lie             C. error         D. agreement

**B. WORD STUDY:** *The root* -know- *means "to understand." Answer each of the following questions using one of these words containing* -know-: *unknowingly, acknowledge, knowledgeable.*

1. How might you *unknowingly* hurt a friend's feelings?

_____

_____

2. How would you *acknowledge* a friend's presence?

_____

_____

3. Why would you ask a *knowledgeable* person a difficult question?

_____

_____

Name _____ Date _____

# Enrichment: Making Plans

Suppose that, like Anansi, you want to own all the stories. Then, you, too, must capture Mmoboro, the hornets; Onini, the great python (a snake); and Osebo, the leopard, but you may not copy Anansi's methods. Will you use trickery or technology? Will you talk the animals into going with you? Unlike Anansi, you must catch all of the animals humanely, and they must be alive when you bring them to Nyame, the Sky God. Like Anansi's plans, yours should be fanciful. How will you do it?

**DIRECTIONS:** *Use this chart to map out your plans for capturing the hornets, the python, and the leopard. Describe your plan for each animal, or draw and label a diagram. Then, list the materials you will need.*

**Mmoboro (the hornets):** _____

_____

_____

**Materials:** _____

_____

**Onini (the python):** _____

_____

_____

**Materials:** _____

_____

**Osebo (the leopard):** _____

_____

_____

_____

**Materials:** _____

_____

Name _____ Date _____

"The People Could Fly" by Virginia Hamilton
"All Stories Are Anansi's" by Harold Courlander
# Integrated Language Skills: Grammar

## Abbreviations

An **abbreviation** is a shortened form of a word or phrase. Most abbreviations end with a period, but many do not, and some may be written either with or without a period. Most dictionaries have entries for abbreviations, so look them up if you are not sure of the correct form. Note which abbreviations are written with periods, which ones are not, and which ones appear in capital letters in these lists:

**Titles of persons:** Mr.  Ms.  Mrs.

**Days of the week:** Sun.  Mon.  Tues.  Wed.  Thurs.  Fri.  Sat.  Sun.

**Months of the year:** Jan.  Feb.  Mar.  Apr.  Aug.  Sept.  Oct.  Nov.  Dec.

**Times of day:** a.m.  p.m.

**Street designations:** Ave.  Blvd.  Pl.  St.

**State postal abbreviations:** AL  AK  AZ  AR  CA  CO  CT  DE  FL  GA  HI  ID  IL  IN  IA  KS  KY  LA  ME  MD  MA  MI  MN  MS  MO  MT  NE  NV  NH  NJ  NM  NY NC  ND  OH  OK  OR  PA  RI  SC  SD  TN  TX  UT  VT  VA  WA  WV  WI  WY

**Organizations:** NAACP  UN  YMCA

**Units of measure:** in.  ft.  yd.  lb.  qt.  gal.  *but* mm  cm  m  mg  g  ml  dl  l

**A. PRACTICE:** *Rewrite each sentence below, and abbreviate the words in italics.*

1. James lives at 115 Elm *Street*, Pleasant Valley, *Nebraska*.

   _____

2. The gardener said that if your yard measures 50 *feet* (16.6 *yards*) by 40 *feet* (13.3 *yards*), you will need 2 *pounds* of fertilizer.

   _____

   _____

3. *Mister* Raymond works for the *United Nations*.

   _____

**B. Writing Application:** *Compose an e-mail message to a friend. Tell about something you have done recently. Use at least five abbreviations. If you are not sure of the correct form, look up the abbreviation in a dictionary.*

   _____

   _____

   _____

   _____

   _____

Name _____ Date _____

"The People Could Fly" by Virginia Hamilton
"All Stories Are Anansi's" by Harold Courlander

# Integrated Language Skills: Support for Writing a Review

Use this chart to take notes for a **review** of "The People Could Fly" or "All Stories Are Anansi's."

## Notes for Review

| Element of the Tale | My Opinion of the Element | Details From the Tale That Support My Opinion |
|---|---|---|
| Characters | | |
| Description | | |
| Dialogue | | |
| Plot | | |

Now, write a draft of your review. Tell readers whether or not you think they will enjoy the folktale. Remember to support your opinions with details from the tale.

**"The People Could Fly"** by Virginia Hamilton
**"All Stories Are Anansi's"** by Harold Courlander

# Integrated Language Skills: Support for Extend Your Learning

### Listening and Speaking: "The People Could Fly"

Use the following prompts to prepare a **television news report** on the amazing events that took place in " The People Could Fly." Respond to the prompts with details from the folktale.

**Where events took place:** _____

_____

**When events took place:** _____

**What happened:** _____

_____

**Question for Eyewitness:** _____

_____

**Eyewitness's answer:** _____

_____

**Question for Eyewitness:** _____

_____

**Eyewitness's answer:** _____

_____

### Listening and Speaking: "All Stories Are Anansi's"

Use the following prompts to prepare a **television news report** about Anansi's amazing deeds. Respond to the prompts with details from "All Stories Are Anansi's."

**Where events took place:** _____

_____

**When events took place:** _____

**What Anansi wanted:** _____

**What happened with the hornets:** _____

_____

**What happened with the python:** _____

_____

**What happened with the leopard:** _____

_____

**What happened in the end:** _____

_____

Name _____  Date _____

### "All Stories Are Anansi's" by Harold Courlander
# Open-Book Test

**Short Answer** *Write your responses to the questions in this section on the lines provided.*

1. Folk tales often use common character types to teach a lesson. How does "All Stories Are Anansi's" fit this definition of a folk tale?

   _____

   _____

2. Anansi makes an offer to buy stories from Nyame, the Sky God. Compare Anansi to the others who have come to the Sky God for the same reason. Use details from the beginning of the selection to support your answer.

   _____

   _____

   _____

3. Anansi yearned to own all of the stories in the world. What did the hornets probably yearn for?

   _____

   _____

4. How does Anansi first reveal himself as a trickster in "All Stories Are Anansi's"?

   _____

   _____

5. In the middle of the tale, Anansi traps Onini the python. What lesson can be learned from the python's experience? Use details from the tale to support your response.

   _____

   _____

   _____

6. Anansi uses the word *foolish* to describe the animals he has tricked. Who do you think is more foolish, the hornets or the python? Use details from the tale to explain your answer.

   _____

   _____

   _____

7. Anansi agrees to help the leopard out of the hole after Osebo swears not to eat Anansi and his children. Consider what then happens to Osebo. Why did Anansi bother to bargain with Osebo?

_____

_____

8. Anansi takes additional steps to make sure that he can bring the leopard back to the Sky God. Describe the steps that Anansi takes, and explain why he takes them.

_____

_____

_____

9. Anansi brings the Sky God what he asks for. Use the graphic organizer to compare the ways in which he captures each animal. Then, tell which animal was the most foolish. Explain your opinion, using support from the organizer.

| Hornets | Python | Leopard |
|---------|--------|---------|
|         |        |         |

_____

_____

_____

10. At the end of the tale, the Sky God says that people must acknowledge Anansi as the owner of all tales. Would you want others to acknowledge a big mistake you had made? Explain why or why not, using the definition of *acknowledge*.

_____

_____

_____

## Essay

*Write an extended response to the question of your choice or to the question or questions your teacher assigns you.*

11. Anansi uses a different method to trap each of his victims. In an essay, explain what methods he uses and what each method shows about his knowledge of that animal. Use details from the folk tale in your response.

12. Think about Anansi the trickster. He is successful, but is he an admirable character? In an essay, explore whether the author means for readers to admire Anansi. Include in your answer an explanation of the lesson of the tale. Use details from the folk tale to support your response.

13. In "All Stories Are Anansi's," there is a high value placed on the ownership of stories. Why is owning stories so important? In an essay, explain why the culture that originally told the story might have seen stories as so important. Consider who does not end up owning them in this folk tale. Use details from the selection to support your opinion.

14. **Thinking About the Big Question: Community or Individual: Which is more important?** Who does Anansi find more important, the individual or the community? Do you agree? Write an essay in which you offer an opinion about whether he or the community is more important in this story. Use information from the selection to support your opinion.

**Oral Response**

15. Go back to question 4, 5, or 9 or to the question your teacher assigns you. Take a few minutes to expand your answer and prepare an oral response. Find additional details in the selection that support your points. If necessary, make notes to guide your oral response.

Name _____ Date _____

**Critical Reading** *Identify the letter of the choice that best answers the question.*

_____ 1. What do folk tales such as "All Stories Are Anansi's" often have in common?
    I.  plot elements
    II.  settings
    III.  character types
    IV.  themes
    **A.** I, II, III
    **B.** II, III, IV
    **C.** I, II, IV
    **D.** I, III, IV

_____ 2. At the beginning of "All Stories Are Anansi's," who owns all the stories?
    **A.** a spider
    **B.** a god
    **C.** a snake
    **D.** a human

_____ 3. Based on "All Stories Are Anansi's," what is important to the people who told this tale?
    **A.** spiders
    **B.** physical strength
    **C.** storytelling
    **D.** wealth

_____ 4. With what tool does Anansi capture the hornets in "All Stories Are Anansi's"?
    **A.** a gourd
    **B.** a pit
    **C.** a bamboo pole
    **D.** a calabash

_____ 5. In "All Stories Are Anansi's," after Anansi catches the hornets, he says, "Oh, yes, but you are really foolish people!"
Why does he say that?
    **A.** because they dislike the rain
    **B.** because they trusted him
    **C.** because they do not sting him
    **D.** because they live in a tree

Unit 6 Resources: Themes in the Oral Tradition
199

_____ 6. In "All Stories Are Anansi's," Anansi takes advantage of the python to capture him. Which character trait of the python does Anansi take advantage of?
   A. his pride
   B. his stupidity
   C. his dishonesty
   D. his physical weakness

_____ 7. In "All Stories Are Anansi's," when the leopard falls into the pit, why does Anansi say that he is "half-foolish"?
   A. The leopard is smart enough to escape.
   B. The leopard has fallen only halfway into the pit.
   C. Anansi's plan to capture the leopard is only half finished.
   D. Anansi does not know how to complete the job of capturing the leopard.

_____ 8. What do all the victims in "All Stories Are Anansi's" have in common?
   A. greed
   B. ambition
   C. strength
   D. foolishness

_____ 9. "All Stories Are Anansi's" is a trickster tale. Who is the trickster in the story?
   A. Nyame
   B. Anansi
   C. the python
   D. Osebo

_____ 10. In "All Stories Are Anansi's," how is Anansi's approach to all of his victims the same?
   A. He overpowers them.
   B. He hides from them.
   C. He fools them.
   D. He pays them.

_____ 11. How is Anansi different from all his victims in "All Stories Are Anansi's"?
   A. He is smaller than they are.
   B. He is weaker than they are.
   C. He is smarter than they are.
   D. He is poorer than they are.

_____ 12. What lesson about life does one learn from "All Stories Are Anansi's"?

    **A.** Do not be too quick to trust.

    **B.** Do not be afraid of the rain.

    **C.** Do not trust spiders.

    **D.** Do not fall into pits.

_____ 13. What lesson about life is suggested by "All Stories Are Anansi's"?

    **A.** Intelligence is more important than strength.

    **B.** Spiders are more powerful than gods.

    **C.** Rulers are stronger than warriors.

    **D.** Animals are essentially foolish.

## Vocabulary and Grammar

_____ 14. In which sentence is the meaning of the word *yearned* expressed?

    **A.** Warriors and kings tried to own the stories, but they failed.

    **B.** Anansi wanted the stories so much he worked hard to get them.

    **C.** The python did not see that Anansi was going to trick him.

    **D.** The hornets hated water so much that they flew into the gourd.

_____ 15. What does the abbreviation M.D. stand for in the following sentence?

    Rosa Gonzales, M.D., posted her hours on her office door.

    **A.** Maryland

    **B.** medical doctor

    **C.** miles per hour

    **D.** minutes after noon

## Essay

16. Is Anansi in "All Stories Are Anansi's" an admirable character? That is, do you look up to him? Would you want to be like him? Why or why not? Present your opinion in an essay. Cite two details from the folk tale to support your main ideas.

17. Which of Anansi's victories in "All Stories Are Anansi's" did you find most impressive? Was it the way Anansi captured the hornets? The way he captured the python? The way he captured the leopard? In an essay, explain your choice. Cite two details from the selection to support your ideas.

18. **Thinking About the Big Question: Community or individual: Which is more important?** In "All Stories Are Anansi's," whom does Anansi find more important, the individual or the community? Do you agree? Explain your opinion in an essay supported by details from the selection.

Name _____ Date _____

## "All Stories Are Anansi's" by Harold Courlander
# Selection Test B

**Critical Reading** *Identify the letter of the choice that best completes the statement or answers the question.*

_____ 1. Folk tales such as "All Stories Are Anansi's" are part of a tradition that includes which of the following kinds of literature?
   I. fairy tales
   II. tall tales
   III. ghost stories
   IV. science fiction
   A. I only
   B. I and II only
   C. I, II, and III only
   D. I, II, III, and IV

_____ 2. Which character owns all the stories when "All Stories Are Anansi's" begins?
   A. Anansi
   B. the Sky God
   C. the python
   D. Osebo

_____ 3. What motivation does the major character have for his actions in "All Stories Are Anansi's"?
   A. Anansi wants to rule the forest.
   B. Anansi wants to impress the Sky God.
   C. Anansi wants to get rid of the hornets.
   D. Anansi wants to own all the stories.

_____ 4. In "All Stories Are Anansi's," the price of owning all the stories is high. What does that tell you about the people who told this story?
   A. They valued storytelling.
   B. They valued trickery.
   C. They valued wealth.
   D. They valued spiders.

_____ 5. In "All Stories Are Anansi's," Anansi approaches the python by
   A. flattering him.
   B. insulting him.
   C. questioning him.
   D. challenging him.

_____ 6. In "All Stories Are Anansi's," how is Anansi's treatment of the leopard different from his treatment of his other victims?
   A. He calls him foolish.
   B. He talks to him.
   C. He tricks him.
   D. He kills him.

_____ 7. In "All Stories Are Anansi's," what is the same about Anansi's approach to all of his victims?
A. He bribes them.
B. He kills them.
C. He outsmarts them.
D. He kidnaps them.

_____ 8. Which attribute does Anansi use to capture all his victims?
A. his ability to spin webs
B. his ability to avoid traps
C. his ability to talk to the Sky God
D. his ability to use his intelligence

_____ 9. Folk tales often show one character taking advantage of other characters. Which character trait of his victims does Anansi take advantage of in "All Stories Are Anansi's"?
A. their intelligence
B. their naivete
C. their greed
D. their anger

_____ 10. Which two traits are contrasted in "All Stories Are Anansi's"?
A. strength and weakness
B. good and evil
C. intelligence and foolishness
D. ambition and laziness

_____ 11. What lesson about life is taught in "All Stories Are Anansi's"?
A. Ambition will make you wealthy.
B. Storytelling can be dangerous.
C. Warriors may be defeated.
D. Trust given quickly is foolish.

_____ 12. Which word best describes Anansi's attitude toward the other animals?
A. respect
B. contempt
C. appreciation
D. puzzlement

_____ 13. Why is Anansi able to do what warriors and chiefs failed to do?
A. He uses thought instead of weapons.
B. He is more powerful than the warriors.
C. He uses words instead of money.
D. He uses the language of animals.

____ 14. What contrast between Anansi and his victims in "All Stories Are Anansi's" makes the victims unable to believe that Anansi poses a danger to them?
   A. They are so much bigger than he is.
   B. They are so much richer than he is.
   C. They are so much smarter than he is.
   D. They are so much prouder than he is.

## Vocabulary and Grammar

____ 15. In which sentence does the word *gourd* make sense?
   A. The thirsty explorer drank from a *gourd*.
   B. We bandaged our wounds with a *gourd*.
   C. The *gourd* escaped and ran to the bushes.
   D. The scientist made notes with a *gourd*.

____ 16. In which sentence is the meaning of the word *acknowledge* expressed?
   A. A representative of the company questioned whether we had paid our bill.
   B. Millions of people vote in every national election in the United States.
   C. The writer gives credit for the ideas he uses from other sources.
   D. Our animals are never let out to roam around the neighborhood.

____ 17. Which of the following abbreviations is correct?
   A. cm. for *centimeter*          C. Penn for *Pennsylvania*
   B. in for *inch*                 D. ml for *milliliter*

____ 18. Which of the following abbreviations is correct?
   A. M.S. for *Mississippi*        C. M.S. for *master of science*
   B. Miss. for *Miss*              D. Ms. for *Mister*

## Essay

19. Anansi pays a high price to gain possession of all the tales and all the stories, but "All Stories Are Anansi's" never explains why Anansi wants those tales and stories in the first place. What do you think motivates Anansi? Does he just want to do something that the wealthiest and most powerful families have failed to do? Does he have some other motive? In an essay, express your ideas. Cite a detail from the story to support your opinion.

20. A folk tale can tell a reader a great deal about the people who traditionally told the tale. In an essay, tell what "All Stories Are Anansi's" tells you about the people who told that tale. What does it tell you about their environment? What does it tell you that they valued? What lessons were they likely to pass on to their children? Cite three details from the tale to support your ideas.

21. **Thinking About the Big Question: Community or individual: Which is more important?** Whom does Anansi find more important, the individual or the community? Do you agree? Write an essay in which you offer an opinion about whether he or the community is more important in this story. Use information from the selection to support your opinion.

**"The Fox Outwits the Crow"** by William Cleary
**"The Fox and the Crow"** by Aesop
# Vocabulary Warm-up Word Lists

*Study these words from "The Fox Outwits the Crow" and "The Fox and the Crow." Then, complete the activities that follow.*

## Word List A

**curves** [KERVZ] *n.* lines or shapes that bend like parts of a circle
   The car hugged the road as it traveled around the mountain <u>curves</u>.

**figure** [FIG yoor] *n.* a person's shape
   The designer's clothes looked great on the model's perfect <u>figure</u>.

**fondly** [FAHND lee] *adv.* in an affectionate manner
   Greta smiled <u>fondly</u> at Grandfather from across the table.

**snatch** [SNACH] *v.* to take or grab something quickly
   I saw two thieves <u>snatch</u> apples from the fruit vendor's cart.

**trust** [TRUST] *v.* to believe that someone is honest and dependable
   The mechanic was the one person Jack could <u>trust</u> to fix his car.

**whiff** [WIF] *n.* a faint smell in the air
   We smelled a <u>whiff</u> of smoke coming from the car engine.

## Word List B

**advice** [ad VYS] *n.* an opinion about what someone should do
   Shelly followed her friends' <u>advice</u> to stay home until she was well.

**exchange** [iks CHAYNJ] *v.* to give one thing for another
   Carter wanted to <u>exchange</u> his new watch for a dirt bike.

**flattery** [FLAT er ee] *n.* insincere or exaggerated praise
   <u>Flattery</u> is the least sincere form of admiration.

**glamorous** [GLAM er uhs] *adj.* attractive and exciting
   The famous actress lived a <u>glamorous</u> lifestyle.

**malice** [MAL is] *n.* the desire to harm or upset someone
   The man accused his innocent neighbor with intentional <u>malice</u>.

**moral** [MAWR uhl] *n.* the lesson taught by a story
   The <u>moral</u> of "The Tortoise and the Hare" is "slow and steady wins the race."

**"The Fox Outwits the Crow"** by William Cleary
**"The Fox and the Crow"** by Aesop
# Vocabulary Warm-up Exercises

**Exercise A** *Fill in each blank in the paragraph below with an appropriate word from Word List A. Use each word only once.*

The firefighters could smell a [1] _____ of smoke as the fire truck sped around the mountainous [2] _____. Just as the truck reached the burning cabin, a woman's [3] _____ emerged from the billowing smoke. She was carrying a small child. One firefighter [4] _____ two oxygen masks out of the truck and rushed toward the woman. He gave one mask to the woman and put the other one over the child's face. When paramedics arrived, the woman handed her child to them, knowing she could [5] _____ them to make sure he was all right. With a sigh of relief, she looked [6] _____ at the firefighters who had helped to ensure their safety.

**Exercise B** *Write a complete sentence to answer each question. Use a word from Word List B to replace each underlined word without changing the meaning.*

**Example:** How do you feel about <u>meaningless compliments</u>?
*I think <u>flattery</u> is insulting.*

1. What is the most <u>exciting</u> thing you have ever done?

   _____

   _____

2. Why would you never act out of <u>meanness</u> toward a friend?

   _____

   _____

3. On what occasion do you <u>trade</u> cards or gifts?

   _____

   _____

4. Why do people like stories with a <u>lesson</u>?

   _____

   _____

5. What <u>opinion</u> would you give someone who is paying too much for an item?

   _____

   _____

**"The Fox Outwits the Crow"** by William Cleary
**"The Fox and the Crow"** by Aesop
# Reading Warm-up A

*Read the following passage. Pay special attention to the underlined words. Then, read it again, and complete the activities. Use a separate sheet of paper for your written answers.*

On her sixteenth birthday, Mira went into the garden wearing the new gown her mother <u>fondly</u> had made for her. Every seam was lovingly stitched so that the fabric perfectly fitted the <u>curves</u> of her body. "Today," she thought dreamily, "I am the prettiest girl in the village."

"That is true," said a musical voice that tickled her ear.

Mira turned to see the <u>figure</u> of a man wearing clothes of purple satin and a peacock-feathered hat. He held a jeweled mirror, and he stared at his own reflection. Mira smelled a <u>whiff</u> of his perfume and sneezed.

"Bless you!" said the figure, never taking his eyes from the mirror.

"Who are you?" asked Mira. "Tell me what is true."

"My name is Vanity," he answered silkily, his eyes still on the mirror, "and you *are* the prettiest girl in the village." With a crook of his finger, he beckoned Mira toward the mirror.

Mira saw a reflection of herself in her new gown. Now, however, the gown was made of gold, and pearls dangled from her earlobes. Her skin glowed like a fresh peach. Her hair shimmered in the sun. She was beautiful!

"Is this a true image of me?" she asked.

"<u>Trust</u> me, it is," said Vanity, "and I tell no lies."

Mira <u>snatched</u> the mirror from Vanity's grasp and stared long at her image. When she looked up, he was gone, but she still held the mirror.

From that day forward, Mira had eyes only for the image in the mirror. She saw herself as no one else ever saw her, and she saw no one else at all. Then one day, the mirror cracked and she was old.

Sadly she saw the truth at last: Vanity had robbed her of her true self, leaving her empty. Vanity had lied.

1. Circle the word that is a synonym for <u>fondly</u>. Use *fondly* in a sentence.

2. Underline the words that tell what <u>curves</u> the fabric fitted. Write the meaning of *curves*.

3. Circle the words that tell what kind of <u>figure</u> Mira saw. Rewrite the sentence using a synonym for *figure*.

4. Underline the words that tell what Mira caught a <u>whiff</u> of. Write about something else you might get a *whiff* of.

5. Circle the word that tells who Mira was asked to <u>trust</u>. Name someone you *trust* and tell why.

6. Circle the word that tells what Mira <u>snatched</u>. Give a synonym for *snatched* and use it in a sentence.

**"The Fox Outwits the Crow"** by William Cleary
**"The Fox and the Crow"** by Aesop
# Reading Warm-up B

*Read the following passage. Pay special attention to the underlined words. Then, read it again, and complete the activities. Use a separate sheet of paper for your written answers.*

*One crow for sorrow, Two crows for mirth . . .*

So begins an old counting rhyme that reflects the different ways in which the crow is viewed in folklore. The crow is a familiar figure. Although it's not as <u>glamorous</u> as many tropical birds, the crow has been both feared and admired since ancient times.

In nature, the crow belongs to a family of birds that includes the raven and the magpie. They are *carrion* birds, meaning they eat dead flesh. Crows, in fact, will eat anything: eggs, fish, acorns, berries, grains, insects. They are good at stealing food, too. Crows will band together to steal another animal's meal; however, they will rarely steal from one another. Within their group, they generously share and <u>exchange</u> bits of food.

In folklore the crow is often an omen of death. The bird's color and carrion diet probably contribute to this association. Crows are sometimes portrayed as creatures of <u>malice</u>, committing acts of evil intent. This is the dark side of the "trickster" crow. In one fable, however, the table is turned. A vain crow is tricked by false words of <u>flattery</u>. The <u>moral</u> of the tale holds this lesson for the crow: *As you trick, so will you be tricked.*

In some cultures, the crow represents laughter and the spirit of mischief. It is still a trickster, but its tricks benefit humankind. Native Americans admire the crow's intelligence and ability to mimic speech. Their stories often cast the crow as a messenger for humans seeking <u>advice</u> from spirits.

*Bird of sorrow, bird of mirth*: the crow is a complex creature both in nature and native lore.

1. Circle the words that tell what the crow is not as <u>glamorous</u> as. Describe something or someone that you think of as *glamorous*.

2. Underline the words that tell what crows sometimes <u>exchange</u>. Write the meaning of *exchange*.

3. Underline the words that mean the same as <u>malice</u>. Write a sentence using the word *malice*.

4. Circle the words that mean the same as <u>flattery</u>. Describe a situation in which someone might use *flattery*.

5. Circle the word that is a synonym for <u>moral</u>. Tell the *moral* of a familiar story and what it means to you.

6. Circle the words that tell from whom humans seek <u>advice</u> in Native American lore. Use *advice* in a sentence.

Name _____ Date _____

# Writing About the Big Question

## Community or individual: Which is more important?

### Big Question Vocabulary

| | | | | |
|---|---|---|---|---|
| common | community | culture | custom | diversity |
| duty | environment | ethnicity | family | group |
| individual | team | tradition | unify | unique |

**A.** *Use one or more words from the list above to complete each sentence.*

1. People enjoyed listening to Leslie's _____ singing voice.

2. She frequently sang at _____ gatherings.

3. She felt it was her _____ to share her gift with others.

4. She did not want to use her talent for _____ gain.

**B.** *Follow the directions in responding to each of the items below.*

1. List two works of literature from which you have learned something significant.
   _____    _____

2. Write two sentences describing one of the works and what it taught you. Use at least two of the Big Question vocabulary words.

   _____

   _____

   _____

   _____

**C.** *Complete the sentence below. Then, write a short paragraph in which you connect this experience to the big question.*

   One of the purposes of literature is to teach individuals how to _____

   _____

   _____

   _____

   _____

   _____

**"The Fox Outwits the Crow"** by William Cleary
**"The Fox and the Crow"** by Aesop
# Literary Analysis: Comparing Tone

The **tone** of a literary work is the writer's attitude toward his or her subject and characters. The tone can often be described by a single adjective, such as *formal, playful,* or *respectful.* To determine the tone of each selection, notice the words and phrases that the authors use to express their ideas.

The theme is a central message in a literary work. A theme can usually be expressed as a general statement about life. Although a theme may be stated directly in the text, it is more often presented indirectly. To figure out the theme of a work, look at what it reveals about people or life.

**A. DIRECTIONS:** *Compare the tone of the two selections by completing this chart. Choose one adjective to describe each passage. Use* serious, formal, informal, *or* playful.

| "The Fox Outwits the Crow" | Adjective | "The Fox and the Crow" | Adjective |
|---|---|---|---|
| **1.** One day a young crow snatched a fat piece of cheese. . . . | | A Fox once saw a Crow fly off with a piece of cheese in its beak. . . . | |
| **2.** A fox . . . got a whiff of the cheese, / The best of his favorite hors d'oeuvres, . . . | | "That's for me, as I am a Fox," said Master Reynard, . . . | |
| **3.** Hey, you glamorous thing, / Does your voice match your beautiful curves? | | "I feel sure your voice must surpass that of other birds, just as your figure does." | |

**B. DIRECTIONS:** *Answer the following questions to determine the theme of each work.*

1. What are the characters' key traits?

   **Poem:** _____

   **Fable:** _____

2. What is the main conflict in the story?

   **Poem:** _____

   **Fable:** _____

3. What happens as a result?

   **Poem:** _____

   **Fable:** _____

4. What general statement about life does this outcome suggest?

   **Poem:** _____

   **Fable:** _____

Name _____ Date _____

# Vocabulary Builder

**Word List**

flatterers    glossy    hors d'oeuvres    malice    surpass    whiff

**A. DIRECTIONS:** *Circle* T *if the statement is true or* F *if the statement is false. Then, explain your answer.*

1. A true bloodhound can follow someone's trail after getting only a *whiff* of the person's odor.

   **T / F** _____

2. *Flatterers* are honest and sincere.

   **T / F** _____

3. Something that is *glossy* has a rough finish.

   **T / F** _____

4. Most people would feel *malice* toward someone who has harmed them.

   **T / F** _____

5. *Hors d'oeuvres* are served after the main course.

   **T / F** _____

6. For a person to *surpass* expectations, he or she must do better than expected.

   **T / F** _____

**B. DIRECTIONS:** *For each pair of words in CAPITAL LETTERS, write the letter of the pair of words that best expresses a similar relationship.*

____ 1. OUTDO : SURPASS ::
    A. lose : win
    B. talk : remember
    C. work : play
    D. throw : toss

____ 2. WHIFF : SCENT ::
    A. sight : hearing
    B. good : bad
    C. love : adoration
    D. eyes : nose

____ 3. MALICE : GOODWILL ::
    A. stroll : walk
    B. painter : artist
    C. large : humongous
    D. blame : praise

Name _____  Date _____

**"The Fox Outwits the Crow"** by William Cleary
**"The Fox and the Crow"** by Aesop
# Support for Writing to Compare Reactions to Tone and Theme

Use this graphic organizer to take notes for an essay that compares your reaction to the tone and theme in "The Fox Outwits the Crow" with your reaction to the tone and theme in "The Fox and the Crow."

**"The Fox Outwits the Crow"**                                      **"The Fox and the Crow"**

| | How is the character presented? | |
|---|---|---|

| | What details help you see whether the writer establishes a personal relationship with readers? | |
|---|---|---|

| | What general statement does the work make about life? | |
|---|---|---|

What is the difference between the tone in the two selections? How does the tone influence your reaction to each work?

Now, use your notes to write an essay in which you compare your reaction to the tone and theme of "The Fox Outwits the Crow" with your reaction to the tone and theme of "The Fox and the Crow."

Name _____ Date _____

**"The Fox Outwits the Crow"** by William Cleary
**"The Fox and the Crow"** by Aesop
# Open-Book Test

**Short Answer** *Write your responses to the questions in this section on the lines provided.*

1. In "The Fox Outwits the Crow," why does the crow fly to the top of a Juniper Tree? Use details from the poem in your answer.

   _____

   _____

   _____

2. Read the crow's thoughts on lines 11 and 12 of "The Fox Outwits the Crow." What does the crow think of herself? Explain.

   _____

   _____

   _____

3. In "The Fox Outwits the Crow," the fox is full of malice. If someone makes a comment out of malice, what is the comment intended to do? Explain your answer.

   _____

   _____

   _____

4. In "The Fox and the Crow," the Fox is sure that the Crow's voice must surpass that of other birds. What would you have to do to surpass someone who gets a B on a report? Explain.

   _____

   _____

   _____

5. At the beginning of "The Fox and the Crow," Master Fox speaks in one way. At the end of the fable, he speaks in quite another way. Fill in the chart to describe his tone and manner at the beginning and end of the fable. Then, on the lines below, explain the change.

| **Beginning** | **End** |
| --- | --- |
| | |

   _____

   _____

6. In "The Fox and the Crow," why does Aesop advise "Do not trust flatterers"? Explain.

_____
_____
_____

7. Which version of the fable has a more playful tone, "The Fox Outwits the Crow" or "The Fox and the Crow"? Use details from the selections to explain.

_____
_____
_____

8. The tone of a literary work is the writer's attitude toward his subject and characters. What is Aesop's tone in "The Fox and the Crow"? Use details from the fable to explain.

_____
_____
_____

9. Compare the fox in "The Fox Outwits the Crow" to the fox in "The Fox and the Crow." Which author's tone makes the fox seem like more of a threat? Explain.

_____
_____
_____

10. Which version of the crow seems sillier, Aesop's or Cleary's? Explain how the author's tone helped you make your choice. Use details from the selection.

_____
_____
_____

**Essay**

*Write an extended response to the question of your choice or to the question or questions your teacher assigns you.*

11. A fox is a common character in fables. Consider what the fox says and does in both "The Fox Outwits the Crow" and "The Fox and the Crow." In an essay, explain how these characters are alike, how they are different, and which one you prefer.

12. A crow appears as a character in many works of literature. In an essay, compare and contrast the crow in "The Fox Outwits the Crow" with the Crow in "The Fox and the Crow." Explain how they are alike and how they are different. Focus on what each crow does and what each learns. Then, explain which crow's attitude seems more extreme. Explain your ideas.

13. Readers can discover the tone of a work by analyzing descriptive details, word choice, and sentence structure. In an essay, analyze the tone of both "The Fox Outwits the Crow" and "The Fox and the Crow." Focus on how the characters speak, the details included, and how the tone of each selection influences the reader's attitude toward the work. Use details from both selections in your essay.

14. **Thinking About the Big Question: Community or Individual: Which is more important?** Think about the two characters in "The Fox Outwits the Crow" and "The Fox and the Crow." Which would they feel is more important—the community or the individual? Explain your answer by using details from the selections.

**Oral Response**

15. Go back to question 2, 6, 7, or 10 or to the question your teacher assigns you. Take a few minutes to expand your answer and prepare an oral response. Find additional details in "The Fox Outwits the Crow" and "The Fox and the Crow" that will support your points. If necessary, make notes to guide your response.

## "The Fox Outwits the Crow" by William Cleary
## "The Fox and the Crow" by Aesop
# Selection Test A

**Critical Reading** *Identify the letter of the choice that best answers the question.*

____ 1. In the poem "The Fox Outwits the Crow," where does the crow get the piece of cheese?
   A. from a porch
   B. from the fox
   C. from a child
   D. from Maria Callas

____ 2. Which word best describes the character of the fox in "The Fox Outwits the Crow"?
   A. irritable
   B. honest
   C. vain
   D. sly

____ 3. How does the crow react when the fox speaks to her in "The Fox Outwits the Crow"?
   A. She does not trust anything about him.
   B. She likes what he says but doubts his honesty.
   C. She is pleased and takes out some music.
   D. She knows that what he is saying is true.

____ 4. What is the tone of these words spoken by the fox in "The Fox Outwits the Crow"?
   Hey, you glamorous thing, / Does your voice match your beautiful curves?
   A. playful
   B. serious
   C. formal
   D. sad

____ 5. In "The Fox Outwits the Crow," the crow thinks to herself,
   "How fondly that fox will listen . . . / To hear how I caw in falsetto."

   What does this show about the crow's character?
   A. She is greedy.
   B. She is angry.
   C. She is happy.
   D. She is proud.

Name _____ Date _____

____ 6. In "The Fox and the Crow," why does the Fox want the Crow to sing?
   **A.** so that he may sing with her
   **B.** so that he can make fun of her voice
   **C.** so that she will drop the piece of cheese she has in her beak
   **D.** so that she can serenade him with beautiful music

____ 7. What word *best* describes the character of the Crow in "The Fox and the Crow"?
   **A.** sly
   **B.** vain
   **C.** honest
   **D.** irritable

____ 8. What is the tone of these words spoken by the Fox in "The Fox and the Crow"?
   "I feel sure your voice must surpass that of other birds, just as your figure does."
   **A.** sad
   **B.** formal
   **C.** angry
   **D.** funny

____ 9. Which statement best expresses the moral of "The Fox and the Crow"?
   **A.** Nothing lasts forever.
   **B.** Value your friends.
   **C.** Do not trust flattery.
   **D.** Friends may turn against you.

____ 10. How might the tone of a literary work such as "The Fox and the Crow" or "The Fox Outwits the Crow" be described?
   **A.** It is the subject of the work.
   **B.** It is the writer's attitude.
   **C.** It is the characters' attitude.
   **D.** It is the message of the work.

____ 11. Which statement best expresses the theme of "The Fox Outwits the Crow"?
   **A.** People do not always mean what they say.
   **B.** Never trust anyone.
   **C.** Always share your food with others.
   **D.** Be careful not to think too little of yourself.

Unit 6 Resources: Themes in the Oral Tradition
© Pearson Education, Inc. All rights reserved.
217

___ 12. How does the tone of "The Fox Outwits the Crow" compare with the tone of "The Fox and the Crow"?
A. The tone of "The Fox Outwits the Crow" is more serious.
B. The tone of "The Fox Outwits the Crow" is more suspenseful.
C. The tone of "The Fox Outwits the Crow" is more playful.
D. The tone of "The Fox Outwits the Crow" is more formal.

**Vocabulary**

___ 13. Where would you most likely find *hors d'oeuvres*?
A. at a concert
B. at school
C. on a train
D. at a party

___ 14. What item is most likely to be described as *glossy*?
A. a rough stone
B. a waxed floor
C. a wool sweater
D. an old frying pan

___ 15. In which sentence is the meaning of *surpass* expressed?
A. In their slyness, foxes are superior to all other animals.
B. If you are fooled by the fox, you will not be alone.
C. Crows are known to have unpleasant voices.
D. Crows are not well known for their vanity.

**Essay**

16. The crow is a character in many literary works. In an essay, compare and contrast the Crow in the fable "The Fox and the Crow" with the crow in the poem "The Fox Outwits the Crow." What does each crow do? What does each crow learn?

17. The fox is a common character in fables and other stories. In an essay, compare and contrast the Fox in the fable "The Fox and the Crow" with the fox in the poem "The Fox Outwits the Crow." What does each fox do? What tone does each fox's words contribute to the selection?

18. **Thinking About the Big Question: Community or individual: Which is more important?** Think about the two characters in "The Fox Outwits the Crow" and "The Fox and the Crow." Which would they feel is more important—the community or the individual? Explain your answer in an essay that uses details from the selections.

**"The Fox Outwits the Crow"** by William Cleary
**"The Fox and the Crow"** by Aesop
# Selection Test B

**Critical Reading** *Identify the letter of the choice that best completes the statement or answers the question.*

_____ 1. In "The Fox Outwits the Crow," the crow gets a piece of cheese from
A. the back yard of a stone house.
B. the front yard of a brick house.
C. the porch of a stone house.
D. the attic of a brick house.

_____ 2. In "The Fox Outwits the Crow," the crow takes the cheese to the top of a tree in order to
A. share it with other birds.
B. show off to the forest what she has.
C. enjoy it by herself.
D. get away from the fox.

_____ 3. What is the tone of these words spoken by the fox in "The Fox Outwits the Crow"?
"Hey, you glamorous thing, / Does your voice match your beautiful curves?"
A. playful
B. serious
C. formal
D. arrogant

_____ 4. In "The Fox Outwits the Crow," what quality of the crow's character is evident as she thinks these thoughts?
"How fondly that fox will listen, . . . / To hear how I caw in falsetto."
A. greed
B. anger
C. happiness
D. pride

_____ 5. The character of the fox in "The Fox Outwits the Crow" could best be described as
A. irritable.
B. honest.
C. vain.
D. sly.

_____ 6. In "The Fox Outwits the Crow," the crow's reaction to the fox shows that the crow
A. is pleased by the fox's flattery.
B. is suspicious of the fox's flattery.
C. is sure of the fox's insincerity.
D. is angered by the fox's insincerity.

____ 7. In "The Fox and the Crow," why does the Fox say that he wants to hear the Crow sing?
A. He wants to hear beautiful music.
B. He wants to make fun of the Crow's voice.
C. He wants to sing with the Crow.
D. He wants to get the cheese the Crow has.

____ 8. How would the Fox's tone *best* be described in this line from "The Fox and the Crow"?
"I feel sure your voice must surpass that of other birds, just as your figure does."
A. informal
B. formal
C. angry
D. amusing

____ 9. Which word *best* describes the character of the Crow in "The Fox and the Crow"?
A. sly
B. vain
C. honest
D. irritable

____ 10. Which statement *best* describes the moral of "The Fox and the Crow"?
A. Birds of a feather flock together.
B. The end justifies the means.
C. Compliments may be used to deceive.
D. You can kill two birds with one stone.

____ 11. In "The Fox and the Crow," why does Aesop advise the reader not to trust flatterers?
A. Flatterers may have hidden motives.
B. Flatterers are liars.
C. Flatterers only want attention.
D. Flatterers are too kind to tell the truth.

____ 12. In a literary work such as "The Fox and the Crow" or "The Fox Outwits the Crow," the tone may be described as the writer's
A. attitude.
B. words.
C. characters.
D. adjectives.

____ 13. Compared with the tone of "The Fox Outwits the Crow," the tone of "The Fox and the Crow" is more
A. serious.
B. comical.
C. playful.
D. informal.

Name _____ Date _____

____ 14. The themes of "The Fox Outwits the Crow" and "The Fox and the Crow," make general statements about
A. love and betrayal.
B. friendship.
C. vanity and greed.
D. generosity.

## Vocabulary

____ 15. In what situation would you most likely encounter *hors d'oeuvres*?
A. at a museum
B. at a concert
C. on a boat
D. at a reception

____ 16. Which item is most likely to be *glossy*?
A. a sweater
B. a magazine
C. a book
D. a piece of cheese

____ 17. People who *surpass* something are most likely to be considered
A. achievers.
B. flatterers.
C. failures.
D. athletes.

## Essay

18. The crow is a character in many literary works. In an essay, compare and contrast the Crow in "The Fox and the Crow" with the crow in "The Fox Outwits the Crow." Describe how they are different and how they are alike. Tell what each crow does and what each crow learns. Is one crow's attitude more extreme than the other? Explain your answer.

19. A reader can discover the tone of a literary work by analyzing descriptive details, word choice, and sentence structure. In an essay, compare and contrast the tone of "The Fox and the Crow" with that of "The Fox Outwits the Crow." Consider these elements: How do the characters speak? What details are included? Finally, answer these questions: How do you think the writer wants you to react to the work? How does the tone of each selection influence your attitude toward the work? Explain your answer.

20. **Thinking About the Big Question: Community or individual: Which is more important?** Think about the two characters in "The Fox Outwits the Crow" and "The Fox and the Crow." Which would they feel is more important—the community or the individual? Explain your answer by using details from the selections.

# Research: Research Report

## Prewriting: Choosing a Topic

To choose the right topic to research, answer the following questions according to your own interests.

| Question: | Answer: |
|---|---|
| What broad subject interests you? | |
| What specific categories of that subject do you find appealing? | |
| What people in history would you like to understand better? | |
| What current event would you like to understand better? | |

## Drafting: Making an Outline

Review your prewriting notes and group them by category; then, complete the following outline to organize your supporting details.

| Your Thesis Statement: |
|---|
| |

I. _____

   A. _____

   B. _____

II. _____

   A. _____

   B. _____

III. _____

   A. _____

   B. _____

Name _____  Date _____

Writing Workshop—Unit 6, Part 2

# Research Report: Integrating Grammar Skills

## Revising for the Correct Case of Pronouns

**Case** is the relationship between a pronoun's form and its role in a sentence. Pronouns can be one of three cases: nominative, objective, or possessive.

| Case | Pronouns | Role in Sentence | Example |
|------|----------|------------------|---------|
| Nominative | I, we<br>you<br>he, she, it, they | subject of a verb<br>predicate pronoun<br>(after a linking verb) | *We* walked to school.<br>The best students were<br>Jan and *I*. |
| Objective | me, us<br>you<br>him, her, it, them | direct object<br>indirect object<br>object of a preposition | The teacher helped us.<br>Get *him* a book.<br>Give that book to *them*. |
| Possessive | my, mine; our, ours<br>your, yours<br>his; her, hers; its; their,<br>theirs | to show ownership | Jo is at *her* locker.<br>That locker is *yours*. |

## Identifying the Correct Case of Pronouns

**A. DIRECTIONS:** *Circle the pronoun that correctly completes each sentence.*

1. Jackie and (them, they) are on the softball team
2. The coach taught Sonya and (she, her) a new pitch.
3. Were you throwing the ball to Tanya or (I, me)?
4. The close game really excited Sally and (we, us).

## Fixing the Incorrect Case of Pronouns

**B. DIRECTIONS:** *On the lines provided, rewrite these sentences so that they use the correct pronouns. If a sentence is correct as presented, write* correct.

1. Wendell, Terry, and me like to play basketball.

_____

2. Terry's brother taught Wendell and I some good moves.

_____

3. Often Wendell's older brother joins Wendell and us in a game.

_____

4. Him and Terry's brother have been playing together for years.

_____

Name _____  Date _____

# Unit 6 Vocabulary Workshop—1
# Figurative Language

**Figurative language** is vivid, imaginative language that is not meant to be interpreted literally. This chart shows three types of figurative language that are used to make comparisons.

| Type of Figurative Language | What It Is | Example |
|---|---|---|
| metaphor | a comparison that is made by stating that one thing is another thing | That football player is a real tiger. |
| simile | a comparison using *like* or *as* | He was so happy that he felt as high as a kite. |
| analogy | an explanation of something unfamiliar through comparison to something familiar | Bake the bread until its crust resembles the color of a penny. |

**DIRECTIONS:** *Identify the type of figurative language appearing in each sentence. On the line, write* **metaphor, simile,** *or* **analogy.**

_____ 1. Life is just a bowl of cherries.

_____ 2. Talking to Jake reminds me of trying to calm a barking dog.

_____ 3. The abstract painting looked like a bowl of green spaghetti.

_____ 4. To do simple waltz steps, make little squares with your feet.

_____ 5. He was as hungry as a bear.

_____ 6. We had a mountain of homework last night.

_____ 7. Unlike most birds, the starling has a fairly unpleasant call that brings to mind the screech of a rusty screen door.

_____ 8. Our opinions on this issue are as far apart as the North Pole and the South Pole.

# Unit 6 Vocabulary Workshop—2
## Figurative Language

Another lively form of figurative language is the **idiom.** These are popular expressions that are unique to a language, a culture, or a geographic region. Like other forms of figurative language, they are not meant to be taken literally. For example, if you said that a joke was so funny that you "almost died laughing," you would not mean that you were literally near death!

**B. DIRECTIONS:** *Write a definition for each of the following idioms. Then use each in a sentence that clearly shows its meaning.*

| Idiom | Meaning | Sentence |
|---|---|---|
| 1. catch her eye | | |
| 2. in the mean time | | |
| 3. kind of | | |
| 4. over the hill | | |
| 5. threw a fit | | |
| 6. under the weather | | |
| 7. happy-go-lucky | | |
| 8. no sweat | | |
| 9. what's up? | | |
| 10. never mind | | |

Name _____   Date _____

# Conducting an Interview

After choosing a person to interview, fill out the following chart to complete the interview and gather the information you need.

**Topic of interview:** _____

| |
|---|
| **What kind of information are you trying to get during the interview?** |
| **What research have you done to prepare for the interview?** |
| **What questions do you plan to ask?** |
| **What follow-up questions might there be?** |

## Unit 6: Themes in the Oral Tradition
# Benchmark Test 12

## MULTIPLE CHOICE

### Reading Skill: Compare and Contrast

1. Which choice best describes a Venn diagram?
   A. two or more circles in a straight line with no points overlapping
   B. two or more circles that overlap one another
   C. two or more circles of exactly the same size right on top of one another
   D. two or more circles having the same center but of increasingly larger size

2. If you are comparing and contrasting two things, how many circles would you need in your Venn diagram?
   A. two
   B. three
   C. four
   D. five

*Read the selection. Then, answer the questions that follow.*

During the Middle Ages, knights wore armor to protect themselves in battle. The armor helped prevent serious injury and death. Arrows, swords, lances, clubs, and spears were the main weapons. A suit of armor was thick and awkward, like an astronaut's spacesuit. It usually included metal plates to protect the body, chain mail worn underneath, and a metal helmet with a hinged visor that could be raised and lowered over the eyes. The chain mail, which was made of thousands of small linked metal rings, moved more easily with the body than the metal plates. It was often worn alone in areas of frequent movement, such as the neck and wrists. Even with chain mail, a suit of armor still made movement very difficult. It was also extremely heavy—the chain mail alone often weighed over fifty pounds.

3. Which of the following comparisons help you "picture" how the knight looked?
   A. It compares the armor to arrows, swords, and other weapons.
   B. It compares a suit of armor to an astronaut's spacesuit.
   C. It compares the metal plates of armor to the helmet worn on the head.
   D. It compares the thickness of the armor to the weight of the chain mail.

4. If you were using a Venn diagram to help you compare and contrast chain mail and the metal plates in a suit of armor, which of these details would you list in the similarities space?
   A. made of metal rings
   B. moves easily with the body
   C. often worn on the neck
   D. very heavy

5. Which of these more familiar modern items would be the most similar kind of armor?
   A. a pair of blue jeans
   B. a helicopter
   C. a bulletproof vest
   D. a computer program

6. Which of these modern jobs would be most similar to a knight in the Middle Ages?
   A. a soldier
   B. a TV newscaster
   C. a bank teller
   D. a big-city mayor

Name _____    Date _____

# Reading Skill: Analyze Point of View

*Read the selection. Then, answer the questions that follow.*

We have a huge waste-management problem in the United States. On average, Americans will throw away 600 times their adult weight in garbage in a lifetime. That translates into a legacy of about 90,000 pounds of trash for a 150-pound adult. Where does all this trash go? Trash is burned, buried, dumped into bodies of water, or recycled. Only the last option is friendly to the environment.

By using materials more than once, we conserve natural resources and the energy needed to create and process new materials. Recycling also reserves landfill space for items that cannot be recycled. Some experts estimate that each ton of recycled paper can save 17 trees, over 300 gallons of oil, 3 cubic yards of landfill space, and 7,000 gallons of water.

How can students help in the recycling effort? For one thing, they can start a recycling program at school. A committee comprising of students, teachers, administrators, and custodians should plan how to best collect, store, and transfer recyclable paper products. Students and teachers could deposit recyclable paper at a specific location in the classroom. After school, someone could transfer the paper from the classrooms to a storage area, where it can be kept for eventual transport to a recycling center. Some day you might be buying paper made from the material you helped recycle. That is what the process is all about.

7. Which is a statement of the author's main point of view?
   A. It is more important to recycle paper than any other product.
   B. Americans must produce less trash to help the environment.
   C. Students are the most important part of the recycling effort.
   D. Recycling is the answer to our waste-management problem.

8. What is the primary intent of this selection?
   A. to describe one way to help the recycling effort
   B. to explain how different items can be recycled
   C. to inform readers how much trash the average American discards
   D. to persuade readers to recycle

9. With which of the following statements would the author most likely agree?
   A. It is the responsibility of adults to lead the recycling effort.
   B. Burning trash is not as harmful to the environment as burying it.
   C. Buying recycled paper is an equally important step in the recycling process.
   D. It is more important to recycle at school than at home.

## Literary Analysis: Folk Tales

10. Which of the following is the best definition of a folk tale?
    A. a story that features human characters who display traits like those of animals
    B. a story that features an ordinary hero or heroine who performs extraordinary deeds
    C. a story that is designed to teach a lesson that does not include any animal characters
    D. a story composed orally and passed down by word of mouth before being written down

11. Which of the following statements is true of folk tales?
    A. Folk tales from different cultures usually have different plot elements.
    B. Folk tales from different cultures usually have different character types.
    C. Folk tales often present a clear separation between good and evil.
    D. Most folk tales are not part of the oral tradition.

12. Which of the following does a textbook usually provide to help you understand the cultural context of a folk tale?
    A. a character description and short summary of the events in the folk tale
    B. a paragraph of background information that introduces the folk tale
    C. a list of vocabulary words that appear in the folk tale
    D. questions that have you compare and contrast characters in the folk tale

*Read this folk tale from Ethiopia. Then, answer the questions that follow.*

Long ago, a young man named Arha found work in Addis Ababa as the servant of a rich man named Haptom Hasei. One day, the rich man made a bet that no one could sleep on Mount Intotto without a fire to stay warm. He offered ten acres of land to anyone who could do it. Deciding to take up the bet, Arha sought advice from a wise old man. The old man said, "I will build a fire far from the mountain but close enough for you to see. Seeing the fire, you can imagine the warmth." So that is what Arha did and he managed to endure the whole night. The next day, however, Haptom Hasei refused to honor the bet since, he argued, a fire had been built. Arha took the matter to a judge, who ruled in favor of the rich man. That night, a friend of the wise man invited Haptom Hasei and the judge to dinner. The guests could smell the wonderful food, but it was never brought out for them to eat. When they complained, the friend got them to agree that food smelled from a distance was not the same as food they could eat. The judge realized his error, and reversed his ruling so that Arha won his bet.

13. What lesson does this Ethiopian folk tale teach about the agreements people make?
    A. Always have at least one witness to any agreement you make.
    B. Be careful to follow all agreements precisely and to pay attention to their wording.
    C. A rich person is more likely to break an agreement than a poor person is.
    D. People should be true to the spirit of an agreement and not escape on a technicality.

14. Which of the following conclusions can you draw about the cultural context of the folk tale?
    A. Everyone in Ethiopia used to live in the city of Addis Ababa.
    B. In Ethiopia, farmers were more prosperous than merchants.
    C. Ethiopians used tribal elders, not judges, to rule on disagreements.
    D. Rural Ethiopians often took advice from wise men in their tribes.

15. Which of the following is an important difference between Addis Ababa and Mount Intotto?
    A. Addis Ababa is a city.
    B. Addis Ababa has more poor people.
    C. Mount Intotto is colder at night.
    D. Mount Intotto is far from Addis Ababa.

16. If you were using a Venn diagram to compare and contrast the characters of Arha and Haptom Hasei, where would you put the word *rich?*
    A. on the part of the Venn diagram that applies to Haptom Hasei only
    B. on the part of the Venn diagram that applies to both Arha and Haptom Hasei
    C. on the part of the Venn diagram that applies to Arha only
    D. on the part of the Venn diagram that applies to neither Arha nor Haptom Hasei

## Literary Analysis: Tone

17. What does the tone of a literary work generally express?
    A. the attitude of the writer
    B. the attitude of the reader
    C. the mood of a character
    D. the atmosphere of a setting

18. Which of the following choices best describes the tone of this sentence?

    The remarkable founders of our nation bravely risked their lives and reputations to fight for the dream of American independence.

    A. angry
    B. humorous
    C. sad
    D. admiring

19. Compare and contrast the tones of these two sentences:

    The store teemed with Christmas spirit as jolly shoppers made last-minute purchases.

    The store teemed with shoppers shoving their way through their last-minute purchases.

    A. The tone of the first sentence is calm and unemotional, while the tone of the second sentence is angry.
    B. The tone of the first sentence is warm and pleasant, while the tone of the second sentence is irritated.
    C. The tone of the first sentence is happy and carefree, while the tone of the second sentence is sad.
    D. The tone of the first sentence is joyful, while the tone of the second sentence is calm and unemotional.

## Vocabulary: Suffixes and Roots

20. What is the meaning of the word formed by adding the suffix *-ity* to *flexible?*
    A. the quality of being easily bent
    B. an act showing great skill
    C. without the ability to change
    D. tending to become rigid

21. What is the meaning of the word formed by adding the suffix *-ity* to *curious?*
    A. a willingness to help others
    B. an eager desire to know
    C. a strong, unwavering belief
    D. a loss of interest

22. Using your knowledge of the suffix -*ity*, what does *integrity* mean in the following sentence?

    President Lincoln defended the integrity of the nation.

    **A.** tending to be broken into parts     **C.** worthy of being honest

    **B.** without the ability to deceive     **D.** the condition of being whole

23. Based on your knowledge of the suffix -*ity*, how would someone showing *humility* act?

    **A.** in a proud way     **C.** in a humble way

    **B.** in a kind way     **D.** in a mean way

24. Using your knowledge of the root -*myst*-, what does the word *mystical* mean in the following sentence?

    Some people believe in the mystical effects of a new moon.

    **A.** having some secret meaning     **C.** being widespread

    **B.** being of great benefit     **D.** having little consequence

25. How does the meaning of the word *knowledgeable* reflect the meaning of the root -*know*-?

    **A.** A knowledgeable person studies much of the time.     **C.** A knowledgeable person is better off than others.

    **B.** A knowledgeable person has a great deal of experience.     **D.** A knowledgeable person understands many things.

## Grammar

26. Which of the following sentences uses capitalization correctly?

    **A.** My brother said, "If you go to the movies, please take me along."     **C.** my brother said, "If you go to the movies, please take me along."

    **B.** My brother said, "if you go to the movies, please take me along."     **D.** my brother said, "if you go to the movies, please take me along."

27. Which of the following sentences is capitalized correctly?

    **A.** Jo and Anne went to a Portuguese Restaurant after they visited the Newark Museum.     **C.** Jo and Anne went to a Portuguese restaurant after they visited the Newark Museum.

    **B.** Jo and Anne went to a portuguese restaurant after they visited the Newark museum.     **D.** Jo and anne went to a Portuguese restaurant after they visited the Newark museum.

28. Which statement about abbreviations is true?

    **A.** Abbreviations are usually longer than the word or words they stand for.     **C.** Abbreviations usually end with a period.

    **B.** Abbreviations always start with a capital letter.     **D.** Abbreviations never include letters that are not in the word they stand for.

29. Which of the following phrases uses abbreviations correctly?

    **A.** Martin Luther King Jr     **C.** 55 San Andreas Bvd.

    **B.** JAN 23, 2007     **D.** Dr. Sheldon L. Greenfarb

30. Which pronoun correctly completes the following sentence?

    Carlos and _____ are planning to read that best seller.

    A. I

    B. me

    C. myself

    D. mine

31. Which of the following sentences uses pronouns correctly?

    A. The stars of the game were Jackie and her.

    B. The stars of the game were Jackie and she.

    C. Larry and him scored some points in the first quarter.

    D. The crowd cheered loudly for Larry and he.

## Spelling

32. Which of the following words is spelled correctly?

    A. oxugen

    B. cematery

    C. catagory

    D. medicine

33. In which sentence is the italic word spelled correctly?

    A. The police officers gathered *evadence* at the crime scene.

    B. If you *multeply* by 2, the answer is always an even number.

    C. Do not *abandon* hope yet; help is on the way.

    D. The teacher knew the subject but had trouble with *disapline*.

34. Which statement about spelling is correct?

    A. The sound of "uh" is usually spelled with an *a*.

    B. The sound of "uh" is usually spelled with an *e*.

    C. The sound of "uh" is usually spelled with an *i* or a *u*.

    D. The sound of "uh" is usually spelled with a vowel.

## ESSAY

### Writing

35. Recall a folk tale or another story from the oral tradition, such as a fairy tale or a myth. It might be a story you read recently or in the past, or even one you had read to you as a child. On your paper or on a separate sheet, write a summary of the tale.

36. Think about why you remembered the tale you summarized in the previous question. Then, on your paper or on a separate sheet, write a one-paragraph review of the tale. Be sure to indicate whether or not you recommend that others read it.

37. Think about subjects that interest you and that you would like to know more about. Then, on your paper, write down your idea for a subject that you could investigate for a research report. Also, list at least three information sources that would probably provide good information on the subject.

# Diagnostic Tests and Vocabulary in Context
## Use and Interpretation

The Diagnostic Tests and Vocabulary in Context were developed to assist teachers in making the most appropriate assignment of *Prentice Hall Literature* program selections to students. The purpose of these assessments is to indicate the degree of difficulty that students are likely to have in reading/comprehending the selections presented in the *following* unit of instruction. Tests are provided at six separate times in each grade level—a *Diagnostic Test* (to be used prior to beginning the year's instruction) and a *Vocabulary in Context*, the final segment of the Benchmark Test, appearing at the end of each of the first five units of instruction. Note that the tests are intended for use not as summative assessments for the prior unit, but as guidance for assigning literature selections in the upcoming unit of instruction.

The structure of all Diagnostic Tests and Vocabulary in Context in this series is the same. All test items are four-option, multiple-choice items. The format is established to assess a student's ability to construct sufficient meaning from the context sentence to choose the only provided word that fits both the semantics (meaning) and syntax (structure) of the context sentence. All words in the context sentences are chosen to be "below-level" words that students reading at this grade level should know. All answer choices fit *either* the meaning or structure of the context sentence, but only the correct choice fits *both* semantics and syntax. All answer choices—both correct answers and incorrect options—are key words chosen from specifically taught words that will occur in the subsequent unit of program instruction. This careful restriction of the assessed words permits a sound diagnosis of students' current reading achievement and prediction of the most appropriate level of readings to assign in the upcoming unit of instruction.

The assessment of vocabulary in context skill has consistently been shown in reading research studies to correlate very highly with "reading comprehension." This is not surprising as the format essentially assesses comprehension, albeit in sentence-length "chunks." Decades of research demonstrate that vocabulary assessment provides a strong, reliable prediction of comprehension achievement— the purpose of these tests. Further, because this format demands very little testing time, these diagnoses can be made efficiently, permitting teachers to move forward with critical instructional tasks rather than devoting excessive time to assessment.

It is important to stress that while the Diagnostic and Vocabulary in Context were carefully developed and will yield sound assignment decisions, they were designed to *reinforce*, not supplant, teacher judgment as to the most appropriate instructional placement for individual students. Teacher judgment should always prevail in making placement—or indeed other important instructional—decisions concerning students.

Name _____  Date _____

# Diagnostic Tests and Vocabulary in Context
# Branching Suggestions

These tests are designed to provide maximum flexibility for teachers. Your *Unit Resources* books contain the 40-question **Diagnostic Test** and 20-question **Vocabulary in Context** tests. At *PHLitOnline,* you can access the Diagnostic Test and complete 40-question Vocabulary in Context tests. Procedures for administering the tests are described below. Choose the procedure based on the time you wish to devote to the activity and your comfort with the assignment decisions relative to the individual students. Remember that your judgment of a student's reading level should always take precedence over the results of a single written test.

Feel free to use different procedures at different times of the year. For example, for early units, you may wish to be more confident in the assignments you make—thus, using the "two-stage" process below. Later, you may choose the quicker diagnosis, confirming the results with your observations of the students' performance built up throughout the year.

The **Diagnostic Test** is composed of a single 40-item assessment. Based on the results of this assessment, make the following assignment of students to the reading selections in Unit 1:

| Diagnostic Test Score | Selection to Use |
| --- | --- |
| If the student's score is 0–25 | more accessible |
| If the student's score is 26–40 | more challenging |

Outlined below are the three basic options for administering **Vocabulary in Context** and basing selection assignments on the results of these assessments.

1. For a one-stage, quicker diagnosis using the *20-item* test in the *Unit Resources:*

| Vocabulary in Context Test Score | Selection to Use |
| --- | --- |
| If the student's score is 0–13 | more accessible |
| If the student's score is 14–20 | more challenging |

2. If you wish to confirm your assignment decisions with a *two-stage* diagnosis:

| Stage 1: Administer the 20-item test in the *Unit Resources* | |
| --- | --- |
| Vocabulary in Context Test Score | Selection to Use |
| If the student's score is 0–9 | more accessible |
| If the student's score is 10–15 | (Go to Stage 2.) |
| If the student's score is 16–20 | more challenging |

| Stage 2: Administer items 21–40 from *PHLitOnline* | |
| --- | --- |
| Vocabulary in Context Test Score | Selection to Use |
| If the student's score is 0–12 | more accessible |
| If the student's score is 13–20 | more challenging |

3. If you base your assignment decisions on the full 40-item **Vocabulary in Context** from *PHLitOnline:*

| Vocabulary in Context Test Score | Selection to Use |
| --- | --- |
| If the student's score is 0–25 | more accessible |
| If the student's score is 26–40 | more challenging |

Unit 6 Resources: Themes in Folk Literature

Name _____   Date _____

# Grade 7—Benchmark Test 11
# Interpretation Guide

*For remediation of specific skills, you may assign students the relevant Reading Kit Practice and Assess pages indicated in the far-right column of this chart. You will find rubrics for evaluating writing samples in the last section of your Professional Development Guidebook.*

| Skill Objective | Test Items | Number Correct | Reading Kit |
|---|---|---|---|
| **Reading Skill** | | | |
| Cause and Effect | 1, 2, 3, 4, 5, 6, 7 | | pp. 244, 245 |
| Analyze Cause-and-Effect Structures | 8, 9, 10 | | pp. 246, 247 |
| **Literary Analysis** | | | |
| Myths | 11, 12, 13, 15, 16, 17 | | pp. 248, 249 |
| Legends | 14, 18, 19, 20 | | pp. 250, 251 |
| Epic Conventions Universal Theme | 21, 22, 23 | | pp. 252, 253 |
| **Vocabulary** | | | |
| Prefixes and Roots -vac-, -dom-, out-, uni- | 24, 25, 26, 27, 28, 29 | | pp. 254, 255 |
| **Grammar** | | | |
| Colon | 30, 31, 34 | | pp. 256, 257 |
| Commas | 32, 33, 35 | | pp. 258, 259, 260, 261 |
| **Writing** | | | |
| Myth | 36 | Use rubric | pp. 262, 263 |
| Description | 37 | Use rubric | pp. 264, 265 |
| Business Letter | 38 | Use rubric | pp. 266, 267 |

# Grade 7—Benchmark Test 12
# Interpretation Guide

*For remediation of specific skills, you may assign students the relevant Reading Kit Practice and Assess pages indicated in the far-right column of this chart. You will find rubrics for evaluating writing samples in the last section of your Professional Development Guidebook.*

| Skill Objective | Test Items | Number Correct | Reading Kit |
|---|---|---|---|
| **Reading Skill** | | | |
| Compare and Contrast | 1, 2, 3, 4, 5, 6 | | pp. 268, 269 |
| Analyze Point of View | 7, 8, 9 | | pp. 270, 271 |
| **Literary Analysis** | | | |
| Cultural Context | 13, 14, 15, 16 | | pp. 272, 273 |
| Folk Tales and Oral Tradition | 10, 11, 12 | | pp. 274, 275 |
| Tone | 17, 18, 19 | | pp. 276, 277 |
| **Vocabulary** | | | |
| Suffixes and Roots *-ity, -myst-, -know-* | 20, 21, 22, 23, 24, 25 | | pp. 278, 279 |
| **Grammar** | | | |
| Capitalization | 26, 27 | | pp. 280, 281 |
| Abbreviations | 28, 29 | | pp. 282, 283 |
| Personal Pronouns in the Nominative and Objective Cases | 30, 31 | | pp. 284, 285 |
| **Spelling** | | | |
| Vowel Sounds in Unstressed Syllables | 32, 33, 34 | | pp. 286, 287 |
| **Writing** | | | |
| Plot Summary | 35 | Use rubric | pp. 288, 289 |
| Review | 36 | Use rubric | pp. 290, 291 |
| Research Report | 37 | Use rubric | pp. 292, 293 |

# ANSWERS

## Big Question Vocabulary—1, p. 1

**A.** Answers will vary. Possible responses are shown.

1. Something that is common is shared by two or more people, such as an interest in photography or a fear of snakes. Something that is unique is one of a kind, such as an individual or a snowflake.

2. An individual is a person. Several individuals live together in a community, a town or neighborhood that they share.

3. A belief in democracy, the value of honesty, and the custom of giving someone gifts on his or her birthday

**B.** Answers will vary. Possible responses are shown.

1. soccer
2. Sydney, Australia
3. Puerto Rico
4. Manny Ramirez
5. my skills as a painter

## Big Question Vocabulary—2, p. 2

Explanations will vary. Possible responses are shown.

1. environment. The animals live together in a specific setting.

2. duty. Sally has the responsibility of caring for her sisters after school.

3. custom. The annual tradition of making May baskets is shared by the members of the family.

4. group. All of these individuals will combine to form a group.

5. diversity. The menu contains a wide assortment of foods from different cultures.

## Big Question Vocabulary—3, p. 3

Explanations will vary. Possible responses are shown.

1. unify. *Unify* means to bring objects together into a group, and *separate* means to pull objects apart.

2. ethnicity. Chico and Manny's ethnicity is Spanish because that is the national group to which their family belongs.

3. team. Each group contained members who were working toward a common goal.

4. tradition. The women's Valentine's Day project is repeated over time.

5. family. The brothers and cousins are all related.

## "Grasshopper Logic," "The Other Frog Prince," and "duckbilled platypus vs. beefsnakstik®"
### by Jon Scieszka and Lane Smith

### Vocabulary Warm-up Exercises, p. 8

**A.** 1. bragged
2. plenty
3. fur
4. pathetic

5. hopped
6. promptly
7. wiped
8. moral

**B.** Sample Answers

1. When the <u>princess</u> arrived, the photographers wanted to take her picture.

2. <u>Mammals</u>, such as horses and dogs, are warm-blooded animals.

3. The <u>wicked</u> boss always treated his employees unfairly.

4. The <u>logic</u> of the witches' spell was not easy to comprehend.

5. If you <u>rewrite</u> your assignment, it is a second draft of your work.

6. The <u>production</u> of the play is meant to be seen live on stage.

## Reading Warm-up A, p. 9

### Sample Answers

1. (doing a dance to celebrate the easy life of summer); *Hopped* means "jumped or leaped in a short, springing motion."

2. (the sweat from his brow); Kristen used the eraser when she *wiped* the chalk off the board.

3. <u>food</u>; In my home, there are *plenty* of towels and cans of soup.

4. (It will help me keep warm during the cold days of winter.); *Fur* is "the soft, thick hair covering many mammals."

5. <u>my comfortable hammock and shady home</u>; Billy *bragged* that he was the best chess player in the county.

6. (continued on his way); I have *promptly* reported for my babysitting job.

7. <u>shivered in the cold. He could find no food anywhere.</u>; It is a *pathetic* sight when people do not have enough warm clothes to wear.

8. <u>Plan ahead for the days of necessity.</u> A *moral* is "a lesson taught by a fable."

## Reading Warm-up B, p. 10

### Sample Answers

1. <u>fairy tales and legends; make-believe stories that have been handed down through time; these fantastic stories</u>; A *princess* is "the daughter of a king or queen."

2. (witch); The evil man told a *wicked* lie.

3. (a wizard); A magician, a witch, or a genie might cast a *spell.*

4. <u>a rabbit and a fox</u>; Other *mammals* are bats, dogs, and opossums.

5. <u>that many similar stories come from different parts of the world</u>; *History* means "a course that studies the recorded past events of the world."

Unit 6 Resources: Themes in the Oral Tradition
© Pearson Education, Inc. All rights reserved.
237

6. (has never been proved); It is not good <u>logic</u> to assume you will pass the test if you do not study.

7. (many old stories that are based on legends and folktales); I once had to *rewrite* a poem and make it into a story for my language arts class.

8. of a play; I have seen a *production* of *Romeo and Juliet*.

## Jon Scieszka

### Listening and Viewing, p. 11

Sample answers and guidelines for evaluation:

Segment 1. Jon Scieszka chose a young audience as a result of his teaching experience, where he found that young readers are involved and enthusiastic about stories. Scieszka read Dr. Seuss books, comics, and adventure and mystery stories as a young student. Students may suggest that his diverse reading helps him to come up with creative ways to retell the information he gathers from reading to a young audience.

Segment 2. Jon Scieszka is amazed that these stories have been around for hundreds of years and are still relevant to today's reader. Students may answer that it is important to tell these stories to ensure the stories' survival and to teach kids lessons and common knowledge often taught in these tales.

Segment 3. Lane Smith illustrates Jon Scieszka's books; Smith comes up with the visual representation of Jon Scieszka's ideas and brings them to life on the page. Students may answer that illustrations are important to these stories because they add excitement and detail.

Segment 4. Jon Scieszka likes being able to connect with a wide audience and teach many people through his stories. Students may suggest that reading is important because it allows people to learn more about the world around them as well as more about themselves. Reading is also a creative activity, which allows readers to use their imaginations more, unlike television and video games.

### Learning About the Oral Tradition, p. 12

**A.** 1. hyperbole
2. myth
3. legend
4. personification
5. moral

**B.** Plot summaries will vary but should include one or more animals with human characteristics. The fable should end with a moral that defines the lesson that the animal or animals learned.

### "Grasshopper Logic," "The Other Frog Prince," and "duckbilled platypus vs. beefsnakstik®" by Jon Scieszka and Lane Smith

### Model Selection: The Oral Tradition, p. 13

**A.** 1. The homework assignment is an example of hyperbole. It is greatly exaggerated.

2. In the traditional fairy tale, the frog turns into a handsome prince when the princess kisses him.

3. They are a mammal and a beef snack food stick. They speak like humans, and they try to outdo each other.

**B.** The grasshopper speaks and acts like a human boy who wants to hang out with his friends after school rather than start his homework. His mother acts like a human mother, wanting her son to complete his assignment.

### "Grasshopper Logic," "The Other Frog Prince," and "Duckbilled Platypus vs. beefsnakstik®" by Jon Scieszka and Lane Smith

### Open-Book Test, p. 14

**Short Answer**

1. Sample answer: The theme of the story might be that sometimes people need courage and patience. The theme represents the central message of the story.
   **Difficulty:** *Average* **Objective:** *Literary Analysis*

2. The technique being used is hyperbole, which is exaggeration or overstatement.
   **Difficulty:** *Easy* **Objective:** *Literary Analysis*

3. The fable will probably end with a moral. The purpose of the moral is to teach a lesson about life.
   **Difficulty:** *Easy* **Objective:** *Literary Analysis*

4. You would expect to hear personification, giving human characteristics to nonhuman subjects because the tale is about talking stones. You would also expect an allusion, or reference to a well-known place, to places in ancient Rome.
   **Difficulty:** *Challenging* **Objective:** *Literary Analysis*

5. Yes; she has read the assignment, which is very long, and he had said he only had "one small thing." He was being unrealistic about how much work he had to do.
   **Difficulty:** *Average* **Objective:** *Interpretation*

6. The story is easy to remember, so it would be easy to tell orally. In addition, it has a message that is universal—children don't always tell their parents everything. Therefore, it would be a story that could be handed down easily from one generation to another.
   **Difficulty:** *Average* **Objective:** *Literary Analysis*

7. The fable says that she "felt sorry" for him because he had a "sad and pathetic voice."
   **Difficulty:** *Average* **Objective:** *Interpretation*

8. When he speaks to the princess, the frog intentionally speaks in his "most sad and pathetic voice." This phrase shows that he is putting on an act.
   **Difficulty:** *Challenging* **Objective:** *Interpretation*

9. Duckbilled Platypus: natural qualities, bill like a duck, webbed feet, fur; BeefSnakStik: rude, filled with artificial ingredients; Both: brag about what they have
   The platypus is more admirable. BeefSnakStik is boasting and totally artificial.
   **Difficulty:** *Average* **Objective:** *Interpretation*

10. The moral says that having stuff does not make you special. Another moral could be "Telling about your stuff just lets people know how fake you are."

**Difficulty:** *Challenging*  **Objective:** *Literary Analysis*

## Essay

11. Students should note that Scieszka uses grasshoppers, a platypus, and a beefstick as characters in the stories. They should explain that the choice of characters adds to the humor in the stories. The bouncy little grasshopper is a good choice for the kid who jumps from one task to another. "Hopping mad" can be used to describe either a grasshopper or a human mom. The platypus and beefstick are such unusual choices that they are both funny and memorable.

**Difficulty:** *Easy*  **Objective:** *Essay*

12. Students should explain that the tale, if told from the princess's point of view, would include her opinion about the frog: first, she is scared of him; then, she feels sorry for him; then, she is disgusted by him. The moral should include some idea about being wary of frogs making promises.

**Difficulty:** *Average*  **Objective:** *Essay*

13. Students should point out several instances of humor in the stories: the ridiculousness of the homework assignment, the moral of the grasshopper story, the frog's slimy lips, the absurdity of BeefSnakStik's bragging (especially "beef lips"). Students should make a case for which story they found most amusing.

**Difficulty:** *Challenging*  **Objective:** *Essay*

14. Students should say that each of the characters would respond that the individual is more important. Grasshopper is concerned only about his own enjoyment. Frog is concerned only about amusing himself by tricking the princess. Neither one cares about the feelings of the community—mother or princess. BeefSnakStik certainly cares only about proving how fabulous he is.

**Difficulty:** *Average*  **Objective:** *Essay*

## Oral Response

15. Oral responses should be clear, well organized, and well supported by appropriate examples from the selections.

**Difficulty:** *Average*  **Objective:** *Oral Interpretation*

## Selection Test A, p. 17

### Learning About the Oral Tradition

| | | |
|---|---|---|
| 1. ANS: A | DIF: Easy | OBJ: Literary Analysis |
| 2. ANS: C | DIF: Easy | OBJ: Literary Analysis |
| 3. ANS: A | DIF: Easy | OBJ: Literary Analysis |
| 4. ANS: D | DIF: Easy | OBJ: Literary Analysis |
| 5. ANS: C | DIF: Easy | OBJ: Literary Analysis |

## Critical Reading

| | | |
|---|---|---|
| 6. ANS: A | DIF: Easy | OBJ: Comprehension |
| 7. ANS: B | DIF: Easy | OBJ: Literary Analysis |
| 8. ANS: B | DIF: Easy | OBJ: Interpretation |
| 9. ANS: C | DIF: Easy | OBJ: Interpretation |
| 10. ANS: D | DIF: Easy | OBJ: Comprehension |
| 11. ANS: A | DIF: Easy | OBJ: Literary Analysis |
| 12. ANS: B | DIF: Easy | OBJ: Comprehension |
| 13. ANS: D | DIF: Easy | OBJ: Comprehension |
| 14. ANS: D | DIF: Easy | OBJ: Literary Analysis |
| 15. ANS: A | DIF: Easy | OBJ: Literary Analysis |

## Essay

16. Answers will vary but should be supported by details from the story. Students may say that the princess feels surprised and maybe a bit foolish. She probably expected the frog to turn into a handsome prince and that they would live "happily ever after" together.

**Difficulty:** *Easy*  **Objective:** *Essay*

17. Students should state that "Grasshopper Logic" is a fable. It features grasshoppers that are personified and speak and act like humans. The moral is directly stated at the end: "There are plenty of things to say to calm a hopping mad Grasshopper mom. 'I don't know' is not one."

**Difficulty:** *Easy*  **Objective:** *Essay*

18. Students might note that each of the characters would respond that the individual is more important. Grasshopper is concerned only about his own enjoyment. Frog is concerned only about amusing himself by tricking the princess. Neither one cares about the feelings of the community—mother or princess. BeefSnakStik cares only about proving how great he is.

**Difficulty:** *Average*  **Objective:** *Essay*

## Selection Test B, p. 20

### Learning About the Oral Tradition

| | | |
|---|---|---|
| 1. ANS: D | DIF: Average | OBJ: Literary Analysis |
| 2. ANS: C | DIF: Challenging | OBJ: Literary Analysis |
| 3. ANS: A | DIF: Average | OBJ: Literary Analysis |
| 4. ANS: C | DIF: Average | OBJ: Literary Analysis |
| 5. ANS: B | DIF: Average | OBJ: Literary Analysis |
| 6. ANS: D | DIF: Challenging | OBJ: Literary Analysis |

## Critical Reading

| | | |
|---|---|---|
| 7. ANS: B | DIF: Average | OBJ: Comprehension |
| 8. ANS: D | DIF: Average | OBJ: Comprehension |
| 9. ANS: A | DIF: Average | OBJ: Comprehension |

| | | |
|---|---|---|
| 10. **ANS:** D | **DIF:** Average | **OBJ:** Literary Analysis |
| 11. **ANS:** C | **DIF:** Challenging | **OBJ:** Interpretation |
| 12. **ANS:** B | **DIF:** Average | **OBJ:** Comprehension |
| 13. **ANS:** A | **DIF:** Average | **OBJ:** Interpretation |
| 14. **ANS:** B | **DIF:** Average | **OBJ:** Literary Analysis |
| 15. **ANS:** A | **DIF:** Challenging | **OBJ:** Interpretation |
| 16. **ANS:** D | **DIF:** Average | **OBJ:** Literary Analysis |
| 17. **ANS:** A | **DIF:** Challenging | **OBJ:** Interpretation |
| 18. **ANS:** B | **DIF:** Challenging | **OBJ:** Literary Analysis |
| 19. **ANS:** C | **DIF:** Average | **OBJ:** Interpretation |

## Essay

20. Answers will vary. Students should effectively retell the main ideas of the story from the princess's point of view, showing her thoughts and feelings regarding the appearance of the frog, the trick he played on her, and her feelings about being tricked into kissing a frog.

   **Difficulty:** *Average*   **Objective:** *Essay*

21. Students may say that the mother will help Grasshopper with his huge assignment, or that she will scold him. Students may predict that Grasshopper will learn his lesson after his mother scolds him. All answers should be logical predictions, based on story events.

   **Difficulty:** *Average*   **Objective:** *Essay*

22. Answers will vary. Students may say that the moral is similar to "Do not believe everything you hear," "Never trust a sad frog," or "Find out more about people before you trust them." All suggested morals should be supported with details from the story.

   **Difficulty:** *Challenging*   **Objective:** *Essay*

23. Students should say that each of the characters would respond that the individual is more important. Grasshopper is concerned only about his own enjoyment. Frog is concerned only about amusing himself by tricking the princess. Neither one cares about the feelings of the community—mother or princess. BeefSnakStik certainly cares only about proving how fabulous he is.

   **Difficulty:** *Average*   **Objective:** *Essay*

## "Icarus and Daedalus"
by Josephine Preston Peabody

## Vocabulary Warm-up Exercises, p. 24

**A.** 1. glimpse
2. captive
3. thirst
4. delay
5. fashioned
6. attempt
7. liberty
8. favor

**B.** Sample Answers

1. The company hired an <u>architect</u> to design a new office building.
2. The <u>imprisoned</u> man missed his freedom.
3. The customer ordered water to <u>quench</u> his thirst.
4. Amy listened to her mom's <u>cautions</u> and always wore a helmet when riding her bike.
5. The acrobat <u>sustained</u> three other acrobats on his shoulders thanks to his upper body strength.
6. The athlete won the race after he <u>overtook</u> the lead runner at the last minute.
7. When the car wheels <u>wavered</u>, Michael decreased the speed.

## Reading Warm-up A, p. 25

### Sample Answers

1. (failed); Every *try* failed, but that did not stop people from trying.
2. (unimaginable freedom); *Glimpse* means "a brief, quick view."
3. *freedom*; My mom gives me the *liberty* to choose my own clothes.
4. (desire); I have a *desire* for travel and adventure.
5. <u>500 years</u>; A *delay* is "a length of time spent waiting."
6. <u>aluminum tubes</u>, <u>synthetic fiber</u>; A synonym for *fashioned* is *created*.
7. (approval); I seek my teacher's *favor*.
8. (set free); Someone might be *captive* during wartime when held by the enemy.

## Reading Warm-up B, p. 26

### Sample Answers

1. (up, up, and up); Smoke billowing from a chimney goes *aloft*; so does a hot-air balloon.
2. <u>in a cramped airplane cabin</u>; I feel *imprisoned* during long drives in a car with my little brother.
3. <u>between flying and taking the train</u>; *Back and forth* means the same thing as *wavered*.
4. (sparkling water); *Quench* means "to satisfy."
5. <u>designed billion-dollar buildings</u>; My mom hired an *architect* to design our new home.
6. <u>He checked his seat belt: buckled. He checked the emergency exit: three rows back.</u> The *cautions* I take most seriously are to buckle my seat belt in a car and to never walk alone once it gets dark.
7. (air); *Supported* is a synonym for *sustained*.
8. (sleep); *Overtook* means "caught up with."

## Writing About the Big Question, p. 27

**A.** 1. team
2. environment

3. duty
4. individual

**B. Sample Answers**

1. I was so obsessed with getting a bicycle for my birthday that I neglected all my other gifts.
2. My **family** had made an effort to choose some really **unique** gifts for me. They felt their efforts were not appreciated. I felt bad for failing to consider their feelings.

**C. Sample Answer**

*When an individual becomes too focused on his or her own desires,* he or she may fail to consider the consequences of his or her actions. This can cause that person to behave in selfish or thoughtless ways and can lead to hurt feelings and guilt. An individual should try to balance his or her desires with those of the individuals or communities around him or her.

## Reading: Ask Questions to Analyze Cause-and-Effect Relationships, p. 28

**Sample Answers**

1. *Effect:* He has Daedalus put in prison. *Effect:* Daedalus escapes from prison.
2. *Question:* What happens as a result of Daedalus' watching the sea-gulls? *Effect:* Daedalus realizes that the only way to escape is by flying. *Effect:* Daedalus makes a set of wings.
3. *Question:* What happens when Icarus ignores the warning? *Effect:* Icarus flies too close to the sun. *Effect:* Icarus wings melt and he falls into the sea.

## Literary Analysis: Myth, p. 29

**Sample Answers**

1. The excerpt shows a human hero with superhuman traits. The excerpt refers to Daedalus as a mortal who "learned the secrets of the gods."
2. The excerpt explores a universal theme. Daedalus is telling Icarus something that every parent might tell a child: Do not go to extremes; act in moderation.
3. The excerpt expresses ideas about right and wrong. Daedalus makes an offering to a god and gives up the idea of flying. This shows that Daedalus admits he was wrong to try to act like a god by doing something humans are not naturally able to do.
*Note:* Students may instead say that the excerpt explains a natural occurrence—how Icaria got its name, or they may link this excerpt to the exploration of a universal theme.

## Vocabulary Builder, p. 30

**A.** 1. C; 2. A; 3. B; 4. A; 5. D; 6. B
**B. Sample Answers**

1. A vacancy sign tells you that a motel or hotel has empty rooms.

2. A vacuum-packed jar has been emptied of air.
3. A vacuous TV show lacks intelligence.

## Enrichment: Greek Gods and Modern English, p. 31

**A.** 1. atlas
2. Herculean
3. *Titanic*
4. chronological
5. chaotic
6. plutonium

**B.** Students should use the words in grammatically correct sentences. Sample answers:

You can look at an atlas if you want to see where the *Titanic* struck the iceberg. If you do not tell what happened in chronological order, your story is likely to be chaotic. The discovery of plutonium was a Herculean undertaking.

## Open-Book Test, p. 32

**Short Answer**

1. He is referred to as a *mortal* who *learned the secrets of the gods,* so he must be a human.
   **Difficulty:** *Easy*   **Objective:** *Literary Analysis*
2. The second paragraph says that the king's feelings *veered with the wind.* He simply changed his mind about how he felt about Daedalus; there was no real reason for his dislike.
   **Difficulty:** *Average*   **Objective:** *Literary Analysis*
3. He sees sea-gulls, who are flying freely in the air. They give him an idea, which is to build wings so that he and his son can fly.
   **Difficulty:** *Average*   **Objective:** *Reading*
4. The immediate effect is that he learns to fly. The long-term effect is that Icarus drowns after flying too high.
   **Difficulty:** *Challenging*   **Objective:** *Reading*
5. Sample answer: Daedalus knew that his son was young and would be excited about flying; he was concerned that Icarus might forget to be cautious.
   **Difficulty:** *Average*   **Objective:** *Interpretation*
6. The author explains that Icarus did not pay much attention to his father's warnings. He felt that since birds weren't careful, he did not need to be careful either.
   **Difficulty:** *Easy*   **Objective:** *Interpretation*
7. The people on the ground assume that the flying pair are the gods Apollo and Cupid. Greek mythology told stories about the gods.
   **Difficulty:** *Challenging*   **Objective:** *Literary Analysis*

8. The word *vacancy* means "emptiness." They are uncomfortable at first because they sense that there is nothing around them.
   **Difficulty:** *Average*  **Objective:** *Vocabulary*

9. [2nd box: flies too high; 3rd box: wax melts and the feathers fall off; 4th box: falls into the sea and drowns.]
   Sample answer: Icarus' main mistake was forgetting his father's warnings.
   **Difficulty:** *Average*  **Objective:** *Reading*

10. The word *sustained* means "supported." The wings of birds are supported, or carried, by the wind.
    **Difficulty:** *Easy*  **Objective:** *Vocabulary*

## Essay

11. Some students will say Daedalus seems more responsible because he controls all of the action. He is the one who thinks of making the wings, and although he cautions his son, he clearly does not take into account how his son will feel once he leaves the island prison. He feels that the responsibility for the disaster is clearly his because he never flies again. Others will say that Icarus is responsible for his own death because he ignored his father's warnings and took off on his own.
    **Difficulty:** *Easy*  **Objective:** *Essay*

12. Students' essays should include some of these points: Icarus' escape made him "forget everything in the world but his joy." His need for freedom overtook his common sense, making him fly too close to the sun. Although he did have some experience practicing with the wings, and his father had warned him not to fly too high or too low, he could not remember what he had been told in the joy of the moment.
    **Difficulty:** *Average*  **Objective:** *Essay*

13. Students may make these points: Daedulus and Icarus were imprisoned on an island; there were only two ways to get off. They could have tried to hide in one of the ships leaving the island, but the ships were well guarded. Since Daedalus was an architect, it makes sense that he would try to construct something to help them fly, and he used the only materials available to him. Based on the building of the labyrinth, he was smart enough to come up with a new invention.
    **Difficulty:** *Challenging*  **Objective:** *Essay*

14. Students may make these points: The communities of both the gods and mortals in "Icarus and Daedalus" control the fate of the two main characters. Daedalus' hunger for knowing "the secrets of the gods" leads him to know things that perhaps he should not know. This knowledge leads eventually to his son's death. In addition, the community of mortals controls the characters' fate because the mortal King Minos imprisons them on a whim.
    **Difficulty:** *Average*  **Objective:** *Essay*

## Oral Response

15. Oral responses should be clear, well organized, and well supported by appropriate examples from the selection.
    **Difficulty:** *Average*  **Objective:** *Oral Interpretation*

## Selection Test A, p. 35

### Critical Reading

| | | |
|---|---|---|
| 1. ANS: B | DIF: Easy | OBJ: Reading |
| 2. ANS: A | DIF: Easy | OBJ: Interpretation |
| 3. ANS: B | DIF: Easy | OBJ: Interpretation |
| 4. ANS: D | DIF: Easy | OBJ: Comprehension |
| 5. ANS: B | DIF: Easy | OBJ: Reading |
| 6. ANS: D | DIF: Easy | OBJ: Reading |
| 7. ANS: B | DIF: Easy | OBJ: Comprehension |
| 8. ANS: C | DIF: Easy | OBJ: Literary Analysis |
| 9. ANS: D | DIF: Easy | OBJ: Interpretation |
| 10. ANS: C | DIF: Easy | OBJ: Interpretation |

### Vocabulary and Grammar

| | | |
|---|---|---|
| 11. ANS: B | DIF: Easy | OBJ: Vocabulary |
| 12. ANS: C | DIF: Easy | OBJ: Vocabulary |
| 13. ANS: D | DIF: Easy | OBJ: Grammar |
| 14. ANS: A | DIF: Easy | OBJ: Grammar |

### Essay

15. Students who prefer Icarus may say that they can relate to his desire to ignore his father's warnings; those who prefer Daedalus may say that they are impressed with his ingenuity. In any case, students should offer a well-thought-out explanation and cite two details from the selection to support their points.
    **Difficulty:** *Easy*  **Objective:** *Essay*

16. In stating whether they believe Daedalus shared in the responsibility for his son's death, students should refer to the warnings Daedalus offers and evaluate whether they were adequate. Students might also comment on whether a lifetime of imprisonment would have been preferable to the risk involved in attempting to flee.
    **Difficulty:** *Easy*  **Objective:** *Essay*

17. Students might note that the communities of both the gods and mortals in "Icarus and Daedalus" control the fate of the two main characters. Daedalus' hunger for knowing "the secrets of the gods" leads him to know things that maybe he should not know. This knowledge leads to his son's death. In addition, the community of mortals controls the characters' fate, because the mortal King Minos imprisons them on a whim.
    **Difficulty:** *Average*  **Objective:** *Essay*

## Selection Test B, p. 38

### Critical Reading

1. ANS: C    DIF: Average    OBJ: Comprehension
2. ANS: B    DIF: Average    OBJ: Interpretation
3. ANS: D    DIF: Average    OBJ: Reading
4. ANS: D    DIF: Average    OBJ: Comprehension
5. ANS: B    DIF: Average    OBJ: Comprehension
6. ANS: D    DIF: Challenging    OBJ: Interpretation
7. ANS: B    DIF: Average    OBJ: Interpretation
8. ANS: B    DIF: Average    OBJ: Comprehension
9. ANS: D    DIF: Average    OBJ: Reading
10. ANS: D    DIF: Challenging    OBJ: Interpretation
11. ANS: C    DIF: Challenging    OBJ: Comprehension
12. ANS: C    DIF: Average    OBJ: Literary Analysis
13. ANS: D    DIF: Challenging    OBJ: Literary Analysis
14. ANS: A    DIF: Challenging    OBJ: Literary Analysis

### Vocabulary and Grammar

15. ANS: C    DIF: Average    OBJ: Vocabulary
16. ANS: D    DIF: Challenging    OBJ: Vocabulary
17. ANS: B    DIF: Average    OBJ: Grammar
18. ANS: C    DIF: Average    OBJ: Grammar

### Essay

19. Students should recognize that Daedalus warns Icarus to fly neither too low (lest he be weighed down by the fog) nor too high (lest the heat of the sun melt the wax that secures the feathers to the wings). They should note that if Icarus had heeded his father's warning and flown a middle course, he would have followed Daedalus to safety.

    **Difficulty:** *Average*    **Objective:** *Essay*

20. If students note that the narrator of the myth suggests that Daedalus was overreaching, they are likely to conclude that he should never have attempted the flight. If they believe that Daedalus was justified in attempting the escape, they should evaluate his warnings to Icarus and provide a credible argument in support of or in opposition to the idea that Daedalus shares in the responsibility for Icarus' death. They may say, for example, that as the father, Daedalus was solely responsible for his son's well-being; or they may say that Icarus received sufficient warning, and a parent can do only so much to protect a child.

    **Difficulty:** *Average*    **Objective:** *Essay*

21. Students should refer to the selection to support their description of Daedalus' character. They might note, for example, that Daedalus "learned the secrets of the gods," which in the context of a Greek myth is considered a negative characteristic. He also invented the Labyrinth, which was meant to fool people, and he may have used deception to escape from the prison cell. As

positive traits, students will likely point to Daedalus' ingenuity in inventing a human-powered means of flight and his great love of his son (although they may argue that he did not do enough to ensure Icarus' safety).

**Difficulty:** *Challenging*    **Objective:** *Essay*

22. Students may make these points: The communities of both the gods and mortals in "Icarus and Daedalus" control the fate of the two main characters. Daedalus' hunger for knowing "the secrets of the gods" leads him to know things that perhaps he should not know. This knowledge leads eventually to his son's death. In addition, the community of mortals controls the characters' fate, because the mortal King Minos imprisons them on a whim.

**Difficulty:** *Average*    **Objective:** *Essay*

## "Demeter and Persephone" by Anne Terry White

### Vocabulary Warm-up Exercises, p. 42

**A.**
1. fertile
2. toiled
3. harvest
4. joyful
5. descend
6. goddess
7. innocent
8. grim

**B.** Sample Answers
1. Parents should not reward a child who *defies* them because he or she is refusing to do as told.
2. You would not call a doctor because a *pang* is a feeling of discomfort, not a health problem.
3. I would wear boots because sandals would not protect my feet from the *thistles*.
4. A man who owns a *chariot* would need hay to feed the horse that pulls it.
5. A heavy *fragrance* will not keep me warm because it is just a smell.
6. A train moving forward *mightily* is moving too fast and too forcefully to jump on.
7. Another *realm* is another place, so you would not be at home.

### Reading Warm-up A, p. 43

**Sample Answers**
1. <u>ruled over humankind</u>; Diana is the goddess of the moon.
2. (cheerful); In fact, he was downright *gloomy* compared with his brothers, Zeus and Poseidon.
3. (barren); *Fertile soil* means "fruitful" or "good for growing crops."
4. <u>fed humankind</u>; The farmer stored his wheat *harvest* inside the barn.
5. <u>into the land of Hades</u>; How can she *descend* the staircase in high heels and a ball gown without tripping?

6. (guilty); *Innocent* means "not guilty of anything."

7. <u>in the fields</u>; I have *toiled* to make my term paper great.

8. (happy-go-lucky); I think holiday music and festive lights are *joyful*.

## Reading Warm-up B, p. 44

### Sample Answers

1. (kingdom); I visited the *realm* of Great Britain.

2. <u>prickly plants</u>; You might find *thistles* growing in a forest or a garden.

3. <u>of stage fright</u>; He was feeling *twinges* of stage fright.

4. (struggled); The lost kitten cried *weakly* for its mother.

5. (in his neck); *Veins* are the tubes that carry blood to all parts of the body.

6. (disobeys); Mom gets angry with my brother when he *defies* her orders.

7. (two-wheeled vehicle); You might have found a *chariot* in the Coliseum during the time of the Roman Empire.

8. (smell); My favorite *fragrance* is the smell of tea roses.

## Writing About the Big Question, p. 45

**A.** 1. tradition
2. community
3. duty
4. common

**B. Sample Answers**

1. My dad, a school principal, had to decide whether to require a school uniform.

2. He decided a uniform would help **unify** the school **community**. Many students were unhappy, but most parents supported the decision.

**C. Sample Answer**

*When making a decision that will affect the greater community, it is one's duty to* weigh the positive and negative consequences of the decision. If it could cause harm, then—if possible—one should reconsider that course of action. At the very least, one needs to let others know if planned actions might place them in danger.

## Reading: Ask Questions to Analyze Cause-and-Effect Relationships, p. 46

### Sample Answers

1. *Effect:* Pluto falls in love with Persephone. *Effect:* Pluto kidnaps Persephone and takes her to the underworld.

2. *Question:* What happens as a result of Persephone's being held captive in the underworld? *Effect:* Demeter blames the earth for Persephone's disappearance. *Effect:* Zeus sends Hermes to bring Persephone back from the underworld.

3. *Question:* What happens as a result of Persephone's eating the pomegranate seeds? *Effect:* She must return to the underworld for four months of every year. *Effect:* Earth experiences winter, the season that Persephone spends in the underworld.

## Literary Analysis: Myth, p. 47

### Sample Answers

1. The excerpt explains a natural occurrence—volcanic activity. The passage refers to a real volcano, Mt. Aetna, and to mythical creatures.

2. The excerpt shows a god with human traits. Pluto, a god, is described as falling in love, just the way a human being might.

3. The excerpt expresses a belief about right and wrong. It refers to the famine that Demeter causes on earth as a result of her grief, and it shows Zeus' reaction. Zeus is saying that it is wrong to punish people for something they did not do.

## Vocabulary Builder, p. 48

### Sample Answers

**A.** 1. Zeus becomes angry when a god or goddess defies his orders.

2. When there is trouble, Zeus is likely to intervene.

3. The subjects bowed before their monarch.

4. Pluto rules supreme within his dominions.

5. Within the realm of fantasy, imagination is unleashed.

6. With its cheerful fire and sweet scent, the Queen's abode gave her a sense of security.

**B. Sample Answers**

1. People live in a domicile.

2. A dominant figure would hold a powerful position.

3. When you domesticate an animal, you tame it.

## Enrichment: Gods and Goddesses in Greek Mythology, p. 49

**A.** 1. Persephone
2. Poseidon
3. Apollo
4. Athena
5. Ares, Nike
6. Zeus
7. Demeter

**B.** Students should name at least two gods and/or goddesses and suggest actors or actresses to play the roles. They should offer logical explanations for their choices.

## "Icarus and Daedalus"
by Josephine Preston Peabody
## "Demeter and Persephone" by Anne Terry White

## Integrated Language Skills: Grammar, p. 50

**A.** 1. All of the characters in "Demeter and Persephone" are gods or goddesses: Aphrodite, Eros, Pluto, Persephone, Demeter, Zeus, and Hermes.

2. Daedalus warns Icarus not to do these things: fly too low, fly too high, and fly too far from him.

**B.** Guidelines for evaluation: Students should write two grammatically correct sentences that include a colon followed by a list of items.

# "Demeter and Persephone" by Anne Terry White

## Open-Book Test, p. 53

### Short Answer

1. Pluto is king of the underworld, the realm of the dead. He does not want light in his dark world of death.
   **Difficulty:** *Average* **Objective:** *Interpretation*

2. *Defies* means "opposes." The story says "never had his heart been touched." He has never been in love, which is part of the goddess of love's power.
   **Difficulty:** *Challenging* **Objective:** *Vocabulary*

3. She is annoyed that Pluto has never been in love. She wants him to "feel the pangs of love," just as others do who live on the earth.
   **Difficulty:** *Easy* **Objective:** *Interpretation*

4. Eros' arrow causes Pluto to fall in love with Persephone.
   **Difficulty:** *Easy* **Objective:** *Reading*

5. Pluto throws Persephone into his golden chariot. They cover lots of ground in moments. He opens the earth with his trident, and the earth then grabs him, Persephone, the horses, and the chariot.
   **Difficulty:** *Average* **Objective:** *Literary Analysis*

6. Demeter sees her daughter's girdle and blames the earth for taking her daughter. She punishes the earth by not letting anything grow. Mankind has nothing to eat.
   **Difficulty:** *Average* **Objective:** *Reading*

7. The word *intervene* means "come between to settle an argument." Zeus sees that all the earth is dying, and he cannot allow humans to die due to a problem among the gods.
   **Difficulty:** *Average* **Objective:** *Vocabulary*

8. Zeus says Persephone may leave forever if she has not eaten any food in the underworld. Because she ate four pomegranate seeds, she must return to the underworld for four months each year.
   **Difficulty:** *Easy* **Objective:** *Reading*

9. Sample answers: Pluto—falls in love; Persephone—picks flowers, screams for her mother
   Sample answer: Persephone seems most human because she is sad and frightened in the underworld.
   **Difficulty:** *Average* **Objective:** *Literary Analysis*

10. Persephone has to spend one third of the year in the underworld. While she is in the underworld, the upper world experiences winter. When she returns, spring returns. This explanation serves one of the functions of a myth, which is to explain natural phenomena.
    **Difficulty:** *Challenging* **Objective:** *Literary Analysis*

### Essay

11. Students should explain Aphrodite and Eros' role. Some may say that Aphrodite and Eros should be punished for causing all of the trouble that follows. Aphrodite took action against Pluto mostly out of spite. She could not stand that he had avoided her power for so long. Others may say the goddess was only doing her job; she was not responsible for Pluto's kidnapping of Persephone.
    **Difficulty:** *Easy* **Objective:** *Essay*

12. Students should explain how Demeter's actions affected humans. They should also note that in the myth, it seems humans have no control over their fate. They were starving because of Demeter's actions, and "men and oxen toiled in vain." Only because another god intervenes are the humans saved.
    **Difficulty:** *Average* **Objective:** *Essay*

13. Students may include the following: Persephone comes from a world of life and energy in which things grow and thrive. Pluto comes from a world where death and darkness surround everything. Nothing is living or growing. The jewels are beautiful and from the underworld, but they too are dead. The author may be hinting that some things that seem valuable are really not.
    **Difficulty:** *Challenging* **Objective:** *Essay*

14. Students may say the individual is more important: the actions of each individual god or goddess cause all of the story events. Eros shoots an arrow; Pluto kidnaps Persephone; Demeter rages; Zeus intervenes. There is no sense of community. Others may say community is important because the community of mankind drives Zeus' action to save the humans. The community of family drives Demeter to avenge her daughter. The community of mankind is affected by the actions of the community of the gods.
    **Difficulty:** *Average* **Objective:** *Essay*

### Oral Response

15. Oral responses should be clear, well organized, and well supported by appropriate examples from the selection.
    **Difficulty:** *Average* **Objective:** *Oral Interpretation*

## Selection Test A, p. 56

### Critical Reading

| | | |
|---|---|---|
| 1. ANS: B | DIF: Easy | OBJ: Reading |
| 2. ANS: B | DIF: Easy | OBJ: Reading |
| 3. ANS: D | DIF: Easy | OBJ: Comprehension |
| 4. ANS: A | DIF: Easy | OBJ: Interpretation |
| 5. ANS: B | DIF: Easy | OBJ: Reading |
| 6. ANS: A | DIF: Easy | OBJ: Comprehension |
| 7. ANS: B | DIF: Easy | OBJ: Interpretation |
| 8. ANS: A | DIF: Easy | OBJ: Reading |

| 9. ANS: C | DIF: Easy | OBJ: Comprehension |
|---|---|---|
| 10. ANS: D | DIF: Easy | OBJ: Literary Analysis |
| 11. ANS: B | DIF: Easy | OBJ: Literary Analysis |
| 12. ANS: C | DIF: Easy | OBJ: Literary Analysis |

## Vocabulary and Grammar

| 13. ANS: A | DIF: Easy | OBJ: Vocabulary |
|---|---|---|
| 14. ANS: B | DIF: Easy | OBJ: Vocabulary |
| 15. ANS: C | DIF: Easy | OBJ: Grammar |

## Essay

16. Students should describe the character they prefer, including two details about the character to support their explanation.
   **Difficulty:** *Easy* **Objective:** *Essay*

17. Students should state a point of view and provide two details from the selection to support their argument.
   **Difficulty:** *Easy* **Objective:** *Essay*

18. Students may say the individual is more important: the actions of each individual god or goddess cause all of the story events. Eros shoots an arrow; Pluto kidnaps Persephone; Demeter rages; Zeus comes onto the scene. There is no sense of community. Others may say community is important because the community of mankind drives Zeus' action to save the humans. The community of family drives Demeter to avenge her daughter.
   **Difficulty:** *Average* **Objective:** *Essay*

### Selection Test B, p. 59

## Critical Reading

| 1. ANS: D | DIF: Challenging | OBJ: Interpretation |
|---|---|---|
| 2. ANS: A | DIF: Average | OBJ: Interpretation |
| 3. ANS: C | DIF: Challenging | OBJ: Comprehension |
| 4. ANS: D | DIF: Average | OBJ: Comprehension |
| 5. ANS: B | DIF: Average | OBJ: Reading |
| 6. ANS: C | DIF: Average | OBJ: Comprehension |
| 7. ANS: C | DIF: Challenging | OBJ: Interpretation |
| 8. ANS: C | DIF: Average | OBJ: Comprehension |
| 9. ANS: A | DIF: Challenging | OBJ: Interpretation |
| 10. ANS: A | DIF: Average | OBJ: Reading |
| 11. ANS: A | DIF: Average | OBJ: Literary Analysis |
| 12. ANS: C | DIF: Average | OBJ: Interpretation |
| 13. ANS: A | DIF: Challenging | OBJ: Literary Analysis |
| 14. ANS: D | DIF: Average | OBJ: Interpretation |
| 15. ANS: D | DIF: Challenging | OBJ: Literary Analysis |
| 16. ANS: C | DIF: Average | OBJ: Literary Analysis |

## Vocabulary and Grammar

| 17. ANS: D | DIF: Average | OBJ: Vocabulary |
|---|---|---|
| 18. ANS: A | DIF: Average | OBJ: Grammar |

| 19. ANS: D | DIF: Average | OBJ: Grammar |
|---|---|---|

## Essay

20. Students who choose Eros should note that if he had not shot Pluto with the arrow of love, Pluto would never have kidnapped Persephone. Students who choose Pluto should note that he acts selfishly by keeping Persephone with him against her will. Students who choose Demeter should note that she need not have punished the earth for Persephone's disappearance.
   **Difficulty:** *Average* **Objective:** *Essay*

21. Students should recognize that the gods share with humans one or more of the following traits: They fall in love, have familial relationships, and possess different skills and abilities. Students should also recognize that, unlike humans, gods have the following characteristics: the power to imprison some beings under the earth, the ability to make gods fall in love, the ability to travel to different realms (such as the underworld), and the ability to affect the natural order of things on earth.
   **Difficulty:** *Challenging* **Objective:** *Essay*

22. Students may say the individual is more important: the actions of each individual god or goddess cause all of the story events. Eros shoots an arrow; Pluto kidnaps Persephone; Demeter rages; Zeus intervenes. There is no sense of community. Others may say community is important because the community of mankind drives Zeus' action to save the humans. The community of family drives Demeter to avenge her daughter. The community of mankind is affected by the actions of the community of the gods.
   **Difficulty:** *Average* **Objective:** *Essay*

### "Tenochtitlan: Inside the Aztec Capital"
by Jacqueline Dineen

### Vocabulary Warm-up Exercises, p. 63

**A.** 1. described
   2. adobe
   3. gaps
   4. fibers
   5. excellent
   6. prevented
   7. included
   8. historical

**B. Sample Answers**

1. On the *site* of an abandoned campground, I might find a picnic table, ashes from a fire, and extra firewood.
2. To plant some flowers, I would use the following *utensils*: a hoe, a trowel, and a spade.
3. The usual cure for an *enchanted* princess is a kiss from the handsome prince.
4. If I had fireplaces but no *chimneys* in a house, the house would fill with smoke whenever a fire was lit.

5. One advantage to living in *compounds* rather than in separate dwellings is companionship.

6. If I joined *households* with my best friend, *(number will vary)* people would be living together.

7. One way *grandchildren* can show their love for grandparents is to spend time with them.

8. I prefer *courtyards* to back yards because I like the idea of having access to the outdoors from all parts of the house.

## Reading Warm-up A, p. 64

**Sample Answers**

1. building material; *Adobe* is commonly seen in the southwestern part of the U.S.

2. (ancient); A *historical* event that I wish I could have seen in person is the inauguration of John F. Kennedy.

3. hay or grass; *Fibers* are threads or threadlike parts, as of a fabric or of animal or plant tissue.

4. (between the bricks); The word *gaps* means "cracks or openings, as in a wall."

5. shrinkage; I once *prevented* a behavior problem with my dog by taking him to obedience school.

6. (Pink or ochre pigments); Access to the pool is *included* with the price of admission.

7. material; I would like to be *described* as friendly and generous.

8. (it needs little maintenance); One *excellent* choice I made recently was to finish my homework rather than watch TV.

## Reading Warm-up B, p. 65

**Sample Answers**

1. their way of life; As the children walked through the *enchanted* forest, the trees came to life.

2. (individual); *Households* means "families; people who live under the same roof."

3. different generations living in different wings of the home and sharing common space in the middle; *Compounds* means "walled yards with buildings in them."

4. (see one another every day); Carl's *grandchildren* all lived at least a hundred miles away from him.

5. picturesque; The *site* for a home I'd like to have would be high on a hill, overlooking the city lights.

6. (gather and visit); *Courtyards* means "open spaces surrounded by walls."

7. fireplaces; Without *chimneys*, we couldn't have fireplaces in our homes.

8. (dishes, glasses); *Utensils* are tools, implements, or containers used to do or make something.

## Writing About the Big Question, p. 66

**A.** 1. group
2. unique
3. unity
4. common

**B. Sample Answers**

1. I took part in the school play. I helped build a community playground.

2. Members of my town worked together to build a **community** playground for local children. It was hard work, but it made me feel good to be part of such a dedicated team and to contribute to such a worthy cause.

**C. Sample Answer**

*Protecting a community sometimes requires that individuals* work together on difficult or time-consuming projects. These projects might require personal sacrifice, but they serve a common interest, such as protecting a community from damage or attack.

## Reading: Reread to Look for Connections That Indicate Cause-and-Effect Relationships, p. 67

1. cause
2. Therefore; cause and effect
3. Because of; cause and effect
4. As a result; effect
5. cause
6. Because; cause and effect
7. cause and effect
8. Because; cause and effect
9. Because; effect
10. cause
11. For that reason; cause and effect
12. effect

## Literary Analysis: Legends and Facts, p. 68

Sample answers follow the designation of fact or speculation:

1. Fact; this information can be proved true based on written records or excavated ruins.

2. Fact; this information can be proved true based on written records or excavated ruins.

3. Fact; this information can be proved true based on Bernal Diaz's description.

4. Fact; this information can be proved true based on excavated ruins and observation.

5. Speculation; the word *think* indicates that the information has not been proved true.

6. Speculation; the words *are not sure* and *think* indicate that the information has not been proved true.

## Vocabulary Builder, p. 69

**A.** Sample answers follow the yes or no designation:

1. No, the outskirts of a city are far from the center, and the Temple Mayor was in the center of Tenochtitlan.

2. No, reeds are grasses, not trees.

3. No, he was serving a beverage; goblets are cups.

4. No, causeways are raised roads. The causeways in Tenochtitlan were built over the swamp.

5. Yes, irrigation involves the use of ditches, canals, or sprinklers to supply water.

6. No, they would be much larger. The nobility were wealthy and could afford large homes.

## B. Sample Answers

1. An outcast is someone people tend to avoid.

2. An outlaw would be wanted for committing a crime.

3. The opposing team wins because they played better.

## Enrichment: Aztec Words in English, p. 70

1. chili
2. ocelot
3. shack
4. chocolate
5. mesquite
6. tomato
7. avocado
8. pulque
9. coyote
10. tamale

## Open-Book Test, p. 71

### Short Answer

1. It was becoming important after 1385. The Aztecs expanded the city with causeways and aqueducts. By the late 1400s, 200,000 people lived in the city.
   **Difficulty:** *Average*   **Objective:** *Interpretation*

2. The selection is factual and can be proved. There are no fictional or fantastic elements or superhuman deeds that would be found in a legend.
   **Difficulty:** *Easy*   **Objective:** *Literary Analysis*

3. The causeways linked the island city to the mainland.
   **Difficulty:** *Easy*   **Objective:** *Reading*

4. The Aztecs built causeways with bridges that could be removed. They built aqueducts. Both required excellent engineering, or building, skills.
   **Difficulty:** *Average*   **Objective:** *Interpretation*

5. Diaz described the city as "an enchanted vision." This could have gradually been turned into a legend that told of an enchanted city rising from the water in the middle of a lake.
   **Difficulty:** *Average*   **Objective:** *Literary Analysis*

6. They built the embankment to keep salt water from the northern lakes out. They knew that the salt water would not be good for irrigating, so they were skilled farmers who understood that salt water would kill their crops.
   **Difficulty:** *Challenging*   **Objective:** *Interpretation*

7. The city was growing. They needed more dry land for farming and for building.
   **Difficulty:** *Easy*   **Objective:** *Reading*

8. The outskirts are "far from the center of a city." The poorer people lived there because they lived on their chinampas, where they farmed.
   **Difficulty:** *Average*   **Objective:** *Vocabulary*

9. *Reeds* are "slender grasses." They could easily and freely be gathered from swamps in the area.
   **Difficulty:** *Challenging*   **Objective:** *Vocabulary*

10. Sample answers: Need: Fresh water; Result: Aqueducts; Need: Protection from enemies; Result: Removable bridges; Need: More land; Result: Drain the lake Students may explain the importance of any of the cause/effect links.
    **Difficulty:** *Average*   **Objective:** *Reading*

### Essay

11. Students should choose any three facts about the city and explain how they could be legendary. For example, students may choose the "gleaming white towers and castles" and tell how that could easily become part of a story about the city.
    **Difficulty:** *Easy*   **Objective:** *Essay*

12. Students' summaries should include at least one element of a legend: a human who is larger than life, fantastic elements, roots or basis in historical fact, events that reflect the culture. Students should also include details about the Aztecs and Tenochtitlan from the selection.
    **Difficulty:** *Average*   **Objective:** *Essay*

13. Students should use details about the ordinary lives of the Aztecs and suggest ways in which those lives could take on legendary qualities.
    **Difficulty:** *Challenging*   **Objective:** *Essay*

14. Students will probably say that the community of Tenochtitlan seems to be much more important than any individual living there. Although individual contributions were vital, such as those of the engineers and the farmers, no one individual seems more important than the accomplishments of the city as a whole.
    **Difficulty:** *Average*   **Objective:** *Essay*

### Oral Response

15. Oral responses should be clear, well organized, and well supported by appropriate examples from the selection.
    **Difficulty:** *Average*   **Objective:** *Oral Interpretation*

## Selection Test A, p. 74

### Critical Reading

1. ANS: B          DIF: Easy          OBJ: Literary Analysis
2. ANS: C          DIF: Easy          OBJ: Comprehension
3. ANS: B          DIF: Easy          OBJ: Reading
4. ANS: D          DIF: Easy          OBJ: Comprehension
5. ANS: A          DIF: Easy          OBJ: Comprehension

| 6. ANS: D | DIF: Easy | OBJ: Comprehension |
|---|---|---|
| 7. ANS: C | DIF: Easy | OBJ: Comprehension |
| 8. ANS: D | DIF: Easy | OBJ: Comprehension |
| 9. ANS: B | DIF: Easy | OBJ: Literary Analysis |
| 10. ANS: A | DIF: Easy | OBJ: Comprehension |
| 11. ANS: B | DIF: Easy | OBJ: Interpretation |
| 12. ANS: B | DIF: Easy | OBJ: Comprehension |

| 7. ANS: A | DIF: Average | OBJ: Literary Analysis |
|---|---|---|
| 8. ANS: D | DIF: Challenging | OBJ: Literary Analysis |
| 9. ANS: B | DIF: Challenging | OBJ: Interpretation |
| 10. ANS: C | DIF: Challenging | OBJ: Interpretation |
| 11. ANS: A | DIF: Average | OBJ: Reading |
| 12. ANS: B | DIF: Average | OBJ: Reading |
| 13. ANS: A | DIF: Average | OBJ: Comprehension |

## Vocabulary and Grammar

| 13. ANS: C | DIF: Easy | OBJ: Vocabulary |
|---|---|---|
| 14. ANS: A | DIF: Easy | OBJ: Grammar |

## Essay

15. Students should conclude that Dineen wrote about Tenochtitlan to inform readers about the city that was the capital of the Aztec empire hundreds of years ago. Evidence should include any fact related to the history of the city, its layout, the skill of the Aztec engineers, and the way in which the Aztecs lived.
Difficulty: *Easy*   Objective: *Essay*

16. Students should describe one solution devised by the Aztecs in response to a problem presented by one of the situations. Students may say, for example, that because Tenochtitlan was built on an island in a lake, the Aztecs built causeways linking the city to the mainland, or they may say that the Aztecs built canals, on which they traveled by canoe. In response to the second situation, they may note that city residents imported food from outside the city, kept turkeys for food and eggs, and drained additional land for farming. The important point is that students should recognize a cause-and-effect relationship, noting something the Aztecs did in response to something else.
Difficulty: *Easy*   Objective: *Essay*

17. Students will probably say that the community of Tenochtitlan seems to be much more important than any individual living there. Although individual contributions were important, such as those of the engineers and the farmers, no one individual seems more important than the work of the city as a whole.
Difficulty: *Average*   Objective: *Essay*

## Selection Test B, p. 77

### Critical Reading

| 1. ANS: B | DIF: Average | OBJ: Literary Analysis |
|---|---|---|
| 2. ANS: D | DIF: Challenging | OBJ: Comprehension |
| 3. ANS: C | DIF: Average | OBJ: Reading |
| 4. ANS: C | DIF: Average | OBJ: Interpretation |
| 5. ANS: B | DIF: Average | OBJ: Comprehension |
| 6. ANS: A | DIF: Average | OBJ: Comprehension |

## Vocabulary and Grammar

| 14. ANS: B | DIF: Challenging | OBJ: Vocabulary |
|---|---|---|
| 15. ANS: A | DIF: Average | OBJ: Vocabulary |
| 16. ANS: A | DIF: Average | OBJ: Grammar |
| 17. ANS: C | DIF: Average | OBJ: Grammar |

## Essay

18. Students should note that in addition to an emperor, there were priests and nobles. They should point out that no more than half the population is thought to have been farmers, and the rest were craftspeople and nobles. Students may cite other details about the distinctions between the homes of the nobles and those of the poorer people.
Difficulty: *Average*   Objective: *Essay*

19. Students should cite at least two of these accomplishments: To irrigate the land, the Aztecs dug ditches; they piled up the earth from the ditches and used it for farming; they built an embankment to keep out salt water and prevent flooding. Students might point out that no more than half the population were farmers, so food was imported, and they may note that farmers grew corn, tomatoes, beans, chili peppers, prickly pears, and maguey cacti and raised turkey for meat and eggs.
Difficulty: *Average*   Objective: *Essay*

20. Students should recall at least two facts relating to the illustration they choose. For example, they should note that the map shows the layout of the causeways, the location of the central temple, and how each group of houses could be reached by a causeway. The photograph of the maguey cactus indicates its size, and the caption describes its many uses. The drawing of the emperor's palace shows its size, and the caption explains the purpose of several of its rooms.
Difficulty: *Challenging*   Objective: *Essay*

21. Students will probably say that the community of Tenochtitlan seems to be much more important than any individual living there. Although individual contributions were vital, such as those of the engineers and the farmers, no one individual seems more important than the accomplishments of the city as a whole.
Difficulty: *Average*   Objective: *Essay*

## "Popocatepetl and Ixtlaccihuatl"
### by Julie Piggott Wood

### Vocabulary Warm-up Exercises, p. 81

**A.** 1. emperor
2. conflict
3. peril
4. behalf
5. coastal
6. capital
7. siege
8. capacity

**B. Sample Answers**

1. No, I would not be proud to take a *bribe* because it is a payment for doing something wrong.
2. If my job were to *reign* over a country, my first act would be to declare longer weekends.
3. A dog who *exhibited* fear might put its tail between its legs and slink away, whining.
4. If I wanted to make a *pyramid* shape out of paper, I would need to cut out a square for the base and four triangles for the sides.
5. I need *approximately* one hour to get ready for school in the morning.
6. An ideal meal that has foods from a *variety* of food groups might include grilled fish, steamed rice, green beans, a green salad, bread, and a fruit assortment with cheese.
7. The *expected* outcome of a series of swim lessons is the ability to swim.
8. At the site of a burned-down house, I might find *fragments* such as broken dishes, shattered mirrors, and broken glass.

### Reading Warm-up A, p. 82

**Sample Answers**

1. Mexico and Central America; A *coastal* area I would especially like to visit is the coast of Oregon because of its rugged beauty.
2. (for adventure); I have a great *capacity* for humor.
3. shipwreck; One *peril* that I have survived is swimming in an area where there were lots of jellyfish.
4. (Montezuma); Once, I acted on my sister's *behalf* when I returned a purchase she didn't want.
5. ruler; *Emperor* means "a person who rules over a group of different states, nations, or territories."
6. (Tenochtitlan); The *capital* of my state is Sacramento.
7. several months; *Siege* means "steady and persistent attempt to win something."
8. (By the spring of the following year); Recently, I had a *conflict* with my best friend over who should be invited to my birthday party.

### Reading Warm-up B, p. 83

**Sample Answers**

1. Aztec; It would be fun to climb to the top of a *pyramid*.
2. (broke off); We used *fragments* of the broken china in our mosaic.
3. Montezuma; *Reign* means "the period during which a monarch rules."
4. (five minutes); *Approximately* means "about or around."
5. of hand signals; A *variety* of hand signals that I use in everyday life include thumbs up for "okay," waving to express good-bye or hello, and holding my thumb and forefinger about an inch apart to mean "just a little."
6. (hostile behavior); Once my neighbor exhibited *hostile* behavior toward me when I accidentally tossed his newspaper at his front window.
7. of his adventure; If this story continued, I think Donnie would get back to the time machine and return home.
8. (guard); Stella tried to *bribe* Maurice to let her copy his homework, but Maurice said no.

### Writing About the Big Question, p. 84

**A.** 1. tradition/custom
2. team
3. duty
4. unify

**B. Sample Answers**

1. celebrating Kwaanza; volunteering in a soup kitchen on Christmas morning
2. Our **family** celebration of Kwaanza gives us an opportunity to focus on our **culture** and also on our larger **community** by emphasizing values that create a sense of **unity**.

**C. Sample Answer**

***Tradition*** and ***duty*** to one's ***community*** should always take priority when a person is responsible for the well-being of others. A leader's own individual desires should never prevent him or her from doing what is right. A leader's actions set an example that other people will follow.

### Reading: Reread to Look for Connections That Indicate Cause-and-Effect Relationships, p. 85

1. cause
2. Therefore; effect
3. because; effect
4. cause
5. As a result; cause and effect
6. Because; cause and effect
7. Because; cause and effect
8. cause
9. effect

10. Because; cause and effect
11. effect
12. effect
13. Therefore; cause and effect
14. effect
15. effect

## Literary Analysis: Legends and Facts, p. 86

1. This passage is rooted in historical fact; it contains facts, information that can be proved true.

2. This passage is probably based on a historical fact; there may have been an emperor like the one described.

3. This passage describes a larger-than-life hero; the description of him as the one responsible for driving off the enemy is probably exaggerated.

4. This passage describes a fantastic event, pyramids turning into mountains.

## Vocabulary Builder, p. 87

**A. Sample Answers**

1. No, he gave an order.

2. Yes, no one would have claimed he was dead, and he and Ixtla would have married.

3. No, he would have shown wisdom by looking ahead to the future.

4. No, they totally defeated the enemy.

5. No, it prevented him from leading them into battle; he was too ill.

6. Yes, she wanted very much to marry him.

**B. Sample Answers**

1. A unicycle would be hard to balance because it has only one wheel.

2. A unicorn is said to have a single horn in the center of its forehead.

3. When two groups unite, they form one group.

## Enrichment: Volcanoes, p. 88

**Sample Answers**

*Cinder cone: Formation and composition*—Formed from violent eruptions through a single vent; largely composed of cinders; *Typical shape and size*—a bowl-shaped crater at the top; usually rises no more than 1,000 feet above surrounding area; *Famous example*—Parícutin in Mexico

*Composite: Formation and composition*—Formed as magma rises to the surface and pushes through a system of conduits that lead to a central vent or a central cluster of vents; composed of alternating layers of lava, volcanic ash, and cinders; *Typical shape and size*—steep sides and symmetrical cones; may rise as high as 8,000 feet above surrounding area; *Famous examples*—Fuji in Japan, Mount St. Helens and Mount Rainier in Washington State

*Shield: Formation and composition*—Formed when small, thick, rounded masses of lava pile up around a vent; *Typical shape and size*—Broad, gentle sloping cone with a slightly rounded top (resembling a warrior's shield); may have a diameter as great as 4 miles and a height of 2,000 feet; *Famous example*—Mauna Loa on Hawaii

*Lava dome: Formation and composition*—Formed almost entirely from fluid lava flows that spread from a central vent or group of vents. *Typical shape and size*—may have a craggy dome or short, steep sides; *Famous example*—Mount Pelée in Martinique, in the Caribbean

## "Tenochtitlan: Inside the Aztec Capital"
### by Jacqueline Dineen
## "Popocatepetl and Ixtlaccihuatl"
### by Juliet Piggott Wood

## Integrated Language Skills: Grammar, p. 89

**A.** 1. The family consisted of a couple, their married children, and their grandchildren.

2. Aztec houses were very plain; everyone slept on mats of reeds.

**B.** Guidelines for evaluation: Students should write two grammatically correct sentences about the Aztecs. In one they should use one or more commas in one of the ways described in the lesson, and in the other they should use one or more semicolons in one of the ways described in the lesson.

## "Popocatepetl and Ixtlaccihuatl"
### by Juliet Piggott Wood

## Open-Book Test, p. 92

**Short Answer**

1. The names of the volcanoes and the cities are facts. They can be checked and verified.
   **Difficulty:** *Easy* **Objective:** *Literary Analysis*

2. The legend begins with the story of the Aztec emperor. The author writes in the preceding paragraph ". . . they possessed a legend about them and their creation." She then tells the legend.
   **Difficulty:** *Average* **Objective:** *Literary Analysis*

3. While he is a good ruler and warrior, some think his decision to forbid his daughter to marry is unwise and shortsighted.
   **Difficulty:** *Average* **Objective:** *Interpretation*

4. [happy, popular, studious]
   Sample answer: The Princess is a loving daughter who takes her parents' commands seriously.
   **Difficulty:** *Average* **Objective:** *Interpretation*

5. He is tall and strong, a brave but gentle warrior. Like Ixtlaccihuatl, he seems to have many good characteristics, including his ability to take on important responsibilities.
   **Difficulty:** *Challenging* **Objective:** *Interpretation*

6. It leaves them unmarried and only "moderately happy."
   **Difficulty:** *Average*   **Objective:** *Reading*

7. The enemies have had time to become "firmly entrenched" around the city, and so the war goes on for a long time.
   **Difficulty:** *Easy*   **Objective:** *Reading*

8. The word *unanimous* means "in complete agreement." Some of the men are jealous of Popo, so although they may have agreed that he was the cause of their victory, they are not in agreement that he should become the new leader.
   **Difficulty:** *Challenging*   **Objective:** *Vocabulary*

9. The word *routed* means "completely defeated." The warriors cheer, which indicates that they have won a victory over their enemies.
   **Difficulty:** *Easy*   **Objective:** *Vocabulary*

10. Fact: The mountain sometimes gives off smoke. Legend: The mountain formed out of a pyramid built by the Aztecs.
    **Difficulty:** *Average*   **Objective:** *Literary Analysis*

## Essay

11. Popocatepetl is an excellent warrior; he is gentle and understanding about Ixtlaccihuatl's sense of obedience and duty to her father. The "larger than life" aspects of his personality emerge when he singlehandedly kills each warrior who betrays him and then dedicates the rest of his life to watching over the tomb of the woman he loves.
    **Difficulty:** *Easy*   **Objective:** *Essay*

12. Students should include these ideas: The jealous warriors hope to spoil Popo's happiness. However, they do not anticipate that the Emperor would ask to see Popo's body, so they have to tell another lie. Then, when he asks who was responsible for the victory, they are unable to answer, since none of them can accept credit without having the others disagree. Their actions result in the death of the princess and their own deaths.
    **Difficulty:** *Average*   **Objective:** *Essay*

13. Students may point out the Emperor's shortsighted decision to forbid his daughter's marriage. He is not only making her unhappy, he is denying the empire another ruler after his daughter—she will not have heirs without a husband. His decision to offer a bribe to all the warriors leads directly to Ixtla's death and Popo's departure. The empire is left without a ruler.
    **Difficulty:** *Challenging*   **Objective:** *Essay*

14. Students can make a case for either answer. Those who say she would have chosen community should point to her obedience to her father's ideas. She chooses the good of the empire, the community, over her own happiness. Those who say she would have chosen individual should point to her death for the love of Popo. She placed him, the individual, over all else and could not live without him.
    **Difficulty:** *Average*   **Objective:** *Essay*

## Oral Response

15. Oral responses should be clear, well organized, and well supported by appropriate examples from the selection.
    **Difficulty:** *Average*   **Objective:** *Oral Interpretation*

## Selection Test A, p. 95

### Critical Reading

| | | |
|---|---|---|
| 1. **ANS:** D | **DIF:** Easy | **OBJ:** Comprehension |
| 2. **ANS:** B | **DIF:** Easy | **OBJ:** Interpretation |
| 3. **ANS:** C | **DIF:** Easy | **OBJ:** Reading |
| 4. **ANS:** C | **DIF:** Easy | **OBJ:** Reading |
| 5. **ANS:** D | **DIF:** Easy | **OBJ:** Comprehension |
| 6. **ANS:** B | **DIF:** Easy | **OBJ:** Comprehension |
| 7. **ANS:** D | **DIF:** Easy | **OBJ:** Reading |
| 8. **ANS:** A | **DIF:** Easy | **OBJ:** Literary Analysis |
| 9. **ANS:** A | **DIF:** Easy | **OBJ:** Interpretation |
| 10. **ANS:** B | **DIF:** Easy | **OBJ:** Literary Analysis |
| 11. **ANS:** C | **DIF:** Easy | **OBJ:** Interpretation |

### Vocabulary and Grammar

| | | |
|---|---|---|
| 12. **ANS:** B | **DIF:** Easy | **OBJ:** Vocabulary |
| 13. **ANS:** A | **DIF:** Easy | **OBJ:** Grammar |
| 14. **ANS:** B | **DIF:** Easy | **OBJ:** Grammar |

### Essay

15. Students will most likely note that Ixtla and Popo are well suited to each other. They should focus on the characters' fierce loyalty to each other and to the Emperor (though they are in love and want to marry, they honor his wishes that they not marry).
    **Difficulty:** *Easy*   **Objective:** *Essay*

16. Students should support their response with a well-reasoned explanation. They may hold that the warriors got the fate they deserved since they had acted selfishly and without regard for human life. Alternatively, students may suggest that the warriors could not have known their lies would lead to Ixtla's death and may regard Popo's behavior as excessive, in which case they might suggest that the warriors could have been exiled or imprisoned instead of killed.
    **Difficulty:** *Easy*   **Objective:** *Essay*

17. Students can make a case for either answer. Those who say she would have chosen "community" should point to her obedience to her father's ideas. She chooses the good of the empire—the community—over her own happiness. Those who say she would have chosen "individual" should point to her death for the love of Popo. She placed him, the individual, over all else and could not live without him.
    **Difficulty:** *Average*   **Objective:** *Essay*

## Selection Test B, p. 98

### Critical Reading

| | | |
|---|---|---|
| 1. ANS: A | DIF: Average | OBJ: Comprehension |
| 2. ANS: C | DIF: Average | OBJ: Comprehension |
| 3. ANS: A | DIF: Average | OBJ: Interpretation |
| 4. ANS: B | DIF: Average | OBJ: Interpretation |
| 5. ANS: D | DIF: Average | OBJ: Comprehension |
| 6. ANS: D | DIF: Average | OBJ: Reading |
| 7. ANS: B | DIF: Average | OBJ: Reading |
| 8. ANS: B | DIF: Challenging | OBJ: Interpretation |
| 9. ANS: C | DIF: Average | OBJ: Interpretation |
| 10. ANS: B | DIF: Challenging | OBJ: Interpretation |
| 11. ANS: C | DIF: Average | OBJ: Interpretation |
| 12. ANS: C | DIF: Challenging | OBJ: Interpretation |
| 13. ANS: A | DIF: Average | OBJ: Literary Analysis |
| 14. ANS: B | DIF: Average | OBJ: Literary Analysis |

### Vocabulary and Grammar

| | | |
|---|---|---|
| 15. ANS: C | DIF: Average | OBJ: Vocabulary |
| 16. ANS: A | DIF: Challenging | OBJ: Vocabulary |
| 17. ANS: B | DIF: Challenging | OBJ: Grammar |
| 18. ANS: A | DIF: Average | OBJ: Grammar |

### Essay

19. Students should recognize that Ixtla is given an education and expected to succeed her father as ruler of the state but is not free to marry or choose the man she will marry.

    **Difficulty:** *Average*  **Objective:** *Essay*

20. Students may mention studiousness, seriousness, obedience, loyalty, courage, and strength in battle, honesty, and "true" wisdom and should cite details from the legend to support their claims.

    **Difficulty:** *Average*  **Objective:** *Essay*

21. Students may point to such universal elements as the idealized love between Popo and Ixtla, the protracted war between the Emperor and his opponents, Popo's success at proving himself the best warrior of all, the other warriors' jealousy, and the tragedy that leads to Ixtla's death.

    **Difficulty:** *Challenging*  **Objective:** *Essay*

22. Students can make a case for either answer. Those who say she would have chosen "community" should point to her obedience to her father's ideas. She chooses the good of the empire—the community—over her own happiness. Those who say she would have chosen "individual" should point to her death for the love of Popo. She placed him, the individual, over all else and could not live without him.

    **Difficulty:** *Average*  **Objective:** *Essay*

## "To the Top of Everest" by Samantha Larson
## "The Voyage from Tales from the Odyssey" by Mary Pope Osborne

### Vocabulary Warm-up Exercises, p. 102

**A.** 1. solar
2. destination
3. scenic
4. previously
5. enchanted
6. outline
7. devour
8. embers

**B. Sample Answers**

1. If a man fell <u>overboard</u>, he would be in the water, so a chair would be of no use to him. It would make more sense to throw him a life preserver and a rope.

2. If you lost <u>consciousness</u>, you would lose awareness of your thoughts and what was happening around you, so you would not know who was standing over you until you came to.

3. A person who is impatient and cannot keep still is unable to relax, so it would make sense to describe him as <u>restless</u>.

4. In order to possess something you must own it or have it as a quality inside you; Sarah has done a nice thing and mailed her artwork to her friend, so Sarah does not <u>possess</u> that drawing any longer.

5. Going <u>ashore</u> means going from the water to the land. If you were driving in a car, you would already be on land, so you would not make that suggestion.

6. That's a tricky question: If you were in a <u>mob</u> of people, you would be surrounded by a crowd of others, so you would not be alone. However, if there were no one in the crowd you knew or felt comfortable being around, you might *feel* very much alone in that <u>mob</u>.

7. <u>Correspondents</u> are people who send or receive information from a distance. Since Alex is sending a letter a long way to Chris, they are <u>correspondents</u>.

8. To <u>recover</u> the ring means getting it back again after it has been lost or stolen. If it is on my finger, that means I have not lost it. Therefore, I could not <u>recover</u> it.

### Reading Warm-up A, p. 103

**Sample Answers**

1. <u>Cousin Isabel's cottage</u>; The sign on the front of the bus stated that its *destination* was the baseball field.

2. <u>(edges)</u>; I recognized the *outline* of his head and shoulders from across the street and knew that it had to be my dear friend, Greg.

3. <u>thought the edges of its roof looked different from the time when he had visited there</u>; *Previously*, she had thought she hated green eggs and ham, but after trying

them for the fifteenth time, she decided she liked them after all.

4. absorbed enough energy from the sun to supply all the power needed to run her water heater; *Solar* panels could be mounted on the roof of our school in order to supply some of the electricity we use in classrooms.

5. the lake and the mountains rising behind it; The sky-scrapers and old buildings of downtown Chicago are interesting and beautiful to look at, which makes them *scenic.*

6. (roasted marshmallows) (graham crackers and choco-late); Dakota wanted to *devour* the delicious-looking cake his little brother had baked, until his brother said, "It's a worm cake with chocolate icing."

7. (the flames died out) (were left, glowing in the dark); When I blew on the hot *embers*, tiny flames flickered up for a second or two.

8. (magically alive); I wish I had an *enchanted* broomstick, but I'm going to have to pick up the broom and do the sweeping myself!

## Reading Warm-up B, p. 104

### Sample Answers

1. (no longer aware of what she was doing); At baseball practice, I got hit in the head with a ball by accident and lost *consciousness* for a few seconds.

2. She soon hired a new coach; A synonym for *restless* is *eager*, or *impatient*.

3. (over the side of the boat); The last time I went for a ride in a rowboat, I dropped an oar *overboard* and had to grab it back out of the water.

4. (journalists); You can hear reports from *correspondents* on radio, television, computer, or anywhere that offers video news reports; you can read reports from *corre-spondents* in magazines, newspapers, or on a computer or another electronic device that delivers printed news.

5. England; That queasy, seasick feeling disappeared as soon as she was back *ashore.*

6. (two million people); You might find a *mob* at a music concert, a political demonstration, or at a store selling a new product that lots of people want to buy.

7. hearing; He is at home with the flu, but expects to *recover* and return to school soon.

8. had that quality; An antonym for *possess* is *lack.*

## Writing About the Big Question, p. 105

**A.** 1. team/group
2. common
3. diversity
4. environment

**B. Sample Answers**

1. I went camping in a state forest. I visited my mother's homeland.

2. Visiting my mother's homeland was the first time I was exposed to an entirely new **culture**. Their **customs** were very different, such as eating a large dinner in the mid-afternoon instead of evening.

**C. Sample Answer**

*Travel enriches an individual's view of the world. A com-munity of travelers* can educate people in their own com-munities about such things as how people live in other areas and the value of preserving our natural resources.

## Literary Analysis: Comparing Universal Themes, p. 106

1. "To the Top of Everest": Mount Everest; "The Voyage": Ancient Greece, at sea

2. "To the Top of Everest": a climb to the summit of Mount Everest; "The Voyage": an attempt to return home

3. "To the Top of Everest": information not mentioned; "The Voyage": Ino the White Goddess

4. "To the Top of Everest": focused; "The Voyage": deter-mined

5. "To the Top of Everest": the cold climate; "The Voyage": the storm at sea

6. "To the Top of Everest: the team reaches the summit; "The Voyage": Odysseus reaches the shore.

## Vocabulary Builder, p. 107

**A.** Sample Answers

1. **Explanation:** It does not make sense because to inflict is to cause pain or suffering.
   **New sentence:** Jenna inflicted pain with her rough grasp.

2. **Explanation:** It makes sense because liquid can easily soak cotton.
   **New sentence:** N/A.

3. **Explanation:** It makes sense because star players are often chosen as captains.
   **New sentence:** N/A.

4. **Explanation:** It does not makes sense because if you were unaffected by compliments, you would not smile.
   **New sentence:** Her blank look suggested she was impervious to our compliments.

**B.** 1. D; 2. A; 3. C

## Open-Book Test, p. 109

**Short Answer**

1. Yes, an area designated safe is a place that has been pointed out or marked as safe.
   **Difficulty:** *Easy* **Objective:** *Vocabulary*

2. The journey at that point was probably very, very difficult. Larson was probably too exhausted to write

more. Students should cite details relating to the arduousness of the trek to support their response.

**Difficulty:** *Easy*  **Objective:** *Interpretation*

3. As the climbers go higher, the amount of oxygen in the air continues to decrease. The climbers must adjust to the altitude a little bit at a time.

**Difficulty:** *Challenging*  **Objective:** *Interpretation*

4. Students should respond that they would want to be unaffected by a dangerous storm.

**Difficulty:** *Average*  **Objective:** *Vocabulary*

5. Sample answers: brave, strong, determined, skillful Odysseus survives because he has traits that are very useful for overcoming hardship.

**Difficulty:** *Average*  **Objective:** *Interpretation*

6. Poseidon's powers are equal to Athena's. She makes the waters calm for a while so that Odysseus can swim to shore, but the angry waves return to make his progress difficult.

**Difficulty:** *Challenging*  **Objective:** *Interpretation*

7. Larson goes on a very dangerous climb at a very high altitude. Odysseus continues to swim to shore even when he thinks Poseidon will dash him against the rocks.

**Difficulty:** *Easy*  **Objective:** *Literary Analysis*

8. Both Larson and Odysseus have experiences that test their courage. Larson is tested by the elements as she climbs Mount Everest. Odysseus is tested by Poseidon's anger as he tries to make his way to the shore.

**Difficulty:** *Average*  **Objective:** *Literary Analysis*

9. Larson has a great deal of support from others and never feels that she is in danger. Odysseus feels that he is in constant danger, and he has help only from Ino and Athena.

**Difficulty:** *Challenging*  **Objective:** *Literary Analysis*

10. Students should recognize that Larson is climbing Mount Everest by choice. Odysseus appears to be in a complicated situation that may not be entirely of his own choosing.

**Difficulty:** *Average*  **Objective:** *Literary Analysis*

## Essay

11. Students should note that both selections suggest that with bravery, one can overcome obstacles. Larson is only eighteen years old, but she does not let her inexperience stop her from climbing Mount Everest. She trains herself physically for the task and is mentally positive about the experience. Although the experience is difficult, she never thinks of giving up. Odysseus faces many obstacles. When Poseidon attacks him from the sea, causing waves to wreck his raft and batter his body, Odysseus calls on his strength to survive.

**Difficulty:** *Easy*  **Objective:** *Essay*

12. Some students may argue that Larson better lives up to the definition. Her climb of Everest is inspiring because it is an extraordinary accomplishment for an eighteen-year-old. Students who argue that Odysseus is the greater hero might note that he faces many more obstacles than Larson does. In fact, the assault on him by Poseidon could have been fatal, whereas Larson never mentions being in grave danger.

**Difficulty:** *Average*  **Objective:** *Essay*

13. Students should recognize that an epic is a long narrative; they should recognize that a narrator outside the story is describing a character. They should also note that Odysseus is a fictional character, his character traits are exaggerated, and the events are not realistic. In contrast, they should recognize that a blog is a first-person account; the subject of the blog is telling her own story, and all the events are true. Students should express their reactions to the differences in the genres.

**Difficulty:** *Challenging*  **Objective:** *Essay*

14. Students should note that "To the Top of the World" describes a group effort. Larson does not tackle Everest alone. She has the support of her father, a team, and the sherpas. Although her achievement is great, it is not an individual effort. Students should recognize that Odysseus efforts in "The Voyage" are largely individual. Odysseus is pitted against the sea in a fight for his life. He makes individual judgments about what action to take. However, students may point out that he is helped by Ino and Athena. Thus, there is some involvement of the community in Odysseus struggles.

**Difficulty:** *Average*  **Objective:** *Essay*

## Oral Response

15. Oral responses should be clear, well organized, and well supported by appropriate examples from the selections.

**Difficulty:** *Average*  **Objective:** *Oral Interpretation*

## Selection Test A, p. 112

### Critical Reading

| | | |
|---|---|---|
| 1. ANS: B | DIF: Easy | OBJ: Comprehension |
| 2. ANS: C | DIF: Easy | OBJ: Comprehension |
| 3. ANS: A | DIF: Easy | OBJ: Comprehension |
| 4. ANS: D | DIF: Easy | OBJ: Interpretation |
| 5. ANS: B | DIF: Easy | OBJ: Comprehension |
| 6. ANS: C | DIF: Easy | OBJ: Comprehension |
| 7. ANS: B | DIF: Easy | OBJ: Interpretation |
| 8. ANS: A | DIF: Easy | OBJ: Interpretation |
| 9. ANS: C | DIF: Easy | OBJ: Literary Analysis |
| 10. ANS: A | DIF: Easy | OBJ: Literary Analysis |
| 11. ANS: D | DIF: Easy | OBJ: Literary Analysis |
| 12. ANS: A | DIF: Easy | OBJ: Literary Analysis |

## Vocabulary

13. ANS: D     DIF: Easy     OBJ: Vocabulary
14. ANS: A     DIF: Easy     OBJ: Vocabulary
15. ANS: B     DIF: Easy     OBJ: Vocabulary

## Essay

16. Students should recognize that in "To the Top of Everest," Samantha faces the challenge of climbing higher than she ever has before in order to reach the summit of Mt. Everest. In "The Voyage," Odysseus journeys across a seemingly endless ocean while facing dangers presented by Poseidon. They should recognize that Samantha achieves her goal with the help of her team and various support crews. Odysseus overcomes his challenges with the help of the gods. Students should present a valid reason for finding one or the other character more successful or heroic.
    Difficulty: *Easy*    Objective: *Essay*

17. Students who choose "The Voyage" should explain that all of the characteristics are present. Students who choose "To the Top of Everest" should explain that the first three characteristics are present. They should note that the style of "To the Top of Everest" has a serious but informal style. For either work, students should cite details or examples that reflect the corresponding characteristics.
    Difficulty: *Easy*    Objective: *Essay*

18. Students should note that "To the Top of the World" describes a group effort. Larson does not tackle Everest alone. She has the support of her father, a team, and the sherpas. Students should recognize that Odysseus' efforts in "The Voyage" are mostly individual. Odysseus is pitted against the sea in a fight for his life. He makes individual judgments about what action to take, but he is helped by Ino and Athena. Thus there is some involvement of the community in Odysseus' struggles.
    Difficulty: *Average*    Objective: *Essay*

## Selection Test B, p. 115

### Critical Reading

1. ANS: B     DIF: Average     OBJ: Comprehension
2. ANS: C     DIF: Average     OBJ: Interpretation
3. ANS: A     DIF: Challenging     OBJ: Comprehension
4. ANS: A     DIF: Average     OBJ: Comprehension
5. ANS: D     DIF: Average     OBJ: Comprehension
6. ANS: A     DIF: Average     OBJ: Interpretation
7. ANS: D     DIF: Average     OBJ: Interpretation
8. ANS: C     DIF: Average     OBJ: Literary Analysis
9. ANS: A     DIF: Average     OBJ: Literary Analysis
10. ANS: B     DIF: Average     OBJ: Literary Analysis
11. ANS: D     DIF: Average     OBJ: Literary Analysis
12. ANS: A     DIF: Challenging     OBJ: Literary Analysis
13. ANS: B     DIF: Average     OBJ: Literary Analysis

## Vocabulary

14. ANS: C     DIF: Challenging     OBJ: Vocabulary
15. ANS: A     DIF: Average     OBJ: Vocabulary
16. ANS: D     DIF: Challenging     OBJ: Vocabulary
17. ANS: C     DIF: Average     OBJ: Vocabulary

## Essay

18. Students should note that both characters are on a quest and that both receive help, Odysseus from the gods and Samantha from her team and various support crews. They should also name two ways in which the characters are different, such as the fact that the sea god is actively creating difficulties for Odysseus, whereas Samantha faces only the natural obstacles presented by altitude and weather conditions. Students should support their opinions of whether one character is more heroic with at least one detail from that selection.
    Difficulty: *Average*    Objective: *Essay*

19. Students should recognize that all of the characteristics are present in "The Voyage." The first three are present in "To the Top of Everest," but the style of "To the Top of Everest" is less formal. They should suggest a sound reason to support their opinion of whether "To the Top of Everest" may be considered an epic.
    Difficulty: *Challenging*    Objective: *Essay*

20. Students should note that "To the Top of the World" describes a group effort. Larson does not tackle Everest alone. She has the support of her father, a team, and the sherpas. Although her achievement is great, it is not an individual effort. Students should recognize that Odysseus' efforts in "The Voyage" are largely individual. Odysseus is pitted against the sea in a fight for his life. He makes individual judgments about what action to take. However, students may point out that he is helped by Ino and Athena. Thus, there is some involvement of the community in Odysseus' struggles.
    Difficulty: *Average*    Objective: *Essay*

## Writing Workshop

### Business Letter: Integrating Grammar Skills, p. 119

**A.** 1. A; 2. A; 3. B

**B.** After the federal government cut money to the states, most state, county, and local governments had budget problems. Many libraries and other local services had to be cut back. Hoping to help, a group of people began Bookworms, an organization that is raising funds for the local library. One of the first things Bookworms organized was an art show. Many creative, talented artists donated their works, and the money from the sales went to the library.

## Benchmark Test 11, p. 120

### MULTIPLE CHOICE

1. ANS: A
2. ANS: C
3. ANS: D
4. ANS: C
5. ANS: D
6. ANS: B
7. ANS: D
8. ANS: B
9. ANS: C
10. ANS: A
11. ANS: B
12. ANS: D
13. ANS: C
14. ANS: D
15. ANS: A
16. ANS: C
17. ANS: D
18. ANS: B
19. ANS: C
20. ANS: A
21. ANS: B
22. ANS: A
23. ANS: B
24. ANS: A
25. ANS: D
26. ANS: B
27. ANS: C
28. ANS: A
29. ANS: C
30. ANS: D
31. ANS: A
32. ANS: B
33. ANS: D
34. ANS: C
35. ANS: D

### ESSAY

36. Students should indicate the action of the myth by identifying a problem or conflict and its solution or resolution. They should also indicate characters in the myth and the traits characters will display. They should indicate time of day and may also provide other setting details.

37. Students should clearly identify the place they are describing and the source from which it comes if it is not of their own invention. They should include in their descriptions details about the time and place as well as the overall environment or atmosphere of the place they describe. They should use vivid verbs and adjectives to make the description interesting.

38. Students should use either block or modified block format and should include a heading (with date), inside address, greeting, body, closing, and signature. They should clearly state their complaint about the product and give details supporting that complaint. They should use formal and polite language. They may suggest how a refund should be handled and include a question about whether or not they should return the product, and to where.

## "Sun and Moon in a Box"
by Richard Erdoes and Alfonso Ortiz

### Vocabulary Warm-up Exercises, p. 128

**A.**
1. eagle
2. cunning
3. reliable
4. relented
5. talons
6. wooded
7. burden
8. lag

**B. Sample Answers**

1. The *grasshoppers* could jump very far with their powerful hind legs.
2. If we lie and *betray* our friends, they will learn they cannot *rely* on us.
3. It is not very pleasant when someone is continuously *pestering* us.
4. The *outer* layer of clothing is the easiest one to remove if you are too warm.
5. The majority of voters *objected* to the proposed law, so it did not pass.
6. Because Tom *regretted* his rudeness, he decided to apologize.

## Reading Warm-up A, p. 129

### Sample Answers

1. (after a lot of pleading on my part); *Relented* means "became less stubborn."
2. The camp; A waterfall or hiking trails might be located in a *wooded* area.
3. (atop the cliffs); An *eagle* is "a large bird of the hawk family."
4. predator; Synonyms for *cunning* are *skillful* or *clever.*
5. The eagle will swoop at the slower bird. . . . The eagle quickly grasps the prey in its sharp talons and flies away with it.; Emily did not sleep well the night before, and so she started to *lag* behind in the race.
6. (the prey); Other animals with *talons* are hawks and dinosaurs.
7. (The prey it carries in its claws); *Burden* means "a load that is carried."
8. who always bring food back to the nest for the hungry chicks; The *reliable* crossing guard was always at her station each morning.

## Reading Warm-up B, p. 130

### Sample Answers

1. housed the families; *Outer* means "located farther out than another spot or place."
2. (The families were used to living together); A synonym for *embarrassed* is *flustered.*
3. (invaders); Spies who sell their country's secrets *betray* their nation.
4. If children wanted to join in the work; I have *objected* to people who do not pick up their litter.
5. The children's questions; A synonym for *pestering* is *bothering.*
6. (on being able to pass traditional skills on to the younger generation); May I *rely* on you to walk the dog for me tonight?
7. Over the years, unfortunately, some traditional skills and cultural activities faded away, as European practices took their place.; I have *regretted* not taking better care of my garden.
8. stones and minerals; *Grasshoppers* are "insects that leap and eat plants and have powerful hind legs."

## Writing About the Big Question, p. 131

**A.** 1. team/group
   2. environment
   3. common
   4. tradition

**B. Sample Answers**
   1. on an oral report; as a member of the debate club
   2. I worked with three classmates as part of a **team** to present an oral history report. Each **individual** had

his or her own unique task to complete. Luckily we were all hard workers; having that in common helped **unify** our group.

**C. Sample Answer**

*In order for people to work together as part of a team, they must* be honest and respectful. They must also each contribute equally to the task. Otherwise, certain individuals might unfairly bear the brunt of the work while others do very little. By being respectful and fair, the needs of both the individuals and the team can be met.

## Reading: Use Prior Knowledge to Compare and Contrast, p. 132

### Sample Answers

2. *Question:* Are the Kachinas like anything I have read about? Are they like the gods and goddesses in Greek myths? *Comparison/Contrast:* The Kachinas do not talk or interact with the Eagle and the Coyote. They seem more spiritual and more connected to nature than the Greek gods and goddesses.
3. *Question:* Is this box going to turn out to be like Pandora's box? *Comparison/Contrast:* Like Coyote, Pandora gets a box and is told not to open it. Like Coyote, Pandora is curious.
4. *Question:* What is the difference between what happens when Coyote opens his box and what happens when Pandora opens hers? *Comparison/Contrast:* When Coyote opens his box, winter comes to the Earth. When Pandora opens hers, all the troubles of the world are released.

## Literary Analysis: Cultural Context, p. 133

1. place; The references to "the west" and "a deep canyon" indicate that the folk tale is set in the American Southwest.
2. beliefs; The passage suggests that the Zuni believed that, at a much earlier time, the Kachinas controlled the sun and the moon. They treated them as if they were precious, using each one only a little at a time.
3. beliefs; The passage suggests that the Zuni believed that borrowing was acceptable but stealing was not.
4. customs *or* beliefs; The passage suggests that the Zuni helped one another with hard work; perhaps they believed it was embarrassing to be seen letting someone else do all the work.

## Vocabulary Builder, p. 134

**A.** 1. F; *Reliable* means "dependable," and a car that starts only half the time is not dependable.
   2. F; *Relented* means "gave in," and someone who refuses to give in to someone else's pleas has not relented.
   3. F; A person skilled in cheating would not get caught repeatedly.

3. F; A person skilled in cheating would not get caught repeatedly.

4. T; If he disliked it so much, he probably wished he hadn't seen it.

5. F; If a child is being annoying, parents would be irritated.

6. F; The neighbor's curiosity would make him want to know what others are up to.

**B. Sample Answers**

1. You test an object's elasticity by seeing how far it will stretch.

2. You might question a person's sincerity when his or her actions contradict his or her words.

3. You might appreciate a coworker's predictability because you can always count on him or her to behave a certain way.

## Enrichment: Coyote, the Character With Many Roles, p. 135

### Sample Answers

1. Coyote does not play the role of a hero. He is not part human, and he does not help any humans.

2. Coyote does play the role of a trickster. He tricks Eagle into letting him have the box, and then he runs off with it. He also is a survivor. Nothing serious happens as a result of his actions. He only has to listen to Eagle criticize him.

3. Coyote plays the role of a fool. He is foolish and greedy when he steals the box, and he is very foolish when he opens it.

4. Coyote teaches at least two lessons: Do not steal, and do not interfere with the harmony of the natural world.

## Open-Book Test, p. 136

### Short Answer

1. Eagle seems more impressive because he catches rabbits, which would be a filling meal. Coyote catches "nothing but grasshoppers."
   **Difficulty:** *Easy* **Objective:** *Reading*

2. Coyote is more of a burden than a companion. He cannot fly over canyons, and he is a bad swimmer.
   **Difficulty:** *Easy* **Objective:** *Interpretation*

3. The setting of the story is in the American West, in a Native American village, when "the earth was still soft and new." It shows a Native American people's version of how the sun and the moon came to be in the sky.
   **Difficulty:** *Challenging* **Objective:** *Literary Analysis*

4. They both believe that the sun and moon are very special and should be kept nearby to keep light and summer always at hand.
   **Difficulty:** *Average* **Objective:** *Literary Analysis*

5. The word *reliable* means "dependable." Because Coyote is not a good hunter or traveler, Eagle has little faith in him.
   **Difficulty:** *Average* **Objective:** *Vocabulary*

6. Coyote really wants to open the box. He says he is "ashamed" in order to persuade Eagle to allow him to carry the box. He is clever enough to know that if he simply asks to carry the box, Eagle will not let him.
   **Difficulty:** *Challenging* **Objective:** *Interpretation*

7. Coyote understands that Eagle is the leader, and he is the follower, just as though they were a Native American tribe with a chief.
   **Difficulty:** *Challenging* **Objective:** *Literary Analysis*

8. Eagle is concerned that Coyote's curiosity will get the better of him and fears that he cannot be trusted. Eagle not only has very little faith in Coyote but also feels superior to Coyote and free to insult him.
   **Difficulty:** *Average* **Objective:** *Interpretation*

9. *Relented* means "gave in." Eagle is not happy about the decision; he's just tired of saying no.
   **Difficulty:** *Average* **Objective:** *Vocabulary*

10. Sample answer: Question: How do we feel about stealing? Comparison: Both the Zuni and modern culture think stealing is wrong.
    **Difficulty:** *Average* **Objective:** *Reading*

### Essay

11. Students should point out that Eagle is smarter and more capable physically. Coyote is unable to hunt or travel very well. He is also completely controlled by his curiosity and has no thought for how opening the box might affect others, while Eagle is smart enough to know that opening the box will create problems for everyone.
    **Difficulty:** *Easy* **Objective:** *Essay*

12. Most students will say Eagle is more admirable. He is smarter and faster. He also understands that it is important not to steal the box. However, in some ways he is a more disappointing character. We expect Coyote to be sneaky and unaware of the damage he would do by opening the box, but it is surprising that Eagle allows himself to be persuaded to give the box to Coyote.
    **Difficulty:** *Average* **Objective:** *Essay*

13. Students may say that to the Kachinas, the effect of his borrowing the box is the same as stealing it. They have lost something precious to their community. Eagle justifies his action by labeling it as "borrowing," and he thinks he is better than Coyote. But he doesn't tell Coyote what he plans to do with the box, other than carry it around, and his action contributes to the problems that eventually occur when the box is opened.
    **Difficulty:** *Challenging* **Objective:** *Essay*

14. Students may say the community is valued more highly than the individual because the entire Kachina community protects the box in which the sun and moon are held, letting out some light carefully and occasionally. Eagle and Coyote do not have enough of an understanding of the impact their actions will have

on others until it is too late. Their actions are important specifically because they affect the community.

**Difficulty:** *Average*   **Objective:** *Essay*

## Oral Response

15. Oral responses should be clear, well organized, and well supported by appropriate examples from the selection.

**Difficulty:** *Average*   **Objective:** *Oral Interpretation*

## Selection Test A, p. 139

### Critical Reading

| | | |
|---|---|---|
| 1. ANS: A | DIF: Easy | OBJ: Literary Analysis |
| 2. ANS: C | DIF: Easy | OBJ: Comprehension |
| 3. ANS: C | DIF: Easy | OBJ: Interpretation |
| 4. ANS: B | DIF: Easy | OBJ: Comprehension |
| 5. ANS: C | DIF: Easy | OBJ: Reading |
| 6. ANS: C | DIF: Easy | OBJ: Reading |
| 7. ANS: C | DIF: Easy | OBJ: Interpretation |
| 8. ANS: A | DIF: Easy | OBJ: Interpretation |
| 9. ANS: C | DIF: Easy | OBJ: Comprehension |
| 10. ANS: A | DIF: Easy | OBJ: Interpretation |
| 11. ANS: C | DIF: Easy | OBJ: Interpretation |
| 12. ANS: B | DIF: Easy | OBJ: Literary Analysis |
| 13. ANS: B | DIF: Easy | OBJ: Literary Analysis |

### Vocabulary and Grammar

| | | |
|---|---|---|
| 14. ANS: C | DIF: Easy | OBJ: Vocabulary |
| 15. ANS: C | DIF: Easy | OBJ: Grammar |

### Essay

16. Students who think that Eagle should not have allowed Coyote to carry the box may cite the line in which Coyote suggests that they steal it. That statement strongly suggests that Coyote is not trustworthy. Students who agree with Eagle's decision to let Coyote carry the box may point to the animals' friendship or to Eagle's compassion for Coyote's claims that he will lose the respect of his family if he does not carry it; they may say that it is a virtue to trust one's fellow creatures.

**Difficulty:** *Easy*   **Objective:** *Essay*

17. Students may point out these similarities: Both are creatures, both are hunters, both are drawn to the box and its contents. They may point out these differences: Eagle is a bird; he travels by flying; Coyote is an animal; he travels by running and, when he has to, swimming. Coyote hunts grasshoppers; Eagle hunts rabbits. Coyote wants to steal the box containing the sun and the moon; Eagle wants only to borrow it. Eagle is reliable; Coyote is cunning and unreliable.

**Difficulty:** *Easy*   **Objective:** *Essay*

18. Students may say the community is valued more highly than the individual because the entire Kachina community protects the box in which the sun and moon are held, carefully letting out some light occasionally. Eagle and Coyote do not have enough of an understanding of the effect their actions will have on others until it is too late. Their actions are important because they affect the whole community.

**Difficulty:** *Average*   **Objective:** *Essay*

## Selection Test B, p. 142

### Critical Reading

| | | |
|---|---|---|
| 1. ANS: D | DIF: Average | OBJ: Literary Analysis |
| 2. ANS: C | DIF: Average | OBJ: Comprehension |
| 3. ANS: A | DIF: Average | OBJ: Comprehension |
| 4. ANS: B | DIF: Challenging | OBJ: Interpretation |
| 5. ANS: D | DIF: Challenging | OBJ: Literary Analysis |
| 6. ANS: C | DIF: Average | OBJ: Interpretation |
| 7. ANS: A | DIF: Average | OBJ: Interpretation |
| 8. ANS: B | DIF: Average | OBJ: Interpretation |
| 9. ANS: D | DIF: Average | OBJ: Interpretation |
| 10. ANS: B | DIF: Challenging | OBJ: Reading |
| 11. ANS: C | DIF: Average | OBJ: Reading |
| 12. ANS: C | DIF: Average | OBJ: Literary Analysis |
| 13. ANS: B | DIF: Average | OBJ: Literary Analysis |
| 14. ANS: C | DIF: Challenging | OBJ: Literary Analysis |

### Vocabulary and Grammar

| | | |
|---|---|---|
| 15. ANS: A | DIF: Average | OBJ: Vocabulary |
| 16. ANS: C | DIF: Average | OBJ: Vocabulary |
| 17. ANS: D | DIF: Average | OBJ: Grammar |
| 18. ANS: C | DIF: Average | OBJ: Grammar |

### Essay

19. Students who hold that Eagle shares in the responsibility should point out that Eagle takes the box in the first place and admits to knowing that Coyote is not reliable. Students who hold that Eagle is not responsible may point out that he meant only to borrow the box and that he is motivated by compassion—by the pity he feels for the arguments Coyote raises—to let Coyote carry the box for a while.

**Difficulty:** *Average*   **Objective:** *Essay*

20. Students should recognize that Coyote is deceitful, greedy, and uncontrollably curious, whereas Eagle is moderate and reliable. They should point out that Eagle's traits are undoubtedly ones the Zuni valued, whereas Coyote's traits are ones seen as undesirable.

**Difficulty:** *Challenging*   **Objective:** *Essay*

21. Students may say the community is valued more highly than the individual because the entire Kachina commu-

nity protects the box in which the sun and moon are held, letting out some light carefully and occasionally. Eagle and Coyote do not have enough of an understanding of the impact their actions will have on others until it is too late. Their actions are important specifically because they affect the community.

**Difficulty:** *Average*   **Objective:** *Essay*

## "How the Snake Got Poison"
by Zora Neale Hurston

## Vocabulary Warm-up Exercises, p. 146

**A.** 1. fight
2. enemy
3. claws
4. snakes
5. belly
6. poison
7. shakes
8. rattles

**B. Sample Answers**

1. vastness; The scope and <u>vastness</u> of the history book are very great.
2. world; We must take care of our <u>world</u> if we want it to survive.
3. decorate; We will <u>decorate</u> the house with flowers for the party.
4. defense; Our <u>defense</u> against burglars is a watch dog.
5. stamped; We <u>stamped</u> out the embers so a fire would not start.
6. relations; Past <u>relations</u> in our family fought in the Civil War.
7. topic; The <u>topic</u> of her term paper is the history of women's suffrage.

## Reading Warm-up A, p. 147

**Sample Answers**

1. (reptiles that have no legs); A few kinds of *snakes* are cobras, garter snakes, and copperheads.
2. (a snake moves along the ground) (Some snakes also use these muscles for climbing trees.); *Belly* means "the stomach or underside of an animal."
3. <u>deadly</u>; Some frogs have *poison* in their skin, which protects them from animals that might eat them.
4. (mountain lions or bears); Other animals that have *claws* are lizards, cats, dogs, and raccoons.
5. <u>rattlesnake</u>; *Fight* means "to take part in a physical struggle or battle."
6. (the series of rings called rattles that grow on its tail); Someone who *shakes* out a rug is usually trying to get the dirt out of it.

7. <u>on its tail</u>; *Rattles* are "rings on a rattlesnake's tail that make a rattling sound."
8. <u>the animals they like to eat. Such prey includes toads, lizards, mice, and birds</u>; *Enemy* means "a foe."

## Reading Warm-up B, p. 148

**Sample Answers**

1. <u>kinds of plants and animals</u>; *Earth* means "this world or the planet we live on."
2. (The growing grass and the graceful antelopes); I would *ornament* my room with posters and pictures of friends and family.
3. (the world's many habitats); An antonym for *immensity* is *smallness*.
4. <u>The immensity of the world's many habitats</u>; I wonder about the *subject* of how to predict earthquakes.
5. <u>a colony of termites</u>; *Stomped* means "to have injured or killed by stamping on or out."
6. (whales could not exist); I hope that future *generations* of my family will inherit a healthy planet earth.
7. (educating others about the importance of the balance of nature); I am working *towards* getting along better with my brothers.
8. <u>preserving the entire habitat in which it lives</u>; What kind of *protection* will we give to the more delicate plants in the garden during winter?

## Writing About the Big Question, p. 149

**A.** 1. individual
2. community
3. environment
4. common

**B. Sample Answers**

1. during a road trip to see my brother's first cross-country meet at college
2. It was a **family tradition** to see my brother's first race of the season. I was feeling car sick and needed to stop. We were running late, but if I got sick, we would be even later, so we took a five-minute break for fresh air.

**C. Sample Answer**

*When the needs of the individual and the needs of the larger group are in conflict,* everyone must be willing to work together to reach a compromise. That way, no one will feel taken advantage of or left out of the decision-making process.

## Reading: Use Prior Knowledge to Compare and Contrast, p. 150

Note: For students to write answers such as these, they would have to have some prior knowledge of snakes or have done some basic research.

## Sample Answers

2. *Question:* How are snakes portrayed in Greek mythology? *Comparison/Contrast:* In Greek mythology, the snake was sacred to medicine. That is why a staff with a snake coiled around it symbolizes medicine.

3. *Question:* How is this snake's behavior like that of the poisonous snakes described in the story "Rattlesnake Hunt"? *Comparison/Contrast:* Those snakes are active only when the weather is warm. Some of them live in gopher holes and will not come out unless they are disturbed.

4. *Question:* How does this solution compare with the way the rattlesnake uses its rattle in real life? *Comparison/Contrast:* I read that not all rattlesnakes use the rattle before they strike.

## Literary Analysis: Cultural Context, p. 151

### Sample Answers

1. The passage suggests that the African Americans who told this tale believed that all creatures have the right to protect themselves. Possibly the passage has a broader meaning: that all people must be able to protect themselves.

2. The passage suggests that the African Americans who told this tale believed that every creature should be allowed to protect itself but that it is wrong to kill every creature without regard to who it is or without first considering whether there is a need to kill.

3. The passage suggests that the African Americans who told this tale believed that friends should be protected from harm, but enemies deserve their fate.

## Vocabulary Builder, p. 152

**A.** 1. T; *Ornament* means "beautify," and those items would make a backyard beautiful.

2. F; *Immensity* is an immeasurably large space, so it could not easily be fenced in.

3. T; Bright colors look good on a person with a rosy complexion.

4. F; Gardeners would not want undesirable animals in their gardens.

**B. Sample Answers**

1. To stay in business, a company must be able to sell its products.

2. People would be reluctant to vote for someone they did not trust.

3. I would try to avoid such a hateful person.

## Enrichment: Snakes Are Not So Bad, p. 153

1. Most snakes avoid humans whenever they can and strike only when they are cornered or harassed.

2. Snakes are an important part of the food chain. They kill rats and mice that eat crops. They also are fed on by hawks, mongooses, and bigger snakes.

3. Snakes are dry and scaly, not slimy.

## "Sun and Moon in a Box"
by Richard Erdoes and Alfonso Ortiz
## "How the Snake Got Poison"
by Zora Neale Hurston

## Integrated Language Skills: Grammar, p. 154

**A.** 1. The character named Coyote suggested that they steal the box.

2. The folk tale takes place in the American Southwest, perhaps in present-day Arizona or New Mexico.

3. Coyote said to Eagle, "This is a wonderful thing."

4. "I do not trust you," Eagle said many times. "You will open that box."

**B.** Students' episodes should describe Coyote's actions after he opens the box containing the sun and the moon. Writing should be grammatically correct and should include at least one quotation, one proper noun, and one proper adjective, all correctly capitalized.

## "How the Snake Got Poison"
by Zora Neale Hurston

## Open-Book Test, p. 157

### Short Answer

1. The word *ornament* means "to beautify." The snake's pattern and colors decorate the ground.
   **Difficulty:** *Easy*   **Objective:** *Vocabulary*

2. The animals approach God by simply climbing up a ladder. This shows that the people who told the tale believed God was easily found.
   **Difficulty:** *Challenging*   **Objective:** *Literary Analysis*

3. God and the animals both speak in the same way ("Good mawnin," "How you makin' it?") to show that they are all connected and all similar.
   **Difficulty:** *Challenging*   **Objective:** *Interpretation*

4. The word *immensity* means "immeasurable vastness." This word is a good choice because it emphasizes the immeasurable vastness of God.
   **Difficulty:** *Average*   **Objective:** *Vocabulary*

5. "Snake's Complaints"—being stomped on, having no protection; "Varmints' Complaints"—being poisoned by the snake

   They both fear that if they are killed, the future of their race is in danger; they fear for their "generations."
   **Difficulty:** *Average*   **Objective:** *Reading*

6. The snake is "strikin' everything dat shakes de bushes," so the varmints are probably all the small animals that live in the bushes and that snakes eat: mice, rabbits, lizards.
   **Difficulty:** *Easy*   **Objective:** *Interpretation*

7. God seems disappointed. He expected that the snake would use the poison more carefully than he seems to be doing.
   **Difficulty:** *Average*   **Objective:** *Interpretation*

8. God gives the snake a bell to put on his tail. When he sees feet coming, the snake is to ring the bell. Friends (the varmints) will know it's the snake and avoid stepping on him. Enemies will have to take their chances.
   **Difficulty:** *Challenging*   **Objective:** *Interpretation*

9. It shows that they felt snakes were not all bad, and that they had the same rights to exist and protect themselves as any other creature.
   **Difficulty:** *Average*   **Objective:** *Literary Analysis*

10. God's attitude toward his creatures is friendly and caring. He wants to be fair to all of them, and he expects them to behave fairly toward one another. His attitude shows that the people who told the tale believed God was loving.
    **Difficulty:** *Challenging*   **Objective:** *Literary Analysis*

## Essay

11. Students should say that God in this story is both caring and helpful. He listens to the complaints of the snake and the other varmints and does not place one above the other. He tries to be fair so that all of the creatures he has created will be properly protected.
    **Difficulty:** *Easy*   **Objective:** *Essay*

12. Students should discuss the use of dialect, the beliefs shown about the ability and willingness of God to solve problems, the need to be able to protect oneself, and the explanation of a natural phenomenon (the snake's poison and rattle).
    **Difficulty:** *Average*   **Objective:** *Essay*

13. Students should point out the snake is lower than the other animals because he is "down in de dust." He also doesn't have the other protective aspects of other animals, such as claws or feet, to help him if there is a conflict between him and others. That is why he asks God twice to protect him. His situation is like that of a person who is not treated well by the rest of society. Humans can learn to think twice about "stepping on" those below them because even the lowliest creature can and will defend itself.
    **Difficulty:** *Challenging*   **Objective:** *Essay*

14. Some students may say the individual is more important: God solves all the problems. Others may say the community is more important because God places a value on each individual's worth to the community. Others may say they are equally important because each individual's needs are met so that the community will continue to thrive as a whole.
    **Difficulty:** *Average*   **Objective:** *Essay*

## Oral Response

15. Oral responses should be clear, well organized, and well supported by appropriate examples from the selection.
    **Difficulty:** *Average*   **Objective:** *Oral Interpretation*

## Selection Test A, p. 160

### Critical Reading

| | | |
|---|---|---|
| 1. ANS: B | DIF: Easy | OBJ: Literary Analysis |
| 2. ANS: B | DIF: Easy | OBJ: Comprehension |
| 3. ANS: C | DIF: Easy | OBJ: Interpretation |
| 4. ANS: A | DIF: Easy | OBJ: Reading |
| 5. ANS: C | DIF: Easy | OBJ: Comprehension |
| 6. ANS: A | DIF: Easy | OBJ: Comprehension |
| 7. ANS: A | DIF: Easy | OBJ: Reading |
| 8. ANS: D | DIF: Easy | OBJ: Comprehension |
| 9. ANS: D | DIF: Easy | OBJ: Comprehension |
| 10. ANS: C | DIF: Easy | OBJ: Interpretation |
| 11. ANS: A | DIF: Easy | OBJ: Literary Analysis |
| 12. ANS: B | DIF: Easy | OBJ: Interpretation |

### Vocabulary and Grammar

| | | |
|---|---|---|
| 13. ANS: B | DIF: Easy | OBJ: Vocabulary |
| 14. ANS: D | DIF: Easy | OBJ: Grammar |
| 15. ANS: C | DIF: Easy | OBJ: Grammar |

### Essay

16. Students who find the snake sneaky may suggest that it might have gotten along without the poison—there are many nonpoisonous snakes—or that it might not have attacked every creature that approached. Students who say the snake was not sneaky will likely argue that its complaints were reasonable. Students should express their opinion of the snake's character and defend it with a reference to at least one detail from the selection.
    **Difficulty:** *Easy*   **Objective:** *Essay*

17. Students may note that the informal style adds humor to the story and that the dialect makes the cultural context especially vivid, or they may object to those characteristics, saying that they detract from the message of the folk tale. Students should state their opinion of the effect of the dialect and informal style on the selection's overall effect and cite two examples to support their ideas.
    **Difficulty:** *Easy*   **Objective:** *Essay*

18. Some students may say the individual is more important: God solves all the problems. Others may say the community is more important because God places a value on each individual's worth to the community. Others may say they are equally important because each individual's needs are met so that the community will continue to thrive as a whole.
    **Difficulty:** *Average*   **Objective:** *Essay*

## Selection Test B, p. 163

### Critical Reading

1. ANS: B    DIF: Average    OBJ: Comprehension
2. ANS: C    DIF: Average    OBJ: Comprehension
3. ANS: A    DIF: Average    OBJ: Comprehension
4. ANS: B    DIF: Challenging    OBJ: Interpretation
5. ANS: B    DIF: Average    OBJ: Literary Analysis
6. ANS: D    DIF: Challenging    OBJ: Interpretation
7. ANS: D    DIF: Challenging    OBJ: Reading
8. ANS: C    DIF: Challenging    OBJ: Reading
9. ANS: A    DIF: Challenging    OBJ: Reading
10. ANS: C    DIF: Average    OBJ: Interpretation
11. ANS: D    DIF: Challenging    OBJ: Interpretation
12. ANS: D    DIF: Average    OBJ: Comprehension
13. ANS: A    DIF: Challenging    OBJ: Literary Analysis
14. ANS: C    DIF: Average    OBJ: Literary Analysis
15. ANS: B    DIF: Challenging    OBJ: Interpretation

### Vocabulary and Grammar

16. ANS: B    DIF: Average    OBJ: Vocabulary
17. ANS: A    DIF: Average    OBJ: Vocabulary
18. ANS: C    DIF: Average    OBJ: Grammar

### Essay

19. Students are likely to say that each argument is valid. Although the animals seem to be bickering, there is a sense that God solved the problem with the rattle, and that resolution suggests that the animals were not arguing for the sake of arguing—had they been, the rattle would not have solved the problem. Students may suggest alternative solutions or express satisfaction with the one described in the selection.

   Difficulty: *Average*    Objective: *Essay*

20. Students will likely recognize the tendency of people to defer to a third party rather than confront an adversary. They might mention the role that courts and labor mediators play in settling disputes.

   Difficulty: *Challenging*    Objective: *Essay*

21. Students should recognize that nature is out of balance because the snake has no natural means of defense. God's statement expresses the belief that every creature must be able to defend itself. Students may point out that God's first solution does not correct the balance—the other creatures are unable to defend themselves against the snake's poison. At last, God provides the snake with the rattle, and then the balance of nature is maintained.

   Difficulty: *Challenging*    Objective: *Essay*

22. Some students may say the individual is more important: God solves all the problems. Others may say the community is more important because God places a value on each individual's worth to the community. Others may say they are equally important because each individual's needs are met so that the community will continue to thrive as a whole.

   Difficulty: *Average*    Objective: *Essay*

## "The People Could Fly" by Virginia Hamilton

### Vocabulary Warm-up Exercises, p. 167

**A.**
1. plantation
2. horseback
3. labored
4. flock
5. firelight
6. hip
7. babe
8. soothe

**B. Sample Answers**

1. T; If one is very familiar with *African* folk tales, one probably knows a lot about Africa because *African* describes anything having to do with Africa.
2. F; *Clumsily* means Carol moves "awkwardly or ungracefully," which means she probably does not have the coordination to ice skate well.
3. T; *Bled* means he "was bleeding" and that is very likely if he cut himself.
4. F; *Misery* means "unhappiness," so the expression "misery loves company" means one wants others to feel unhappy, too.
5. T; *Souls* means "people," so if there were a lot of souls at the meeting, it means a lot of people were there.
6. F; *Sundown* is when the sun is setting at the end of the day, so one would not be waking up early at that time.
7. T; *Bawling* means "crying or wailing loudly," so if someone if crying she or he is not very happy.
8. T; *Slavery* means owning people as property and using the slaves as workers.

### Reading Warm-up A, p. 168

**Sample Answers**

1. (cotton); *Plantation* means "a farm or estate, sometimes cultivated by the workers who live there."
2. (she was not given enough time to care for me. Instead, she was sent back to the fields to work. The night was her favorite time, for then we were together again.); My mother said that when I was a *babe* I slept during the day instead of during the night.
3. the glow and warmth; I like how the *firelight* makes the room seem so cozy.
4. (I remember how my mother sometimes carried her in a sort of hip cloth tied to her body like a sling.); *Hip*

means "located by someone's hip bone at the top of the leg."

5. Being carried that way; Listening to soft music or going on a walk can *soothe* me.

6. (The overseer); People who ride on *horseback* often know how to make their horses trot and gallop.

7. Like a flock of birds or animals; A *flock* is "a large group of animals, people, or things that are found together."

8. Picking cotton was hard, hot work. It cut our hands. . . . Sometimes we sang songs to keep our spirits alive.; I have *labored* at finishing my homework assignment on time.

## Reading Warm-up B, p. 169

**Sample Answers**

1. large numbers of African people were captured by slave traders; The slaves brought their *African* heritage with them.

2. (were shipped like cargo, under terrible conditions. They were taken to the West Indies and to the Americas to be sold into slavery.); *Souls* means "people."

3. (Slave traders realized there was a great need for cheap labor in the West Indian and British colonies. They saw the taking of Africans as a way to fill this need and to profit by it.); *Slavery* is wrong because it is against the law and it is a bad way to treat other human beings; it treats a person as a piece of property and takes away his or her freedom, which is that person's right.

4. The captives' freedom and their culture were savagely stripped away from them. . . . they realized they would never see another sunrise or sundown as a free man or woman; *Misery* means "sorrow or discomfort."

5. The *sundown* takes place at dusk every day, so they realized that as slaves, every day, they would experience bondage, and the sunrises and sundowns would never be the same for them as when they were free.

6. (They were mercilessly chained together, causing them to move clumsily.); Yes, I have moved *clumsily* when I took part in a three-legged sack race.

7. Those who rebelled were beaten or whipped until they bled; The puppy bled when it cut its paw on a piece of glass.

8. (Unclean conditions and lack of food caused much illness, and the bawling of the suffering captives could be heard.); *Bawling* means "noisy crying or wailing."

## Writing About the Big Question, p. 170

**A.** 1. diversity
2. ethnicity
3. community/group
4. unity

**B. Sample Answers**

1. African Americans, Native Americans

2. African Americans came together as a **community** to fight for their civil rights. They were **unified** by the

philosophies of powerful leaders, such as Martin Luther King, Jr., and Malcolm X.

**C. Sample Answer**

*In order to unify people who share a common struggle, there needs to be a way to communicate a message of hope. If people feel hopeful as a group, it can inspire them as individuals because they feel they are moving toward the common goal of improving their lot, if not for themselves, then for future generations.*

## Reading: Use a Venn Diagram to Compare and Contrast, p. 171

1. *Toby:* is old, has no family, has learned to survive oppression, still remembers the magic words; *Both:* are descended from Africans, are enslaved, can fly; *Sarah:* is young, has a child, is being destroyed by oppression, no longer remembers the magic words

2. *Enslaved People:* are descended from Africans, are forced to work, may be whipped, are not free; *Both:* are human beings, work for the so-called master; *Overseer and Driver:* are descended from Europeans, choose to work, force the enslaved people to work, are free

## Literary Analysis: Folk Tale, p. 172

**Sample Answers**

1. The passage clearly presents evil. The people have been enslaved, and they are miserable.

2. The passage clearly presents evil. The Driver is cruelly whipping the people and causing them terrible pain.

3. The passage presents a clear distinction between good and evil. The woman has been hurt by the evil Driver. Toby represents good.

4. The passage presents a clear distinction between good and evil. Again the Driver represents evil, and Toby represents good.

5. This passage teaches a lesson about life. It suggests that you have to wait your turn, and when your turn comes, you must take it.

6. The passage teaches a lesson about life. It teaches that it is important to keep your heritage by teaching your children about the past.

## Vocabulary Builder, p. 173

**A.** 1. C; 2. D; 3. B; 4. C; 5. A; 6. D

**B. Sample Answers**

1. I would ask for an explanation or the reason for the request.

2. An ancient artifact might be considered mystical if it is thought to have some secret or spiritual meaning.

3. A person might see a mystic to find answers they cannot get from an ordinary person.

## Enrichment: Oral Tradition, p. 174

Students should commit to memory at least the story line and main ideas of a short, simple folk tale and be able to present it to a small audience.

## Open-Book Test, p. 175

### Short Answer

1. Sample answers: "Say that long ago in Africa . . ."; "Too crowded, don't you know."
   **Difficulty:** *Easy*   **Objective:** *Literary Analysis*

2. They had been "captured for Slavery" and crowded into ships. They were seasick and miserable "when they could no longer breathe the sweet scent of Africa."
   **Difficulty:** *Easy*   **Objective:** *Interpretation*

3. It was not possible to tell them apart. The people who could fly looked the same as the other slaves, with the same "dark skin."
   **Difficulty:** *Average*   **Objective:** *Reading*

4. The word *scorned* means "looked down upon." Sarah is one of the people who can fly, so she has always been free and respected. Being scorned is unbearable.
   **Difficulty:** *Challenging*   **Objective:** *Vocabulary*

5. Calling himself their Master does not make him their Master. He is in charge of their bodies but not their spirits. He is nothing but a "hard lump of clay."
   **Difficulty:** *Average*   **Objective:** *Interpretation*

6. The word *croon* means "to sing or hum soothingly." Sarah is unable to stop her work to take care of the baby. She also "had no heart" to do it. She is so upset that she cannot act in a soothing way.
   **Difficulty:** *Average*   **Objective:** *Vocabulary*

7. Toby helps and comforts Sarah. He tells her that she will be able to leave "soon." She looks to him for the magic words. The word "Father" is used by her to show love and respect.
   **Difficulty:** *Challenging*   **Objective:** *Interpretation*

8. Toby: strong, wise, calm, willing to wait until the right moment; Sarah: young, ready to give up, losing heart; both: can fly, want to escape to freedom

   Students should make a reasonable case for the character they choose. Toby is important because he leads them to freedom. Sarah is important because she carries the next generation with her to freedom.
   **Difficulty:** *Average*   **Objective:** *Reading*

9. This folk tale is a freedom tale told by enslaved Africans. The listeners were probably those enslaved people. The tale was meant to show them that some people had already escaped to freedom (the people who could fly) and that their chance would come.
   **Difficulty:** *Challenging*   **Objective:** *Literary Analysis*

10. The narrator says the slaves told the story to their children and the children told their children. The last line is "And now, me, I have told it to you."
    **Difficulty:** *Easy*   **Objective:** *Literary Analysis*

### Essay

11. Students should say that by using names for the slaves and titles for those who practice slavery, the author shows that the slaves are more human than those who control them. Sarah and Toby are more important to the message of the story, which is that they were greater and more important than the Master, the Overseer, and the Driver.
    **Difficulty:** *Easy*   **Objective:** *Essay*

12. Students should make these points: When they are in Africa, the people who can fly are like "blackbirds" with black shining wings. Once they are captured, they shed their wings for the long journey across the sea. Sarah flies like an eagle when she makes her escape, and when Toby helps the others, they rise on the air like black crows. The people who can fly are most like birds when they are free and least like birds when they are slaves.
    **Difficulty:** *Average*   **Objective:** *Essay*

13. Students may make these observations: The author may have chosen to describe the flying slaves—as they join hands in a circle, rise, and fly "against the heavenly blue"—to plant a clear picture in the minds of those on the ground who view the spectacular event. The author makes the image very special so the story will be told again and again through the generations, in order to preserve hope.
    **Difficulty:** *Challenging*   **Objective:** *Essay*

14. Some students may say that Toby is the most important character, so the individual is more important than the community. Toby is the only one who remembers the magic words and can thus help the community to freedom. Others may say the community is more important because they need each other to survive. The ones who can fly serve as a symbol of hope to the ones who are left on the ground. The story is handed down from one generation to the next in order to preserve the community.
    **Difficulty:** *Average*   **Objective:** *Essay*

### Oral Response

15. Oral responses should be clear, well organized, and well supported by appropriate examples from the selection.
    **Difficulty:** *Average*   **Objective:** *Oral Interpretation*

## Selection Test A, p. 178

### Critical Reading

| | | |
|---|---|---|
| 1. **ANS:** A | **DIF:** Easy | **OBJ:** Comprehension |
| 2. **ANS:** B | **DIF:** Easy | **OBJ:** Comprehension |
| 3. **ANS:** C | **DIF:** Easy | **OBJ:** Interpretation |
| 4. **ANS:** D | **DIF:** Easy | **OBJ:** Comprehension |
| 5. **ANS:** B | **DIF:** Easy | **OBJ:** Reading |
| 6. **ANS:** B | **DIF:** Easy | **OBJ:** Comprehension |

| 7. ANS: A | DIF: Easy | OBJ: Literary Analysis |
| 8. ANS: C | DIF: Easy | OBJ: Reading |
| 9. ANS: D | DIF: Easy | OBJ: Interpretation |
| 10. ANS: C | DIF: Easy | OBJ: Interpretation |
| 11. ANS: D | DIF: Easy | OBJ: Literary Analysis |
| 12. ANS: C | DIF: Easy | OBJ: Literary Analysis |
| 13. ANS: A | DIF: Easy | OBJ: Literary Analysis |

## Vocabulary and Grammar

| 14. ANS: B | DIF: Easy | OBJ: Vocabulary |
| 15. ANS: D | DIF: Easy | OBJ: Grammar |

## Essay

16. Students should recognize Toby's kindness, generosity, knowledge of magic, and willingness to help other slaves escape to freedom and the Overseer's cruelty, use of physical punishment to control the slaves, and willingness to try to prevent the slaves from escaping.
   Difficulty: *Easy* Objective: *Essay*

17. Students should recognize that the folk tale depicts the degradation and injustice of slavery as well as the importance of freedom and the importance of not giving up hope for freedom.
   Difficulty: *Easy* Objective: *Essay*

18. Some students may say that Toby is the most important character, so the individual is more important than the community. Toby is the only one who remembers the magic words and can thus help the community to freedom. Others may say the community is more important because they need one another to survive. The ones who can fly serve as a symbol of hope to the ones who are left on the ground. The story is handed down from one generation to the next in order to preserve the community.
   Difficulty: *Average* Objective: *Essay*

### Selection Test B, p. 181

## Critical Reading

| 1. ANS: C | DIF: Average | OBJ: Comprehension |
| 2. ANS: C | DIF: Average | OBJ: Interpretation |
| 3. ANS: D | DIF: Average | OBJ: Reading |
| 4. ANS: A | DIF: Average | OBJ: Interpretation |
| 5. ANS: A | DIF: Average | OBJ: Comprehension |
| 6. ANS: D | DIF: Challenging | OBJ: Reading |
| 7. ANS: C | DIF: Average | OBJ: Interpretation |
| 8. ANS: B | DIF: Average | OBJ: Reading |
| 9. ANS: C | DIF: Average | OBJ: Interpretation |
| 10. ANS: D | DIF: Challenging | OBJ: Interpretation |
| 11. ANS: B | DIF: Average | OBJ: Literary Analysis |
| 12. ANS: B | DIF: Average | OBJ: Interpretation |
| 13. ANS: D | DIF: Challenging | OBJ: Literary Analysis |

| 14. ANS: B | DIF: Challenging | OBJ: Literary Analysis |
| 15. ANS: A | DIF: Average | OBJ: Literary Analysis |

## Vocabulary and Grammar

| 16. ANS: B | DIF: Average | OBJ: Vocabulary |
| 17. ANS: A | DIF: Average | OBJ: Vocabulary |
| 18. ANS: C | DIF: Challenging | OBJ: Vocabulary |
| 19. ANS: B | DIF: Challenging | OBJ: Grammar |

## Essay

20. Students should offer a well-reasoned explanation of the purpose of the folk tale—for example, that it gave the people hope by showing them triumphing over their enslavement or that it strengthened the community by maintaining their cultural heritage.
   Difficulty: *Average* Objective: *Essay*

21. Students should note that both characters are enslaved and both are among those who could fly. They might point out that Sarah is young whereas Toby is old, and Sarah is a mother whereas Toby is not said to have any family. More important, students may realize that Toby has somehow learned to survive the oppression of the Overseer, whereas Sarah appears to be destroyed by it. Toby also has remembered the magic words that allow him to fly, whereas Sarah has forgotten them. Students may suggest that whereas Toby is a savior of sorts, Sarah is a person worthy of being saved.
   Difficulty: *Challenging* Objective: *Essay*

22. Some students may say that Toby is the most important character, so the individual is more important than the community. Toby is the only one who remembers the magic words and can thus help the community to freedom. Others may say the community is more important because they need one another to survive. The ones who can fly serve as a symbol of hope to the ones who are left on the ground. The story is handed down from one generation to the next in order to preserve the community.
   Difficulty: *Average* Objective: *Essay*

## "All Stories Are Anansi's" by Harold Courlander

### Vocabulary Warm-up Exercises, p. 185

**A.** 1. accepted
   2. respect
   3. offering
   4. opinion
   5. protect
   6. therefore

**B. Sample Answers**

1. (argument); The <u>argument</u> between two guests ruined the party.

2. (captive); The captive tried to escape, but he got caught.

3. (admit); Peter had to admit that his brother was better-looking than he.

4. (in the habit of); I'm in the habit of taking a shortcut through the mall to get home.

5. (soldiers); Some soldiers seem too young to fight in a war.

## Reading Warm-up A, p. 186

**Sample Answers**

1. as a gift from the gods; I *accepted* the invitation to Pam's party.

2. storytelling is just for children; In my *opinion*, children watch too much television.

3. insights into what we as a group admire and fear; Traditional tales teach us about ourselves by *providing* insights into what we as a group admire and fear.

4. (folk stories); *Respect* means "to feel admiration for someone or something."

5. (dying out); I think that our community should *protect* and preserve the old historic section of town, declare it a landmark, and prevent it from being torn down.

6. each listener imagines the world in a personal way; I am good in math and study hard, *therefore*, I always get As in the subject.

## Reading Warm-up B, p. 187

**Sample Answers**

1. (this claim); Some people may *argue* this claim.

2. spiders do keep the insect population in check. *Acknowledge* means "to admit."

3. (used to); I'm *accustomed to* seeing my sister putting on makeup in the morning.

4. cast its small flat web down upon its prey; A synonym for *prisoner* is *captive*.

5. around in the dirt; Spiders are often *prowling* along the walls and ceiling of my house.

6. secretly watching, silently capturing, and steadily devouring the earth's smallest enemies; I've read about the Greek *warriors* who fought over Helen of Troy.

## Writing About the Big Question, p. 188

**A.** 1. group
   2. team
   3. environment
   4. individuals
   5. community

**B.** **Sample Answers**

1. Enron executives; Local car dealer

2. A local car dealer was arrested for selling cars that had been flooded during Hurricane Katrina. People in the **community** were unaware of the cars' histories. When they found out, they hired a **team** of lawyers and took the dealer to court.

**C.** **Sample Answer**

*When an individual exploits others for personal gain,* that individual endangers the community by causing people to lose faith in their fellow citizens. People may become suspicious of one another's motives. These individuals should seek other ways to achieve their goals so that everyone benefits.

## Reading: Use a Venn Diagram to Compare and Contrast, p. 189

1. *Anansi:* is a spider, wants to own all stories, is deceitful; *Both:* are animals in the same jungle; *Onini:* is a snake, is proud; is trusting

2. *Hornets:* are small, are insects, are taken live to the Sky God; *Both:* are dwellers in the same jungle, trust Anansi, are fooled by Anansi, are captured by Anansi; *Leopard:* is huge, is a mammal, is killed by Anansi

## Literary Analysis: Folk Tale, p. 190

**Sample Answers**

1. The passage shows that storytelling was highly valued.

2. The passage teaches the lesson that it is dangerous to be too trusting.

3. This passage also shows that storytelling was highly valued. OR This passage teaches the lesson that if you work hard to achieve something, you will be rewarded.

## Vocabulary Builder, p. 191

**A.** 1. C; 2. A; 3. C; 4. B; 5. D; 6. A

**B.** **Sample Answers**

1. You might fail to notice a new haircut or other recent change.

2. I would say "hello" or wave to let my friend know I see him or her.

3. His or her intelligence makes him or her likely to know—or be able to guess at—the answer.

## Enrichment: Making Plans, p. 192

Students should describe a plan for catching each creature—for example, they might suggest putting honey in a jar, waiting for the hornets to fly into it, and putting a lid on the jar. Their plans need not be practical, but their descriptions should demonstrate some understanding of what might be involved in trapping the animals named.

**"The People Could Fly"** by Virginia Hamilton
**"All Stories Are Anansi's"** by Harold Courlander

## Integrated Language Skills: Grammar, p. 193

**A.** 1. James lives at 115 Elm St., Pleasant Valley, NE.

   2. The gardener said that if your yard measures 50 ft. (16.6 yds.) by 40 ft. (13.3 yds.), you will need 2 lbs. of fertilizer.

3. Mr. Raymond works for the UN.
**B.** Students should write a grammatically correct message that contains at least five correctly formed abbreviations.

## "All Stories Are Anansi's" by Harold Courlander
### Open-Book Test, p. 196
### Short Answer
1. Anansi is a trickster, a common folk tale character. He plays tricks on other animals to get what he wants.
   **Difficulty:** *Average*  **Objective:** *Literary Analysis*
2. Anansi is a spider, a small and seemingly weak creature. The others who have come to the Sky God were rich and powerful.
   **Difficulty:** *Average*  **Objective:** *Reading*
3. The word *yearned* means "wanted very much." The hornets probably yearned to get out of the gourd and sting Anansi.
   **Difficulty:** *Average*  **Objective:** *Vocabulary*
4. He tricks the hornets by pretending it is raining so he can trap them in a gourd.
   **Difficulty:** *Easy*  **Objective:** *Literary Analysis*
5. The python was fooled because he wanted to prove that he was longer, stronger, and deserved respect. The lesson is to beware of flatterers.
   **Difficulty:** *Challenging*  **Objective:** *Literary Analysis*
6. Students should make a reasonable case for either. The hornets simply had to check to see if it was really raining. The python should not have allowed himself to be tied up.
   **Difficulty:** *Average*  **Objective:** *Interpretation*
7. Sample answer: It is another way to show his cleverness and what a trickster he is. He tricked the leopard, who is much bigger and stronger, twice.
   **Difficulty:** *Challenging*  **Objective:** *Interpretation*
8. Anansi traps and kills the leopard. He fears the leopard because of his strength and the fact that he eats spiders. He cannot carry a live leopard to the Sky God.
   **Difficulty:** *Easy*  **Objective:** *Interpretation*
9. Hornets: tricks them into flying into a gourd to stay dry; Python: flatters him into being measured and then tied to a pole; Leopard: traps him, tricks him into being tied to a tree, kills him.
   Sample answer: The python was the most foolish because he allowed himself to be flattered. The other animals were at least trying to save themselves from something.
   **Difficulty:** *Average*  **Objective:** *Reading*
10. The word *acknowledge* means "to recognize and admit." Most people would not want others to recognize a mistake they had made.
    **Difficulty:** *Easy*  **Objective:** *Vocabulary*

### Essay
11. Anansi easily tricks the hornets into thinking it was raining and traps them in a gourd. He knows the foolish hornets will move in a group without checking the situation. He flatters the python into being tied to a bamboo pole, obviously knowing that the python is vain and would want to be thought of as longest and strongest. Anansi treats the leopard with the most care. He traps him indirectly and then tricks him again by bargaining with him. However, he obviously fears the leopard and kills him before taking him to the Sky God.
    **Difficulty:** *Easy*  **Objective:** *Essay*
12. Students may say that Anansi is not an admirable character. He tricks the other animals and even kills the leopard all in order to get what he wants. He is, however, successful even though he is smaller and less powerful than others who have tried to buy the stories. The author may be pointing out that being bigger, richer, and stronger is not always the road to success. The author is also teaching the lesson to be wary of tricksters.
    **Difficulty:** *Average*  **Objective:** *Essay*
13. Students may say that whoever "owns" the stories controls what information is passed down from generation to generation in a culture. Traditions, lessons, and beliefs that were important to a culture were often told in folk tales that were handed down over time. The culture probably believed that stories were not meant for the rich and powerful to have—Anansi the lowly spider succeeds where "rich and powerful families have not been able to pay." Stories were for everyone, particularly those who did not have much else.
    **Difficulty:** *Challenging*  **Objective:** *Essay*
14. Students will probably say Anansi sees himself as most important, as he is willing to sacrifice others for his own success. They may or may not agree with him. He is important as an individual because he does look out for himself first. However, as owner of the stories, he plays an important role in the community.
    **Difficulty:** *Average*  **Objective:** *Essay*

### Oral Response
15. Oral responses should be clear, well organized, and well supported by appropriate examples from the selection.
    **Difficulty:** *Average*  **Objective:** *Oral Interpretation*

### Selection Test A, p. 199
### Critical Reading
| | | |
|---|---|---|
| 1. ANS: D | DIF: Easy | OBJ: Literary Analysis |
| 2. ANS: B | DIF: Easy | OBJ: Comprehension |
| 3. ANS: C | DIF: Easy | OBJ: Interpretation |
| 4. ANS: A | DIF: Easy | OBJ: Comprehension |
| 5. ANS: B | DIF: Easy | OBJ: Interpretation |

| | | |
|---|---|---|
| 6. ANS: A | DIF: Easy | OBJ: Interpretation |
| 7. ANS: C | DIF: Easy | OBJ: Interpretation |
| 8. ANS: D | DIF: Easy | OBJ: Interpretation |
| 9. ANS: B | DIF: Easy | OBJ: Interpretation |
| 10. ANS: C | DIF: Easy | OBJ: Reading |
| 11. ANS: C | DIF: Easy | OBJ: Reading |
| 12. ANS: A | DIF: Easy | OBJ: Literary Analysis |
| 13. ANS: A | DIF: Easy | OBJ: Literary Analysis |

## Vocabulary and Grammar

| | | |
|---|---|---|
| 14. ANS: B | DIF: Easy | OBJ: Vocabulary |
| 15. ANS: B | DIF: Easy | OBJ: Grammar |

## Essay

16. Students who admire Anansi should point out that he is a tiny spider who uses his intelligence to get the better of animals who are bigger, stronger, and more powerful than he; students who do not admire him may point out that Anansi should not be respected because he uses trickery and takes advantage of his victims' weaknesses to get what he wants.

    **Difficulty:** *Easy*  **Objective:** *Essay*

17. Students' responses should reflect their understanding of Anansi's trick in each case, taking advantage of the hornets' dislike or fear of rain, the python's pride in his length, and the leopard's habit of walking along the ground. Students are likely to choose the hornets' or the python's capture if they are inclined to appreciate Anansi's verbal skills; they will choose the leopard's capture if they enjoy the physical trickery and the image of a tiny spider causing a leopard to be hung from a tree.

    **Difficulty:** *Easy*  **Objective:** *Essay*

18. Students will probably say Anansi sees himself as most important because he is willing to sacrifice others for his own success. They may or may not agree with him. He is important as an individual because he does look out for himself first. However, as owner of the stories, he plays an important role in the community.

    **Difficulty:** *Average*  **Objective:** *Essay*

## Selection Test B, p. 202

### Critical Reading

| | | |
|---|---|---|
| 1. ANS: C | DIF: Average | OBJ: Literary Analysis |
| 2. ANS: B | DIF: Average | OBJ: Comprehension |
| 3. ANS: D | DIF: Average | OBJ: Comprehension |
| 4. ANS: A | DIF: Challenging | OBJ: Literary Analysis |
| 5. ANS: A | DIF: Average | OBJ: Interpretation |
| 6. ANS: D | DIF: Average | OBJ: Reading |
| 7. ANS: C | DIF: Average | OBJ: Reading |
| 8. ANS: D | DIF: Average | OBJ: Interpretation |

| | | |
|---|---|---|
| 9. ANS: B | DIF: Challenging | OBJ: Literary Analysis |
| 10. ANS: C | DIF: Average | OBJ: Reading |
| 11. ANS: D | DIF: Average | OBJ: Literary Analysis |
| 12. ANS: B | DIF: Challenging | OBJ: Interpretation |
| 13. ANS: A | DIF: Challenging | OBJ: Interpretation |
| 14. ANS: A | DIF: Average | OBJ: Reading |

## Vocabulary and Grammar

| | | |
|---|---|---|
| 15. ANS: A | DIF: Average | OBJ: Vocabulary |
| 16. ANS: C | DIF: Average | OBJ: Vocabulary |
| 17. ANS: D | DIF: Average | OBJ: Grammar |
| 18. ANS: C | DIF: Challenging | OBJ: Grammar |

## Essay

19. Students may argue that Anansi is simply out to prove that he is craftier than the most powerful families, the great warriors, and the great chiefs. Alternatively, they may point out that storytelling must have been highly prized by the people who told this tale, and Anansi wants the everlasting glory that his achievement wins for him: Everyone who tells a story from then on must acknowledge that the story belongs to Anansi.

    **Difficulty:** *Average*  **Objective:** *Essay*

20. Among the elements that students might mention are these: The Africans who told "All Stories Are Anansi's" lived in a forest and were very familiar with the habits of wild animals; they valued intelligence and enjoyed the exploits of trickster characters; they respected small creatures that are able to defeat those who are stronger and more powerful than they; they prized the tradition of storytelling; they taught their children that naivete and foolishness are potentially dangerous character traits.

    **Difficulty:** *Challenging*  **Objective:** *Essay*

21. Students will probably say Anansi sees himself as most important, as he is willing to sacrifice others for his own success. They may or may not agree with him. He is important as an individual because he does look out for himself first. However, as owner of the stories, he plays an important role in the community.

    **Difficulty:** *Average*  **Objective:** *Essay*

## "The Fox Outwits the Crow" by William Cleary
## "The Fox and the Crow" by Aesop

### Vocabulary Warm-up Exercises, p. 206

**A.** 1. whiff
  2. curves
  3. figure
  4. snatched
  5. trust
  6. fondly

**B.** Sample Answers

1. The most <u>glamorous</u> thing I have ever done is ride in a convertible with the top down.

2. I would never act out of <u>malice</u> toward a friend because I value the friendship and would never want to hurt someone I care about.

3. I <u>exchange</u> cards and sometimes gifts with my friends on Valentine's Day.

4. People like stories with a <u>moral</u> because that lesson can usually be applied to something in their daily lives.

5. My <u>advice</u> to that person would be "Shop around until you find the best value for your money!"

## Reading Warm-up A, p. 207

**Sample Answers**

1. (lovingly); She *fondly* kissed her mother goodbye.

2. <u>of her body</u>; *Curves* are round, bending lines.

3. (of a man); Mira turned to see the *shape* of a man wearing clothes of purple satin and a peacock-feathered hat.

4. <u>his perfume</u>; Sometimes I get a *whiff* of the fresh coffee my mom is making in the morning.

5. (Vanity); I *trust* my dad because he is smart and honest.

6. (mirror); Jack *grabbed* hold of the Golden Goose and raced down the ladder with the Giant behind him.

## Reading Warm-up B, p. 208

**Sample Answers**

1. (many tropical birds); I think movie stars are *glamorous*.

2. <u>bits of food</u>; *Exchange* means "trade one thing for another."

3. <u>acts of evil intent</u>; The evil alien in the sci-fi movie looked at his victim with *malice*.

4. (false words); People use *flattery* to trick other people into giving them something they want.

5. (lesson); I like the *moral* that says, "Don't count your chickens before they hatch!" which to me means, "Don't expect things that might not happen."

6. (from spirits); My friend always asks for my *advice*, but she never follows it.

## Writing About the Big Question, p. 209

**A.** 1. unique

2. community, family, group

3. duty

4. individual

**B.** **Sample Answers**

1. "Saving Shiloh"; "Tuck Everlasting."

2. "Saving Shiloh," a story about a boy, his **family**, and an abused dog, taught me to try to understand what it is that might be causing a person to act cruelly. The **individual** who owned Shiloh could have been seen only as a ruthless villain, but he is actually a sad, complicated, lonely man.

**C.** **Sample Answer**

*One of the purposes of literature is to teach individuals how to* analyze human behavior. It reminds us that people are motivated by many different things. Before we can understand their actions, we need to understand their circumstances.

## Literary Analysis: Comparing Tone, p. 210

**Sample Answers**

Note that students may use *serious* instead of *formal* and *informal* instead of *playful*, and vice versa, but not *serious* instead of *playful*, and so on:

**A.** 1. informal / formal

2. playful / serious

3. playful / formal

**B.** 1. Poem: The crow is vain and the fox is witty and greedy; Fable: The crow is vain and the fox is self-important and deceptive.

2. Poem: The fox wants the crow's cheese; Fable: The fox feels he is more deserving of the crow's cheese.

3. Poem: The fox uses lighthearted flattery to trick the crow into dropping her cheese; Fable: The fox uses formal and effusive flattery to trick the crow into dropping her cheese.

4. Both stories suggest that vanity can have negative consequences and greed can motivate people to say things they do not mean.

## Vocabulary Builder, p. 211

**A.** **Sample answers follow the true or false designations:**

1. T; A bloodhound's sense of smell is very strong.

2. F; *Flatterers* are dishonest and insincere.

3. F; Something that is *glossy* has a smooth, shiny finish.

4. T; Most people would feel ill will toward someone who has harmed them.

5. F; *Hors d'oeuvres* are served before a main course.

6. T; To exceed expectations, one must do better than expected.

**B.** 1. D; 2. C; 3. D

## Open-Book Test, p. 213

**Short Answer**

1. The crow takes the cheese to the top of the tree to eat it by herself. The poem says that she wants "To enjoy her good fortune alone."
   **Difficulty:** *Average*   **Objective:** *Interpretation*

2. The crow is proud. She thinks that the fox will enjoy listening to her voice.
   **Difficulty:** *Easy*   **Objective:** *Interpretation*

3. *Malice* means "ill will." A comment made out of malice is intended to hurt or offend.
   **Difficulty:** *Challenging*   **Objective:** *Vocabulary*

4. *Surpass* means "be superior to." In order to be superior to someone who gets a B on a report, you would have to get a B+ or better.
   **Difficulty:** *Average*   **Objective:** *Vocabulary*

5. Beginning: kind, flattering, tells crow she is beautiful; End: cold, not nice to crow anymore
   Once he gets what he wants (the cheese), he doesn't have to be nice to the crow.
   **Difficulty:** *Average*   **Objective:** *Interpretation*

6. Like the Fox, flatterers do not mean what they say. They have hidden purposes.
   **Difficulty:** *Challenging*   **Objective:** *Interpretation*

7. "The Fox Outwits the Crow" is more playful. The fox says things like "Hey, you glamorous thing . . ." He gets a "whiff of the cheese."
   **Difficulty:** *Average*   **Objective:** *Literary Analysis*

8. Aesop's tone is formal or serious. Master Fox speaks formally to the crow, as when he says "How well you are looking today: how glossy your feathers; how bright your eye."
   **Difficulty:** *Easy*   **Objective:** *Literary Analysis*

9. Aesop's fox is more of a threat. The tone of the fable is serious, so the author seems to take the fox more seriously. Aesop's fox is more cold-hearted than the laughing fox in Cleary's version.
   **Difficulty:** *Challenging*   **Objective:** *Literary Analysis*

10. Cleary's crow is sillier. She takes out a libretto and tries to caw in falsetto. Cleary's light-hearted tone makes the crow seem ridiculous.
    **Difficulty:** *Average*   **Objective:** *Literary Analysis*

## Essay

11. Students should note that both characters flatter a crow to get her to drop some cheese, so they are both clever. They differ in that the fox in the poem seems slightly more evil, as he is full of malice. The Fox in the fable bears the Crow no ill will—he just wants the cheese. In addition, the two characters differ in the tone of their speech. The fox in the poem speaks playfully, while the Fox in the fable speaks formally. Some students might prefer the fox in the poem because he is a more humorous character. Others might prefer the Fox in the fable because he is more persuasive.
    **Difficulty:** *Easy*   **Objective:** *Essay*

12. Students should note that both characters are very much alike: both find a piece of cheese; both are vain; both fall victim to the fox's flattery and lose the cheese; both learn that flatterers are not to be trusted. For differences, students may point to the additional details in "The Fox Outwits the Crow," such as those about opera. They should note that the additional details in the selection make the crow's attitude seem more extreme—she seems more vain and arrogant than the Crow in "The Fox and the Crow."
    **Difficulty:** *Average*   **Objective:** *Essay*

13. Students should point to the playfulness and informality of the poem and the seriousness and formality of the fable. They might note that the fox in the poem is more aggressive and that the poem includes more details, such as those about opera. Students should recognize that Aesop seems to want only that his readers learn a lesson, while Cleary seems to want to amuse his readers as well and perhaps impress them with his cleverness. Students might note that the tone of the poem does not allow the reader to take it too seriously, just as the author himself does not take the subject matter too seriously. On the other hand, the formal fable was meant to be taken seriously, so the reader gives it more credibility.
    **Difficulty:** *Challenging*   **Objective:** *Essay*

14. Students should indicate that both the fox and the crow think only of themselves, not of the community. The crow finds a piece of cheese, which she intends to eat alone. She had no thought about sharing her food with other birds. The fox comes up with a plan to steal the cheese for himself. Again, the character thinks only of his personal needs. Neither one seems concerned with the good of the community, but only with self-interest. As a result, they would feel that the individual is more important than the community.
    **Difficulty:** *Average*   **Objective:** *Essay*

## Oral Response

15. Oral responses should be clear, well organized, and well supported by appropriate examples from the selections.
    **Difficulty:** *Average*   **Objective:** *Oral Interpretation*

### Selection Test A, p. 216

## Critical Reading

| | | |
|---|---|---|
| 1. ANS: A | DIF: Easy | OBJ: Comprehension |
| 2. ANS: D | DIF: Easy | OBJ: Interpretation |
| 3. ANS: C | DIF: Easy | OBJ: Comprehension |
| 4. ANS: A | DIF: Easy | OBJ: Literary Analysis |
| 5. ANS: D | DIF: Easy | OBJ: Interpretation |
| 6. ANS: C | DIF: Easy | OBJ: Interpretation |
| 7. ANS: B | DIF: Easy | OBJ: Interpretation |
| 8. ANS: B | DIF: Easy | OBJ: Literary Analysis |
| 9. ANS: C | DIF: Easy | OBJ: Interpretation |
| 10. ANS: B | DIF: Easy | OBJ: Literary Analysis |
| 11. ANS: A | DIF: Easy | OBJ: Literary Analysis |
| 12. ANS: C | DIF: Easy | OBJ: Literary Analysis |

## Vocabulary

| | | |
|---|---|---|
| 13. ANS: D | DIF: Easy | OBJ: Vocabulary |
| 14. ANS: B | DIF: Easy | OBJ: Vocabulary |
| 15. ANS: A | DIF: Easy | OBJ: Vocabulary |

## Essay

16. Students should recognize that both characters are much the same: both find a piece of cheese; both, because of their vanity, fall victim to the fox's flattery and lose the cheese; both learn that believing in flattery comes at a high price. For differences, students may point to the additional details in "The Fox Outwits the Crow," such as those about opera.

**Difficulty:** *Easy* **Objective:** *Essay*

17. Students should recognize that both characters are similar: Both flatter a crow to get the crow to drop the cheese she is holding in her beak. They differ in the tone of their speech: The Fox in the fable speaks formally; the fox in the poem speaks playfully.

**Difficulty:** *Easy* **Objective:** *Essay*

18. Students might note that both the fox and the crow think only of themselves, not of the community. The crow finds a piece of cheese, which she intends to eat alone. She had no thought about sharing her food with other birds. The fox comes up with a plan to steal the cheese for himself. Again, the character thinks only of his selfish needs. Both seem more concerned with their individual selfish needs, not the good of the community.

**Difficulty:** *Average* **Objective:** *Essay*

## Selection Test B, p. 219

### Critical Reading

| | | |
|---|---|---|
| 1. ANS: C | DIF: Average | OBJ: Comprehension |
| 2. ANS: C | DIF: Challenging | OBJ: Interpretation |
| 3. ANS: A | DIF: Average | OBJ: Literary Analysis |
| 4. ANS: D | DIF: Average | OBJ: Interpretation |
| 5. ANS: D | DIF: Average | OBJ: Interpretation |
| 6. ANS: A | DIF: Average | OBJ: Comprehension |
| 7. ANS: D | DIF: Average | OBJ: Interpretation |
| 8. ANS: B | DIF: Average | OBJ: Literary Analysis |
| 9. ANS: B | DIF: Average | OBJ: Interpretation |
| 10. ANS: C | DIF: Average | OBJ: Interpretation |
| 11. ANS: A | DIF: Challenging | OBJ: Interpretation |
| 12. ANS: A | DIF: Average | OBJ: Literary Analysis |
| 13. ANS: A | DIF: Average | OBJ: Literary Analysis |
| 14. ANS: C | DIF: Average | OBJ: Literary Analysis |

### Vocabulary

| | | |
|---|---|---|
| 15. ANS: D | DIF: Average | OBJ: Vocabulary |
| 16. ANS: B | DIF: Average | OBJ: Vocabulary |
| 17. ANS: A | DIF: Average | OBJ: Vocabulary |

### Essay

18. Students should recognize that the crows are similar. Both find a piece of cheese and lose it when they fall victim to the cunning and flattery of a fox. Both are vain, arrogant creatures. Both are advised not to trust a flatterer. In citing differences, students may point to the additional details in "The Fox Outwits the Crow," such as the crow's belief that she is Maria Callas. They should note that the additional details in that selection make the crow's attitude seem more extreme—she seems more vain and more arrogant than the Crow in "The Fox and the Crow."

**Difficulty:** *Average* **Objective:** *Essay*

19. Students should point to the seriousness and formality of "The Fox and the Crow" and the playfulness and informality of "The Fox Outwits the Crow." They might note that the fox in the poem is more provocative and that the poem includes more details, such as those about opera. Students should recognize that Aesop seems to want only that his readers learn a lesson, whereas Cleary seems to want not just to teach a lesson but to amuse his readers and perhaps impress them with his own cleverness. Students' explanations of the way the tone influenced their attitude should reflect their descriptions of how they thought the writer wanted them to react.

**Difficulty:** *Challenging* **Objective:** *Essay*

20. Students should indicate that both the fox and the crow think only of themselves, not of the community. The crow finds a piece of cheese, which she intends to eat alone. She had no thought about sharing her food with other birds. The fox comes up with a plan to steal the cheese for himself. Again, the character thinks only of his personal needs. Neither one seems concerned with the good of the community, but only with self-interest. As a result, they would feel that the individual is more important than the community.

**Difficulty:** *Average* **Objective:** *Essay*

### Writing Workshop

### Research Report: Integrating Grammar Skills, p. 223

**A.** 1. they; 2. her; 3. me; 4. us;

**B.** 1. Wendell, Terry, and I like to play basketball.

2. Terry's brother taught Wendell and me some good moves.

3. correct

4. He and Terry's brother have been playing together for years.

### Vocabulary Workshop—1, p. 224

### Sample Answers

**A.** 1. metaphor

2. analogy

3. simile

4. analogy

5. simile

6. metaphor

7. analogy

8. simile

**B.** Sentences will vary. Possible responses are shown.

1. get her to notice me; If I see Caryl at the meeting, I'll try to catch her eye.

2. meanwhile; We'll leave in an hour or so. In the mean time, please wash the dishes.

3. almost or in a slight way; I was kind of scared by that movie.

4. old or out-of-date; This old coat of mine is really over the hill.

5. got very upset; Mrs. Haines threw a fit when the dog put his muddy paws on her new chair.

6. not feeling well; After I ate all those pickles, I really felt under the weather.

7. easygoing; Some people worry about the future, but Sharon remains happy-go-lucky.

8. It's not a problem; If you can't come to the meeting, no sweat. I'll see you afterwards.

9. "What's new?" or "What's happening?"; "What's up?" he asked. "Tell me your news!"

10. "Don't bother" or "Cancel that"; "Never mind about that picnic," she said. "It's raining."

## Benchmark Test 12, p. 227

### MULTIPLE CHOICE

1. ANS: B

2. ANS: A

3. ANS: B

4. ANS: D

5. ANS: C

6. ANS: A

7. ANS: D

8. ANS: D

9. ANS: C

10. ANS: D

11. ANS: C

12. ANS: B

13. ANS: D

14. ANS: D

15. ANS: C

16. ANS: A

17. ANS: A

18. ANS: D

19. ANS: B

20. ANS: A

21. ANS: B

22. ANS: D

23. ANS: C

24. ANS: A

25. ANS: D

26. ANS: A

27. ANS: C

28. ANS: C

29. ANS: D

30. ANS: A

31. ANS: B

32. ANS: D

33. ANS: C

34. ANS: D

### ESSAY

35. Students' summaries should be reasonably short and should focus on main ideas. They should give information on the setting or main settings, the major characters, the main events, the central conflict, and the final outcome of that conflict.

36. Students' reviews should give their opinion of the characters, the plot, and other details in the work. They should support their opinions with details from the work. They should open or conclude with a recommendation about whether or not others should read the tale.

37. Students should identify a subject that is neither too narrow nor too broad. They should list information sources that seem useful for investigating the subject—for example, if their subject is a person, they might list biographical references; if their subject is a place, they might list an atlas or a book of maps.